CAN NORWAY LEARN FROM CHINA?

CAN NORWAY LEARN FROM CHINA?

School Quality

ELI PUBLISHING
2016

Arild Tjeldvoll

© 2016 ELI Publishing
Oslo (Norway)
ISBN: 8291953139
ISBN 13: 9788291953137

National Library of Norway Database

All rights reserved. No part of this publication may be reproduced, stored, in a retrieval system or transmitted in any form or by any means, electronic, mechanical, photocopying, recording or otherwise, without the written permission of the publisher.

ELI Publishing
(Educational Leadership International)

2016

Contents

Preface··vii

1 Norwegian School Patriotism Inspired by China················1
2 Where Does School Quality Come From?·····················10
3 The Hong Kong School Synthesis··························27

CHINA

4 The Chinese Source of School Quality······················35
5 Curriculum for Social Harmony··························42
6 The Imperial Examination······························50
7 China's Humiliation and Revival·························56
8 Rich Emigrants Building Knowledge at Home················65
9 A Rice-Cake Baker Graduating from University··············73
10 A New Subject and a New Institute······················82
11 The Saloon···89
12 Deng Xiaoping's Education Policies······················97
13 University Leadership with Confucian Features·············105
14 The Taiwan Miracle··································112
15 Norwegians Facing an Elite School in China···············118
16 A Waitress Building Elite Schools······················126
17 An Elite School's Curriculum, Grades and Resources·········132
18 Elite Shool Leadership································138

19	Elite Teachers · 145
20	Koreans and Swedes Do Not See the Same School · · · · · · · · · · 152
21	Modernization and Culture Export · · · · · · · · · · · · · · · · · · 161

NORWAY

22	Norway Switching Curriculum Tradition · · · · · · · · · · · · · · 171
23	The Golden Age of Norwegian Schooling · · · · · · · · · · · · · · 177
24	Good Will for a Unified School · · · · · · · · · · · · · · · · · · · 188
25	Signs of Crises · 200
26	Misunderstandings of Human Nature · · · · · · · · · · · · · · · · 213
27	Invalid Teacher Training · 220
28	Norwegian School and Other Schools in Norway · · · · · · · · · · · 226
29	A Glossy Image of Norway Seducing Foreigners · · · · · · · · · · · 235
30	Headache in Norwegian School Leadership · · · · · · · · · · · · · 243
31	The Minister of Education and the Minister of Magic · · · · · · · · 252
32	The Essence of Schooling and Social Justice · · · · · · · · · · · · · 261

WHAT CAN NORWAY LEARN FROM OTHERS?

33	What can Norway Learn from China? · · · · · · · · · · · · · · · · 269
34	The Finnish School Code · 279
35	England - Elite Schools for All? · · · · · · · · · · · · · · · · · · · 286
36	An Optimal Knowledge School for All · · · · · · · · · · · · · · · · 294

Background Literature · 303
Can Norway Learn From China? · 309

Preface

ENGLISH EDITION

Two particular experiences, one negative and one positive, caused this educational travelogue. During my seventy years' participation in and observations of Norwegian education, I have seen a sad decline of quality. It started when Norway switched to a US American curriculum tradition after WWII. The positive experience is my familiarizing with the education culture of East Asia over the last twenty-five years. In this culture, there is an enormous respect for learning and knowledge, rooted in Confucius' moral philosophy. Willingness to learn and respect for knowledge is now the super soft power of economically successful East Asian countries. My two opposite experiences resulted in the following question: *What can Norway learn from China in terms of school quality?* The question is also relevant for many other countries, today facing stiff competition in the global knowledge economy.

The book's purpose is to reach parents and grandparents worldwide, and inspire them to be conscious about the quality of their loved-ones' schooling. Quality education is their primary life insurance in a changing global world. From my experiences with East Asia, Finland and England, I present some ideas to enhance school quality.

Many people have inspired me and helped me make this book reality. Primarily there are my Chinese colleagues and students, and, in particular Professor Pan Maoyuan at Xiamen University. Two colleagues at

Shenzhen University were instrumental in making the Chinese edition possible; Xiang Chun, 向春and Xiao Haitao,肖海涛.

In Norway, Inger Lise Walle, Viggo Torbergsen, Anne-Katrine Brun Norbye and Svein Høvik did a great job in giving feedback on the very first Norwegian edition. Anne Welle-Strand, wife and professor, provided a daily encouraging environment. Above all, the children, Dyre, Vetle, Kristin, Erling, Emma and Myrthle, made the greatest inspiration. Thanks to all.

Antibes, France, April 2016

Arild Tjeldvoll

China will soon have the world's largest economy. Is a substantial explanation the population's strong willingness to learn? When China joined the Pisa surveys (2009), Shanghai's 15-year-olds were top in the world. The same was true for Pisa 2013. Chinese students overseas are those completing the fastest. Is willingness to learn China's strongest soft power? Can Norway, with declining school quality for decades, learn something from China? The common denominator for those who analyse the global economic competition is that individuals and nations' level of knowledge is the number one source of power. The overriding framework for this book is the significance of knowledge for individuals, companies and nations' identity and mastery. Focus is on a culture of learning that provides education both as morality and as competence. Special attention is on education policies, curriculum traditions and schools as tools for achieving a culture comprising both moral education and training. The book is an educational travelogue of my experiences with education in East Asia for 25 years, and my Norwegian school experiences over the past 70 years.

1

Norwegian School Patriotism Inspired by China

School patriotism is one crucial inspiration for this book. I believe that the academic quality of the Norwegian school has decayed over the past forty years. The purpose of the book is, therefore, to reach those whom I think are most deeply concerned with quality in Norwegian schools, namely parents and grandparents. I would like to convey my own experiences with schooling in China and Norway, to those who are most motivated to give their most precious the best form of life insurance - an education that provides safe identity and solid mastery. Internationally, we see parents and grandparents who sacrifice everything to ensure their loved ones this best possible life insurance in a challenging global world. Solid basic education also makes it easier to continue to learn new knowledge and skills when the environment is changing. It is no longer enough to have a traditional good education «just in case». Education must be constantly updated, so that the person has «the right skills at the right time and place», when the job market is changing. For the students, the parents and grandparents are more important than the state, the municipality and the school. The very most important person in a person's educational life is the mother. The child's early experiences of her expectations are the start of a child's life-long education. The mother is the child's first teacher, said the famous Czech educator Comenius (1592-1670). He is the father of the unified school for all.

Of course, some politicians, bureaucrats and business people may also be interested in my thoughts. Not least the latter group. In a time where it becomes essential for any business to have the «right qualifications at the right time and place», the company's own learning policies may be critically important for both the employee, the business and, as accumulated impact - for the nation. Especially for people with modest motivation for learning at regular school age, a company's "educational policy" is crucial. Consciousness on the learning dimension of work life might increase the employees' quality of life, at the same time as the company improves its expertise and competitiveness. The least important of my potential readers are politicians, bureaucrats, educational researchers and teachers in Norway. These have so far failed in their efforts to increase the quality of Norwegian schools. Most reprehensible are the educational researchers. They have to some extent crucially provided premises to the politicians. They have trained the bureaucrats to run the school system, and the lecturers to the teacher training colleges. With Norwegian schooling presently in a poor condition, it is understandable that politicians now tend to overlook the academic advice from «school researchers». Their advice has not worked. Politicians' current sesame is in-service training.

In the Norwegian general election campaign of 2013, the political parties competed to outbid each other with billions to the in-service training of teachers. Is it certain that such training is the magic tool to raise quality? I am in doubt. At all times learning results have been dependent on the real motivation and intellectual capability. Do Norwegian teachers, now invited to participate in the billion programme, meet these preconditions? I am in doubt. I think it is a myth that in-service training necessarily will increase teachers' professional competence.

It is strange that people who have undergone four years of teacher education needs in-service training in e.g. «classroom management». What is it the teacher student has studied for four years - if not exactly - classroom management? Politicians' oracular belief in in-service training may be response to a presumption that the teachers before in-service training are frightening poor. Professionally weak teachers are a main reason why Norway is doing poorly in international comparisons. If we follow the politicians' reasoning, further, we could ask, how likely is it that these presently poorly qualified teachers have real motivation for in-service training. Moreover, how sure is it that they have sufficient intellectual capacity to improve? Over a number of years, teacher education colleges recruited academically weak graduates from upper secondary school. Is there any reason to believe that these persons' intellectual power has increased while in practice? I am in doubt. Public billions spent on in-service training may be wasted.

How is the quality of those who are going to conduct in-service training – the professors at the teacher education colleges? Norwegian teacher education was in an evaluation report a few years ago virtually declared invalid. What dictates that teacher training now should be able to provide high quality in-service training? Many years ago, I myself attended several in-service training courses for teachers. Later I led an extensive research project evaluating a national school leadership programme. In-service training was a key dimension of the programme. In conclusion, we observed very modest motivation among participants for the learning objectives of the programme. Main reason to attend was for many to get a break from dreary everyday life, and enjoy a nice social gathering with course colleagues. The organizing of the courses was questionable. Often, the courses' main component was entertaining lectures by gurus in the field, followed by a bit of group work, a short discussion and plenary feedback. It was a happening. The feedback was a quasi-evaluation, where the participants were supposed to respond to questions like, *what do you feel that you have learned?* In other words, there was no objective control (test/examination) of what participants had actually learned in relation to the stated learning objectives. Systematic control of learning achievement would be a sign of distrust to the participants.

Massive in-service training is a questionable strategy. Do alternatives exist? Hardly. Norway is trapped with a teaching profession - based on recruitment over a number of years of academically weak graduates from secondary school, to teacher colleges with questionable quality. To get the best candidates from secondary school to apply for teacher education will require a miracle. Better than waiting for miracles may be to take an educational glance outside the country's borders, trying to understand why other countries have succeeded in achieving secondary school quality. Is it possible for Norway to learn from them?

The other sources of inspiration for the book all come from East Asia - hardworking students, respected teachers, committed parents, the philosopher Confucius, as well as the impressive economic development and social cohesion in China and its cultural neighbouring countries. My very first educational meeting with this part of the world was on a roundtrip to Japanese primary and secondary schools in 1991. In hindsight, I see that impressions from these visits were the seed for my interest in Confucian educational thinking. My next meeting with East Asia was a trip to China in 1995, to study reforms in higher education. There appeared to be a very close connection between theory and practice. Not infrequently, universities had their own factories on campus, where theories from the laboratories immediately found practical application - to products, which they could sell, and thus strengthening the university's finances. The pace easily impressed you, when it came to new infrastructure. Highways and high-rise buildings were completed before one had turned around. However, the image was also frightening for a Scandinavian. Workers up at the high building structures in the Guangzhou (formerly Canton) did not come down from the scaffolds at night. They slept up there. I saw no Labour Inspectorate.

China has in the course of thirty years grown from being a poor, collectivist agricultural country to become the world's second-largest economy. The country is already the world's largest in foreign trade. Economic experts assume that it will not take many years before the country is economic world champion. As a visiting professor at Xiamen University in South China between 2003 and 2005, I got a better understanding of the country and different groups of people. This happened both in my role as a university teacher and by having an 11-year-old son as student at Xiamen international school. Longer research stays in Hong Kong and Taiwan between 2006 and 2010 filled into the bigger picture of China (Taiwan, Hong Kong and Macao included).

In East Asia, I experienced a fundamentally different learning culture than in Norway. Pupils in schools, university students and, in particular, parents are extremely motivated for learning efforts. In a Japanese primary school, I experienced that when little Yoko was ill, and had to be absent from school, then her mother turned up. She asked the teacher to tell her exactly what Yoko had missed in the time she was away. Then the mother found a private teacher who ensured that the girl did not have any "holes" in her learning. This is normal in East Asia. The parents' ambitions have made commercial private schools lighthouses for the public school. In 2013, there was 120 000 private schools, comprising 22% (34 millions) of the country's students. Many parents are ready to pay extra for quality. Surveys of commercially based international schools in China show that they have very high academic and pedagogical quality. The owners are spending money to find the best teachers and school leaders, hiring them on contract and paying them generously. There are no signs that «schools as business» have negative effects on school quality. Rather the contrary. If the school is to be profitable as a business, it needs to deliver school quality that parents are willing to pay for. The ultimate goal for parents is the university and an assumed good life afterwards. Vocational education has traditionally low status.

Already on my first day's walking on Xiamen university campus, I discovered that two students were following me. When I stopped, they asked me politely, in English, about where I came from, and what I was going to teach. As a visiting professor I had no teaching obligations, my primary interest was research on higher education. However, since my research theme was university development internationally, meeting with students in a teaching situation would be a unique opportunity for getting exciting data. I therefore, had asked the university to let me conduct a seminar on my research topic - for master and doctoral students. The two students that had stopped me turned out to be master students.

They became eager participants in my seminar. Many students flocked to my class, and I was pleased to see so much interest for my theme. The joy was somewhat reduced, when I overheard that the seminar was called «The English Class», and that it was the opportunity to practice English, more than the theme, that motivated. However, all worked conscientiously with the written home assignment they had to do every week. Many of them asked to be my unpaid research assistants. They calculated they would then learn even more.

At the university, there was hardly any difference between weekdays and weekend, and every day there is often teaching to late evening. Saturday and Sunday, the campus bustles as much as in the rest of the week. This is in stark contrast to Norway, where campus is dead between Friday afternoon and Monday morning. In Xiamen, there was also no long summer holiday for students. Many had poor economy, and survived by some extra paid work, in addition to support from parents. Liu Li came from a poor family in Western China. She was clever. Her teacher in lower secondary school had explained to her how she could get on with distance education. After upper secondary school examinations, she got into preschool teacher education. When I met her, she was a master student in Xiamen university, with education in other countries as a special interest. She had learned English by self-studies. Since, I know she has taken a doctoral degree and is now working as a professor at a university in Western China.

To be a university teacher (and, a man, with grey hair) in China is very comfortable. I am experiencing great respect, students are listening carefully to what I say, read what I write and ask for advice on how they can learn even better. There is a special Teachers' Day in September every year, which is marked clearly, both in public, and at individual schools. Students and parents show their gratitude towards those who have contributed to «lifting the talent», as their great philosopher Confucius himself expressed it. On Taiwan, teachers were for many years exempted from paying tax, because their efforts were so important for competence development on the island. Teachers' efforts in developing "power of knowledge" for the whole population had important economic and political consequences for the island. Taiwan is influenced by traditional Chinese culture, more strongly than what is the case in Mainland China. Taiwan is "more Chinese". However, politically and economically the island is in practice an independent state - as long as USA finds it expedient.

Education culture in China is a focus of this book. However, it is relevant to recall that equivalent educational culture exists in the other countries also characterized by the ideas of the philosopher Confucius. His ideas are basic culture elements in Japan, Korea, Singapore, and Taiwan, Macao and Hong Kong, the latter a part of China since 1997, but with great autonomy in self-government. Historically, Japan is the first "Confucian country" in modern times to impress with dramatically effective economic and technological development. When Japan in the mid-1800's was pushed by the Americans to open the country for Western trade, the Japanese were horrified, discovering how financially and technologically backward the country was, compared to the West. Japan so that the danger to fall victim to Western colonialism was imminent. Exactly that was what neighbouring China got a bitter taste of during the 1800's, when Western powers and Japan controlled large parts of the country. Thus, Japan launched an economic and technological reform process that history has barely seen before, in terms of efficiency. So strong was the power increase that the country itself turned a colonial power. Already in 1895, China had to cede Taiwan to Japan. Ten years later (1905), Japan was the first non-European power that militarily managed to defeat a European empire - Russia. Later, disaster hit Japan - World War II and atomic bombs. Nevertheless, it did not take a long time after the war until Japan had the world's second-strongest economy, and retained the position until China a few years ago took over.

The economic development in the other «East Asian Dragons» is just as remarkable. Korea (South), Taiwan and Singapore are also Confucian cultural countries, with similar dramatic growth. From being poor dictatorships after WW II, they politically developed democracy and grew up to be among the world's strongest economies. They have universities ranking among the world's best. Hong Kong, with less population than Sweden, has three universities among the forty best in the world, with the University of Hong Kong in 19th place, according to a Times' ranking a few years ago.

The common denominators for these countries are strong economic and technological development as well as market economy. They have shown unusual ability to learn, and to use resources in a way that gives economic return and social levelling. The difference between them is political systems. Japan, South Korea, Taiwan and Singapore are reasonably liberal democracies. They meet certain Western criteria, such as regularly holding free elections, and that the political power can shift between position and opposition. The US can take a lot of honour for «forced democratization» of the former dictatorships of South Korea and Taiwan, and for forcing Japan to adopt a new constitution based on democratic principles. Many in the West would argue that these countries lack considerably on meeting Western ideal requirements for being democratic. Some also fear a reversal in Japan, after Prime Minister Abe recently indicating a desire to change the constitution, in order to be more in accordance with Japanese cultural uniqueness. China and North Korea, however, are communist one-party states, with a communist definition of democracy, with, respectively, Chinese and Korean special features.

The similarity between the East Asian, liberal democracies and China is market economy. North Korea has a planned economy, and is penniless, but everyone gets education, and it has engineers able to develop nuclear weapons. That may be one indication of their abilities and motivation for learning, when it comes to technology. Thus, we can now summarize a central cultural common denominator for the population as a whole, in the East Asian countries: strong motivation to learn. Where does it come from? I think the source is the moral philosopher Confucius, who lived 2500 years ago. He hailed learning as the greatest of all virtues to develop human moral character and social harmony. I assume that his philosophy is a key cultural foundation of the economic miracles in East Asia. The pedagogy following from his thinking may be the soft power that is the core of China's current development to economic superpower, and cultural expansion globally.

Can a country like Norway learn something from China? Before I can answer that question, I will elaborate on the nature of the particular learning culture, which originated from Confucius. In the first part of the book, the China Section, I start by trying to identify what sort of specific *curriculum* that Confucianism has effected. Furthermore, I will present the examination system that has been associated with Confucianism, *The Imperial Examination*. I then reflect on China's brutal awakening to Western and Japanese attempts of colonizing the country, and, to how political history relates to education and examination system. I then turn to unique individuals at various levels of society, showing how they have been inspired to take patriotic knowledge initiatives, due to their Confucian cultural roots with an emphasis on education. In conclusion, on the China Section of the book, I show how China is now trying to use its Confucian, educational soft power to strengthen its cultural influence internationally.

Following, in the Norway Section, I begin with a review of Norwegian school development after World War II. After trying to highlight reasons why Norwegian schools increasingly have lost professional quality, I wonder what Norway can learn from China and some other countries, to regain the academic school quality we once had. In the next chapter, I start with an educational narrative from the reality in Hong Kong. I use it as a starting point to bring up a picture of the perception of school quality, within various educational traditions internationally. Then follows a contrasting of the particular learning culture of «The Confucian Lands» to the four primary learning cultures that have dominated in the West, from Plato in ancient times and up until today.

Chapters 2 and 3 attempt to provide a basic understanding of what is school quality, and why this understanding varies between countries and cultural areas. Some readers might find these two chapters a bit too abstract. My more concrete pedagogical travelogue starts in Chapter 4.

2

Where Does School Quality Come From?

A newspaper spread in Hong Kong in November 2005 was a reminder of differences in the perception of quality in education, between Mainland China and Hong Kong. A more relaxed learning environment in Hong Kong's universities seems like a magnet on the very best students graduating from secondary schools in China. "In China we don't have so much choice as in Hong Kong, when it comes to choice of courses at the university. In Hong Kong, I can use time more efficiently, on what I'm really interested in", says Liu Yang from Shenzhen to the *South China Morning Post*. The 18-year-old had earned the highest score among the 450 000 students at graduation from secondary school in Guangdong, China's largest province with more than 100 million inhabitants, and neighbour to Hong Kong. She could get right into the prestige university Tsinghua in Beijing, but she chose Hong Kong. This notice in the Hong Kong newspaper gives signals about what is quality at basic and secondary schools in both China and Hong Kong, and that produces a Liu Yang. In China, quality of secondary school examinations is key to everything that parents and students see as most important in life. Moreover, level of examination achievements is depending on the quality of teaching and students' work effort in the subjects, in basic and secondary school. However, what is quality?

Two prominent sociologists are of help, when we try to understand the concept of school quality in a context of economic globalization.

Sociology Classic, Max Weber, can help us to clarify this diffuse concept, through his distinction between value- and instrument-aspects of quality. The word quality has long flown high, not least in Norway, where we are constantly implementing a Quality Reform in higher education. A common sense-perception of quality is that it is something that most people perceive as positive. A popular way to explain 'quality' is that it is something relative, and attached to the individual's subjective perception of a high standard. The way I interpret Weber, the quality concept turns clearer from his distinction between value goals and instrumental goals. Value goals revolve around what people perceive as basic, universal qualities or properties, e.g. freedom. Instrumental goals revolve around economic and practical phenomena, often crucial as means to achieve value goals. For example, it is important for a university to have a solid economy, as an instrument, to be able to hire «useless» sociologists or philosophers, who can do research on the conditions that makes the university able to achieve the value goal of «speaking truth to power». Freedom of speech is an important value in a democratic society, whether the power is the state, the market, or powerful trade unions. The university will then be able to help create more of the value freedom, in society as a whole.

The distinction between the value dimension and the instrument dimension of quality illustrates by the terms «quality as fitness *for* something» and «quality as fitness *of* something». The first notion involves the issue of the quality of a remedy to use to achieve something else, such as the quality of a school. The school is an instrument for students to reach certain learning targets. In the second case, quality as «fitness of something», the concern is about whether the case in itself is valuable or not, whether *the purpose* to be reached by the instrument is important. Is the purpose of the school primarily to teach students knowledge and skills, or is the primary purpose of the school "to be a place to stay together» in order to achieve social integration of all the students, and where the goals of knowledge and skills come second? "The school is, in general, a means of poor quality in order to achieve the purpose of authentic learning of knowledge and skills", claims Ivan Illich, in his famous book,

De-schooling Society. He believes that the school, in its distinctive character, is more harmful than beneficial for the many students who do not have a cultural background that matches the school's culture. A school as a high-quality instrument must therefore be able to achieve the value of knowledge and skills learning for all students, their different intellectual preconditions taken into account. Conversely, a school that is not able to provide good knowledge and skills acquisition for all students is a bad school. A school with quality gives students knowledge that is vital to their identity and self-esteem. It also gives the students skills important to master the struggle of the real world, e.g. languages and mathematics.

When parents want to assess whether a particular school has high quality, two different approaches are possible. The first is a principled assessment of different alternatives. The second is to follow traditional mainstream. The principled way involves examining of the curriculum tradition a particular school is based on. Curriculum traditions have a starting point in specific curriculum philosophies. They are expressions of ideal perceptions of school quality. Specific examples are Montessori and Waldorf schools (Steiner). The traditional way is to assume that the regular public school has sufficient quality. The rational basis for the public school is the country's education policy goals, and strategies to achieve these goals. A country's education policies seldom explain evidence for which curriculum philosophy that forms its basis. Concretely, parents' perception of school quality becomes visible when they have the opportunity to choose between alternatives. That is what happened when the parents of former Norwegian prime minister, Jens Stoltenberg, chose the Waldorf (Steiner) school for their son.

Various curriculum traditions emphasize the learning of *knowledge* differently. Typical of our time, internationally, is however, that the learning of knowledge has got increased value, as expressed by many, parents, politicians and businesses. All groups see efficient learning of knowledge as the key characteristic of school quality. In his three-volumes work, *The Information Age: Economy, Society and Culture*, the sociologist Manuel Castells discusses how information and communication technology (ICT) affect the global economy. He argues that ICT brings a revolution on par with the industrial revolution, that ICT is converting the economy's material basis, as well as profoundly changing society and culture. He defines the information in its widest meaning as «communication of knowledge». Historically, this is not something new.

What is new is that ICT brings a new form of social organization where creation, processing and transfer of knowledge is the fundamental source of productivity and power. These processes are penetrating all areas, first in dominant economy activities and military systems, and, eventually, to all areas of everyday life. Innovations in the time after the industrial revolution were based on investment in cheap energy. Innovations now have cheap investments in information as their basis. This follows as an effect of the progress in the microelectronics and telecommunications technology. The most effective knowledge acquisition for as many as possible is vital to a society's economic competitiveness and survivability. Thus, the educational policy turns a vital prerequisite for the economic development and the country's ability to maintain a welfare state. Basic and secondary schools that «produce» students with high level of knowledge is becoming the decisive competence base for any country.

On such a nation-wide foundation of knowledge, the robust «power stations in the knowledge society» can be built – *the research universities*, or in Castell's' own words; «When knowledge is the electricity in the new international information economy, then the universities are the power sources that the economy depends on». For self-assertion and survival, it is crucial for countries, companies and individuals to have effective production and acquisition of knowledge. Knowledge is necessary both for immediate application and as a base for continuous learning, as well as a prerequisite to be an educated, moral human being. The "knowledge school" becomes essential for the population's identity and the country's economy.

Globalization involves mass communication that makes meaning to how people compare the school offers in different parts of the world. People learn about school alternatives through tourism, internet and the international job market. The quality education offers available are important, when people are looking for attractive jobs internationally. Globalization harmonizes the perception of school quality around the world. Parents from different cultural spheres, regardless of country, seems increasingly concerned about what kind of school offers the hopefuls will get when the family moves to a another country, and the children must attend a school different from home. The posting in the Hong Kong newspaper made me wonder about what parents, teachers, school leaders and school politicians in East Asia perceive as school with quality, when globalization comes ever closer into their lives. The parents' perception is the driving force for what is actually going on. What they think is school quality is characterized by strong academic subject-centring, high teacher status and heavy school leader authority. Rooted in parents' opinion, this is the foundation for how people in East Asia think about schooling. As part of the globalization process, I suppose further, that this view of quality will get ever more influential in the West, simultaneously with Western ideas about student centring trickling eastward.

That same year, 2005, there was published a unique research report about the value of education in Europe, Norway included. It hardly received any attention at all in Norway, although, the findings were dramatic for the country. The title of the report was *Norwegians would enjoy, Europeans would provide.* The study was on Europeans' opinion on central values in life. One of the questions was about *education as a value.* Norway is the only country in Europe where the majority of the population does not think education is an important value. I read the report with impressions from my stay in East Asia in fresh memory. Maybe that background was the reason for my first experience of shock. Colleagues from other countries, with whom I discussed the report, could not believe that the majority of such a developed and modern country like Norway did not value education. How could it be possible? In addition, what consequences could this have for the students' motivation, for teachers' opportunities to succeed in teaching and, in a longer perspective, for the nation's knowledge-based skill level, not least after offshore oil and gas are finished?

Can Norway learn from China?

My second shock was that the study did not receive attention in Norwegian media or education professional circles. In a number of newspaper letters to the editor in the years since, I have referred to this study, because it clearly tells something very important about why the Norwegian school under-perform fiercely, both absolutely, but worse still, relatively, since hardly any country in the world spend more money per student. No one has responded, not until July 2013, when I had a call from the Rector (the president) of the University of Oslo, after I had mentioned the report in a chronicle in Norwegian business daily *Dagens Næringsliv*. I have not heard his reasoning for his interest, but it is natural to guess that it has something to do with the motivation of students at the university. The fact that the majority of the population actually do not see schoolwork as important may be linked to moderate study efforts, and a big drop-off percent among students in Norwegian higher education.

Back to China. Obviously, there are big differences within China. The quality of schools in rural areas in Yunnan in the South West is lower than in Shenzhen. Shenzhen is one of a handful of special economic zones on the coast, which the government has granted exclusive good framework conditions to develop. In this group, we also find Xiamen and Shanghai. When Shanghai first participated in the Pisa survey in 2009, its schools scored top in the world in mathematics, reading and science. For those who have kept an eye on education in East Asia over some years, this is coming as no surprise. On the previous Pisa surveys, Japan, South Korea, Taiwan and Singapore have been in the top group. What can be the reason why 15-year-olds in these East Asian countries is so much more academically proficient than same age students in Scandinavia, minus Finland? (In Pisa 2013 Finland, however, decreased significantly, and it will be interesting to see if the country is on a track to the «school fatigue», you have in the neighbouring Scandinavian countries). Of course, explanations are complicated. Yet, when I use my best judgment, from practical experiences, text studies and research, the answer is *pedagogy*. In this term, I include the value and character that learning and education have in a society, expressed in a curriculum that specifies the objectives, content, methodology and rules for examinations. Moreover, I include in the term the character of the school organization, with teachers, management and resources/equipment - and the school's surroundings, e.g. parental expectations and whether the school faces competition.

Pisa does not tell the full truth about any country's school achievements. Nevertheless, it can hardly be any doubt that the study has very high validity and reliability, when it comes to the measurement of the same subjects in different countries. Not only schools in Finland, but also the former English colonies, Australia, New Zealand and Canada are doing very well in the Pisa surveys. In addition, the schools in former European communist countries, such as the Baltics, are doing better than schools in Norway. The world's number one superpower, United States, is consistently doing poorly, at the same time as the country, increasingly, has about eight of the ten best universities in the world. Why do we find such regional differences? A historical glance at dominant curriculum traditions, and the learning culture and teaching practices they have resulted in, many give an answer.

East Asia is also no homogeneous cultural region. Indonesia and Malaysia are rather different from Korea and Japan. Yet, when it comes to school and education, you may to a fair degree claim that the impact from the Confucius philosophy not only include Korea, Japan, China, Taiwan, Hong Kong, Macao and Singapore, but also influences thinking in other countries in the region. Chinese business people throughout history have had important positions in many countries outside China, and brought with them Confucian educational thinking. Hong Kong and Singapore are special cases, because here the English learning culture merged with Confucian ideas. Common to the Confucian countries is that they are economic great powers. It is not hard to find indications of relationship between educational tradition and economic growth.

A deliberate strategy for the import of investment capital, associated with specific requirements to also investment in education, partly explain Taiwan's economic miracle. At the same time as all educational policies reflect competence needed in a given society, one or more *curriculum traditions* are also influencing national education policies. The latter is especially true for the content and method of the basic school (primary and lower secondary). Attitude to education as a value is varying in the different curriculum traditions. Unlike the West, East Asia also has the Confucius-tradition. Learning is the pivotal point in this tradition. Summing up, school quality is, thus, determined both by the curriculum tradition dominating in the country, and by competence needs from the economic sphere of the particular country.

In the West, four curriculum traditions, *essentialism*, *encyclopaedism*, *polytechnicalism* and *progressivism* determine perception of school quality. Each tradition claims to have the best understanding of how students should be educated to obtain such identity and mastery that they can optimally organize their own lives, and be constructive members of society. The teacher role and, implicitly, teacher quality, comes out differently in the four different traditions.

Essentialism is the oldest. It has its root in Plato's social model, and in his theories of individual differences from 2500 years back. In this model, only the academic talented men should be educated. Education should make them capable and wise in governing the state. From Plato's theories of individual differences, there developed a learning psychology and knowledge understanding, which resulted in the earliest known curriculum - the Seven Liberal Arts (Septem Artes Liberales), with four science and three humanities subjects. The humanistic subjects were grammar, rhetoric and dialectic. Science subjects were music, arithmetic, geometry and astronomy. Typical of the essentialist curriculum tradition was to learn subjects thoroughly, in depth.

This curriculum tradition dominated in Europe up to the 1600's. It is still influential in England, and appears now to have gained new relevance internationally, expressed in the international elite schools, and their popularity among wealthy and education-conscious parents. Essentialism has both dominated educational practice, given the criteria for what is the optimal benefit of organized learning and, thus, inspired teachers' efforts to provide students with quality education. A picture of the good teacher in this tradition is *the wise tutor*. The teacher's authority rests in his professional weight and human wisdom. The student's formation to be a morally conscious and responsible human being is as important as acquisition of subject knowledge.

The most significant criticism raised against essentialism during history was that it was education just for the elite. Its concept of relevant schooling has as preconception, students who have good ability to think abstractly. As the ideas of human equality and equal rights emerged, essentialism became less relevant for the society as a whole. Nevertheless, even today it is apparent that the perception of the school's essence, created by essentialism, still is highly influential when it comes to what many politicians and parents consider quality education.

The encyclopaedic tradition appeared in the 1600's, and is the first curriculum tradition that seriously challenges the elitism of essentialism. This tradition is a synthesis of the thinking of the Czech educator, Comenius, and the French Enlightenment-philosophers. Encyclopaedic entails dictionary, that is, a collection of all existing knowledge. Comenius is the founding father of *the unified school model*. All children should learn the most of existing knowledge. This is important for each individual and for the community. In addition, practical subjects are good for developing creativity. The French philosophers, however, emphasized that the school system should also pay attention to particular needs of gifted students. They were important, because they would be the nation's future leaders. The French would thus retain some of the legacy of essentialism. After the French revolution in 1789, encyclopaedism spread all over Europe, except England, where essentialism continued to dominate.

The criticisms against encyclopaedism were two-fold. First, since the curriculum contained many subjects, the learning would be superficial. Second, it was argued that the model implied «knowledge-hierarchies», and thus helped to reproduce an educationally class society. Some knowledge areas, e.g. mathematics had higher status than other subjects did. Encyclopaedism heavily influenced educational policies in the Central, Western and Northern Europe. How effectively the teacher teaches all students, to an optimal level of knowledge, in many subjects is the key indication of teacher quality. The teacher's authority depends on how knowledgeable he is.

In the 20th Century two ideologically radical curriculum traditions occurred. They challenged both essentialism and encyclopaedism. They were polytechnicalism and progressivism. The first has roots in socialism and communism, while the other, which originated in the United States, had philosophical starting points in pragmatist philosophy and democratic liberalism.

The main principle of polytechnicalism is that education shall provide the competencies needed by society for its efficient production of goods and services. Especially important is the practical subjects and technology. The educational system is the main means to give all people the knowledge-based expertise and the values that are required to be constructive in creating the communist society, where everybody could develop their capabilities and facilities optimally. In a society without social classes, every individual have equal access to resources and to the same curriculum.

After the Russian revolution in 1917, polytechnicalism became the curriculum basis of Soviet education policies. The teachers demanded high standards for the students, and many did very well in the humanities, sciences, technology and the fine arts. However, the school became a horrible experience for students without strong capabilities for abstract thinking. Teacher quality in this tradition has many similarities with the encyclopaedic tradition. The impressive learning achievements, especially in technology, made polytechnicalism popular in several countries. A highlight was the Sputnik-shock in 1957, when the Russians were first in space. It led to the United States making its education policies part of their defence policies, particularly after the publishing of a report called *A Nation at Risk*. What the US perceived as a risk, was that Soviet education appeared superior to the American.

Polytechnicalism met strong criticism, because of its uniform, ideological understanding. It entailed restrictions in terms of educating people able to think independently. Marx had decided finally, what was valuable knowledge. The school's mission was simply to transmit knowledge that was relevant in educating students to create the communist, ideal society.

Progressivism is also a radical and distinctly democratic curriculum tradition. Education is an important tool to change society in step with the changes in science and economics. This is the same as with polytechnicalism. In particular, two aspects of progressivism make it different not only from polytechnicalism, but also from the two older traditions, essentialism and encyclopaedism. In the first three traditions, a country's ministry of education normally determines the content of the curriculum, and teachers loyally convey the content to the students. In progressivism, especially in primary school, the contents of the subjects develop in a continuous process of problem solving. The students themselves create the content of the subject area by solving problems. The familiar slogan, *learning by doing*, illustrates the idea well.

The second difference between progressivism and the three other traditions concerns the school organization and its relation to the surrounding environment. All activities in school shall be democratic. *School democracy* is an illustrative label. Thus, the teacher role becomes fundamentally different in progressivism, when compared to the other three traditions. How well the teacher guides the student in the student's own problem solving, is a primary indicator of teacher quality.

Progressivism quickly became popular, especially in politically radical circles. Its significance on education policy making internationally was still limited. The earlier traditions continued to be cultural cornerstones in their respective parts of Europe. Outside of the United States, progressivism had influence in two regions. It had some impact on primary schools in England, and it came largely to replace encyclopaedism in Scandinavia, except Finland. In the United States and Scandinavia, progressivism also had decisive influence on both lower and upper secondary schools. Within the United States, there emerged strong critique of progressivism.

The critique came from academic circles and from parents who had high academic aspirations for their children. In terms of academic professional level of US secondary school, several researchers internationally have termed it «a disaster». The teacher's skills in guiding the students in their «discovery of new knowledge», or their «learning by discovery» determine teacher quality. Practical problem solving becomes the main issue of classroom work. Subjects and the academic aspect of schooling have less attention. This is also a clear difference to essentialism's emphasis on morality and character formation. Contrary to encyclopaedism, the traditional subjects are not important learning goals. In this tradition, there may be fatal consequences if the teacher, just acting as a guide, does not have sufficient authority to control the class. Then there may be poor learning and waste of time. Vice versa, if the teacher is knowledgeable, wise and have solid authority and respect, progressivism can give amazing results for the student. The teaching profession in the public American school has low social status. This is an effect of recruitment to teacher training of weak candidates, the quality of teacher training and the relative lack of authority that teachers have in relation to both students and parents.

These four Western curriculum traditions are still influencing politicians and parents in the areas where they have taken root, and affected particular cultures of learning. The four have their different core areas. Essentialism dominates in England. Encyclopaedism is dominant in continental Europe, as well as in Finland. Both essentialism and encyclopaedism are influential in former English colonies such as Canada, Australia and New Zealand. Russia and countries affected by the Soviet Union are in the polytechnical tradition. Progressivism dominates in the United States and Scandinavia. China's enormous growth and global strength inevitably makes Confucian curriculum tradition interesting for the rest of the world. Many assume that there is a link between China's economic growth and their home grown curriculum tradition.

The moral philosopher Confucius stands for much more than being the founder of a separate curriculum tradition. He is both creator of the

Chinese civilization and its primary maintainer. In his main work, *Analects* (Conversations), he says that the purpose of education is to create social reforms. Cultivating ideal ways of living result in good social order. Optimal development of the individual's personality contributes in similar ways, to create a harmonious society. An ideal life is to be able to learn all life in a society without class distinctions. In Confucianism, there is a deep respect for teacher authority. Accept and respect of authority involves acceptance of social hierarchies, extensive use of competition and strict examinations. In the curriculum tradition following from Confucianism, there is a general high respect for education and work effort.

Financial success in Japan, China and the four little dragons (South Korea, Taiwan, Hong Kong and Singapore), as well as their high performance in the Pisa surveys, have affected international attention to the educational ideas of Confucianism. The Confucian curriculum tradition has similarities with both essentialism and encyclopaedism. In modern China, the country's relationship with the former Soviet Union made polytechnicalism somewhat influential. There is less similarity between Confucianism and progressivism, although the Hong Kong school now seems to experience some influence from progressivism.

Initially, in this chapter, I asked, «where does school quality come from?» The answer varies in relation to the five curriculum traditions I have presented. The deviant is progressivism with its emphasis on students discovering knowledge themselves, and that the teacher primarily is a guide for the students. The significance given to education as a value in itself, and as instrument for other purposes, decide what people in different cultures mean by school quality. Simplified, two factors determine school quality in practice. The parents' expectations to the school and the teachers' perception of their role. Both factors are under control of the current society's culture (education as value and instrument), underlying curriculum tradition and educational policies inspired by economical thinking. Students themselves do not have much choice. They are educated the way parents and teachers want. The exceptions are United States and Scandinavia. There, students can determine quite a lot.

I began my wonderings about what is school quality by telling the story of a top graduate from Shenzhen secondary school. She had decided to take higher education not in China, but in Hong Kong, the former English crown colony. The interview with her in *South China Morning Post* inspired me to take a closer look at the education system and education culture of this particular city. I found that there in Hong Kong, during the last 160 years, had developed a unique education culture – a creative synthesis of different curriculum traditions.

China

3

The Hong Kong School Synthesis

The academically excellent 18-year-old graduate from Shenzhen chose to study at a university with Western characteristics in neighbouring Hong Kong, and not in China. For 12 years, she studied in basic and secondary schools with a curriculum rooted in the Confucian tradition. She had worked hard, competed, and never accepted that she could not improve her scores. Shenzhen is close to Hong Kong. She had probably visited the city several times. Hong Kong is at the same time a typical Chinese city and an international metropolis. Maybe young Liu was attracted by the city's international and more liberal lifestyle. Maybe she saw the study time in Hong Kong as a useful bridge to further studies or work in the West. In a global education policy perspective, Hong Kong is of particular interest. There are several indications that there has been going on an integration of different curriculum traditions in a unique and productive way. The Hong Kong education synthesis can prove to be particularly inspiring model for other countries with ambitions to become globally competitive, in terms of knowledge-based school quality.

Before observing Hong Kong's distinctiveness more closely, it is useful to cast a glance at the backdrop of the educational culture, where the Shenzhen student had spent her 18-years life. Commitment to learning is a key word for this culture. In East Asia, there is a tight link between school motivation and academic results documented by examination. A school is good, if it is an effective means to reach parents' aspirations of academic results for their children. Strong motivation for education is a part of the identity of people in East Asia. The parents themselves were, as students, taught to see education as an important value. This motivation legacy strongly influences expectations to their own children from an early age. Learning is crucially important. The source of the respect for education is Confucius' ideas about the necessity of learning. They have affected the identity of people in East Asia for 2500 years.

Education is both a general value in life, and, simultaneously, an important instrumental value. From early Chinese history, education was a central means of social mobility, for « climbing the social ladder». In principle, everybody in China who passed *The Imperial Examination* could become a privileged state civil servant (a mandarin). For the emperor, the primary intent was to acquire a highly educated, loyal bureaucracy, as a means to ensure power and effectively control a very large country. A key element of Confucianism is respect for authorities. Respect for the father (and his expectations) in the family, and respect for the teacher at school is a main reason why students in East Asia are performing best in the world. When those students get to elite universities, in e.g. California, they are so motivated and study so hard that that there must be specific quota to ensure room for the Americans.

Observing the East Asian countries' successful economic development (China and Japan as the world's, respectively, 2nd and 3rd economy), the rest of the world has been forced to wonder what impact the Confucian educational philosophy has in this context. Simultaneously, there has been a Western review tune that East Asian culture and education are not good at producing autonomy and creativity. For example, critics have clamed Japan's technological success was mainly due to their great skills in copying Western innovations. However, this criticism maybe somewhat rejected, when in reality observing quite a lot of creativity in Japan, China and South Korea, both in technology and in the field of culture. Still, East Asians have themselves expressed concern for the possible lack of innovation capacity. Pragmatism is also a particular characteristic of the Confucian culture area. Like the Americans, East Asians are concerned about what works well in practice. Therefore, they are mentally open to learn from where things do work. It is in this pragmatic perspective Hong Kong turn especially interesting. When on a barren island in the South China Sea, without any natural resources, there has developed a financial centre of global importance and universities in the world's top, creativity cannot have been completely absent.

When the English started colonizing the island 160 years ago, they met a population brought up and educated in a Confucian cultural tradition. They met people who were motivated for learning, diligent, used to competition and with a deep respect for authorities. Several of the colonizers were themselves educated at English elite schools like Eaton and Harrow (private basic and secondary schools in England) and Oxford and Cambridge universities. They had learned respect for authority. A humanistic education culture, where thorough insight and wisdom were important goals, had shaped their character. The English had also, however, democratic ideals, so along with economic development, they extended access to schools to the entire population of Hong Kong. Chinese language (mandarin) and culture were key elements of the curriculum. Outside of the public school, there were *The English Foundation Schools*. They were independent schools, but with public financial support. Their curriculum reflected the English essentialist tradition. Moreover, a growing number of other independent schools appeared. They represented both countries, such as *The French School* and international organizations, such as *United World College*. Already in the colonial era, Hong Kong established an education system, which included both mass education and elite education, both with clear-cut academic focus. The strong academic legacy still makes vocational education reforms difficult to achieve. Hong Kong's system with mass and elite academic education, and a struggling vocational education, is similar to present school development in Mainland China.

Even before the reunification with China in 1997, Hong Kong was an international metropolis. The city had many international companies and thus foreign families with children in school age. Therefore, there appeared many international schools. Even before the reunification, local

Hong Kong Chinese administered the education system, including the implementation of education reform policies. The Hong Kong Chinese were satisfied with their school achievements, not least the way they appeared in international comparisons. Still, the school authorities worried that their schools might be too little innovative and creative. Hong Kong has no raw materials, and is completely dependent on what the brain produces. They assumed that future survival, in the economic competition, not least with Shanghai, depends on innovative thinking. Therefore, Hong Kong's education authorities started thinking that a profound reform was necessary. They wondered if it was something in particular to retrieve from the progressivist curriculum tradition («learning by doing»). Such inspiration came, not at least, from the international financial institutions in Hong Kong, which often had American management.

The Hong Kong Educational Reform of 2004 involved an attempt to soften the position of the traditional academic subjects, and to switch teacher-centred teaching in student-centred direction. One of the reformers' main argument for softening the traditional model was that it was too academic. This was by critics claimed to have a double negative effect for the students who do not have natural prerequisites for theoretical subjects. They struggle to keep up with the rest of the class, and feel they are losers. They risk developing permanent disbelief in themselves in terms of handling education. Complementary to these sad facts at the individual level, the authorities thought it a deficiency, that the school not already at regular school age, facilitated conditions for lifelong learning. The 2004 Reform assumes that effective lifelong learning is vital for Hong Kong to maintain its economic position as a financial world centre in the future. As in the past, trade and finance will be the main commercial basis for this special Chinese province, completely without natural raw materials. Hong Kong's human resources are critical for keeping up the economy and a high standard of living.

The other main argument for reform was an assumption that the current school is not good enough at making students creative. American progressivist pedagogy, and «human resource-thinking» in the business world, which emphasize that everyone can become more creative by learning through «discovery» and problem solving has had influence, not least via the international companies in Hong Kong. In addition to effective lifelong learning, the authorities assume that teaching promoting the students' creativity is important for Hong Kong's future international competitiveness.

Apparently, it seems as that Hong Kong wants to take cautious reform steps in direction of student-centred teaching. However, it will not happen at high speed. Because, the traditional culture and traditional understanding of «what schooling is all about», is deeply rooted in the two main actors who determine what is actually happening in the classroom: Parents and teachers. Angry Letters to the Editor in the *South China Morning Post*, when the reform was launched, clearly indicated broad resistance to the progressivist leaning reform. Moreover, teachers and parents have strong, historical educational experts on their side; Confucius and Plato, the sources of Chinese and English curriculum traditions, respectively. Parents and teachers have more trust in the two ancient philosophers thinking than in our time's leading Western educational philosopher, John Dewey, the founding father of American educational progressivism. In contrast to Norway, where less than half of the population believes that education is an important value, everyone in Hong Kong seem to rate teacher-centred, academic education as a primary asset for a good and secure life.

It will be exciting to follow Hong Kong's educational system in the years ahead. On a historic foundation of solid knowledge conveyed by highly respected teachers and organized by professional school leaders - an opening up for more problem-oriented, student-centred and project-based teaching may cause a creative synthesis of curriculum traditions. Such a synthesis may result in students being particularly competent, creative and morally conscious. However, Hong Kong parents and students think otherwise. They continue to give preference to teaching based in Confucianism and English essentialism.

Parents and teachers in Hong Kong think differently from their education politicians in the issue of school reform as a means to increase school quality. Even if the reform argues well for why it is important to let Western progressivist ideas inspire change, traditional thinking remains strong. The key stakeholders of the school, parents and teachers, continue to believe, strongly, in academic subjects, strict teachers and credible school leader authority. This is the foundation of what parents and teachers perceive as school quality. There are also indications that this view is gaining more weight internationally. A growing number of countries, international organizations (e.g. enterprises), and «elite parents» believe that the East Asian school model is a substantial reason for the successful economic development in East Asia. According to international education policy trendsetters, effective education of a highly qualified labour force with built-in ability "to learn to learn" when surroundings are changing, is the number one productivity factor of the global, economic competition.

Simultaneously, the Chinese modifies its Confucian tradition. More and more Chinese people are students and tourists in the West. They bring Western progressivist ideas home. This has already happened in Hong Kong, where the ground was somewhat prepared by the English curriculum tradition. For Hong Kong, the quality measure was to try to make traditional teaching more problem-and project-based, assuming that the school would then also produce creativity and innovative thinking. Many would argue that this is going to be particularly difficult in countries such as China and Singapore, because of undemocratic political conditions. It remains to see. It is not carved in stone that the Western democratic political model is an absolute condition to get a school where creativity flourishes. In addition, the Chinese will realize that a dynamic economy is dependent on creativity. To figure out how to do this in practice, is a pragmatic challenge for the Chinese.

At the same time, the United States and Scandinavia are good examples of countries where there is put heavy emphasis preparing for creative learning in school. Simultaneously, academic knowledge teaching has become victim. The teachers have turned mainly into a facilitator's role with limited academic authority and respect. Over forty years, school quality has declined. In Norway, there is now close to panic-stricken attempts "to regain the knowledge school". The tricky question is whether regaining is possible, when the school's deep culture has turned dominantly progressivist. School development challenges in Hong Kong and Norway seem to be opposites. In Hong Kong, they have a solid knowledge basis and want to include more student centred teaching practices. In Norway, they have strong student centring, such as illustrated by the principle of «the student's responsibility for his own learning». The country is also struggling to in-service-train teachers from being mainly facilitators to become respected teachers of academic subjects, like they were forty years ago. The optimal solution is of course a synthesis of both respected teacher-centred teaching and student-centred problem solving. It is exactly in this perspective where Hong Kong turns particularly interesting. The schools' context is also of relevance for the climate of learning. The city today probably has the most active democracy debate in the whole world, because they do not think they have as much democracy as they had when the city was a British colony before 1997.

The historic English cultural and curricular influence, recent international currents with an emphasis on student centred learning and the actual social dynamics that follow from an intense struggle for more democracy — make Hong Kong schooling particularly interesting. In Hong Kong, there may appear a constructive and creative synergy effect of three different curriculum traditions, and their understandings of school quality: Confucianism, essentialism and progressivism. The very foundation is, still, the legacy of Confucius; the solid basis of knowledge that comes from years' hard work, respect for the school, the teacher, and documented by a rather strict examination. In the beginning of this chapter, I told about the Shenzhen student, Liu Yang. She was an academic elite product from Shenzhen secondary school in China. She could have marched right into an elite university in Beijing, but preferred to study at a Hong Kong university, with greater freedom of choice. She has solid academic knowledge, ambition and shows initiative. She may be an example of a «globalization's mandarin» - a future winner in the global competition for exciting jobs.

Thus, the Hong Kong synthesis of Confucianism, English essentialism and American progressivism may turn out to be an ideal type for future education policy and curriculum design. However, Confucianism is the foundation. This philosophy has inspired a culture of learning that has brought East Asia to the financial world's top. It is such culture that the rest of the world has become curious about, both in order to understand China better, and, for other countries themselves to take advantage of the old Master's thoughts about education. Therefore, the purpose of the next chapter to become better acquainted with the old master.

4

The Chinese Source of School Quality

Confucius' educational philosophy sprang out of societal problems. In his time, 2500 years ago, civil war ravaged in China. His thought was that only through education that refined man morally, could a peaceful and harmonious society develop. He himself became the great teacher and role model for teachers in East Asia ever since. One of his main theses was that everyone should accept their place in the social hierarchy, and do their duty. Confucius believed he had found the way to create the great social harmony. The students were to learn respect for others, and themselves do what they expected that others would do to them. Only when you have done your own duties, you deserve the respect of others. Everybody benefit from a harmonious society.

During my four years postgraduate study of education at the University of Oslo in the 1970s, there was hardly any mentioning of Confucius. The modules on educational philosophy and history of educational ideas primarily focused on education in Europe, followed by a strong focus on what happened in the United States in the 20th Century. It was during my studies in the discipline of history, I first became aware of Confucius, and I got a first sense of what he has meant for individuals' identity and mastery in East Asia's population over the last 2500 years. My insights, however, were diffuse in terms of whether he was a philosopher or founder of a religion. It was only during my longer research stays in East Asia in the early 2000's, I began to grasp the significance of Confucius' thinking. I discovered that he was the source of how most people perceived a meaningful life, and basic values associated with how to live justly in a harmonious society. The first and strongest signal I met about his existence was the countless Confucius temples I observed and visited. The word temple pointed in the direction that he had created a religion. The great respect people showed, when they visited the temples reinforced the sense of religion.

The first more rigorous introduction to Confucianism, I got September 28, my first autumn in China. This day my students showed me special attention, and I noticed that celebrations took place all around campus. What happened? It turned out to be Teachers' Day, and it was Confucius' birthday. The celebration occurred not only in universities, but also in all schools in the whole country. The Prime Minister's speech to all the country's teachers was the day's main spread in the leading TV channels. The experience of this celebration and obvious respect for the teaching profession made me start questioning both my colleagues and students. My students worked with masters and doctoral degrees in the field of education, and most were simultaneously in full time positions as teachers or school leaders. The Department Chair, my host, had written his doctoral thesis on The Imperial Examination in China.

In total, I got a thorough introduction to how teachers, students and parents perceived the old master. Conversations with my colleagues expanded my insights. They explained the nature of his ideas, justified why he continued to have such great importance, and not least, how he constantly seemed to influence educational theory and practice, even today. It was impossible to not notice how proud both students and professors were of this greatest of all legends in the field of Chinese education. It is an admiration and respect also observed in neighbouring countries. Confucius' philosophy is a value common denominator for people in Korea, Japan, Taiwan, Singapore, Hong Kong, Macao and China, as well as for significant proportions of the population of Vietnam, Thailand, Laos, Myanmar and Malaysia. Back in Norway, I came across the philosopher there too. The occasion was the establishment of the first Confucius Institute in Norway. I was involved in a friendly competition between the Norwegian University of Science and Technology and Bergen University College, who both wanted to host the Institute. The Chinese ministry of education, which organizes the establishing of institutes in foreign countries, requires that one or more local higher education institutions to be included in the Institute's board of directors. Bergen University College won.

Who was Confucius? He was a civil servant, philosopher and teacher, born 551 BC, in Qufu in Shandong province in East China. He died in 479 BC, 71 years old. He came from a fallen noble family, and grew up in poverty. He received a very good education and training by his mother. She died when he was 23. Confucius mourned her for three years. In his youth, he had a variety of jobs, including as a shepherd and a bookkeeper. Eventually he made a public career as minister of justice in his home state, Lu. However, he resigned quickly, after disappointment over how badly the king led the state. He then turned an itinerant teacher in surrounding states, and presented his thoughts on how a well-organized society looked like. It was a way to try to influence the political leaders of the neighbouring states. However, no one listened to him. After travelling for 13 years, he went back to his home state. The rest of his life, he concentrated on his main work, *Lynyu* (Analects in English, meaning Conversations). At the same time, he taught and talked with a group of students. As his disciples, they brought his thoughts on after his death. He died broken down and disappointed after the loss of a son and his favourite student.

Lynyu consists of twenty short chapters with short paragraphs. As the title says, the chapters render talks between the master and his disciples. Through his answers, Confucius make clear what he thinks is a good society, and how to realize it. Lynyu appeared in writing several hundreds of years after his death, and there is an infinite amount of interpretations of what the master is supposed to have said. When you read the book today, it is not difficult to see that many of the statements are ambiguous, and may give rise to quite different interpretations.

Confucius lived in the era before China unified into one kingdom under its first imperial dynasty, Qin. It was a time of social unrest and civil war. Confucius' project was to try to contribute to a better and more harmonious societal development. His main criticism was that the old customs and practices, which had previously ensured social harmony, they were no longer obeyed. In particular, he was critical of the leaders in society. When they did not set a good example, it was the beginning of destruction of social harmony. Confucius emphasized strongly that the social stratification had to be respected and maintained. Each had to accept his place and do what was right for that position, according to tradition. Confucius is therefore, seen as a strong defender of the old social order. Many find him very conservative. However, he emphasized it was the good aspects of the old order he wanted preserved. He expressed an almost revolutionary opinion, when he stressed that people should rebel against immoral leaders, who do not take care of and protect their subjects.

One of his main ideas was that only through education that refined man you can achieve a moral, peaceful, and harmonious society. Humanism is the core of Confucianism. He puts the family at the centre, and, according to most interpreters, he does not believe in gods or a life after death. His teaching is not a religion, but a moral philosophy. The society can improve, because man can learn, improve and perfect himself and in relation to others. Through self-development and self-cultivation, man can be a better member of society. Confucianism focuses on developing virtues and compliance with a code of ethics. The primary basis and function of Confucianism is a series of virtues sought by all members of society. The development of virtues has five distinctive conditions. One of the conditions, justice, is also one of the virtues. The five conditions are: 1) humanity, 2) justice, 3) rules for proper behaviour, 4) knowledge and 5) integrity. From this follows Confucianism's four core virtues: a) loyalty, b) respect for the parents (and superiors), c) self control and d) justice.

Learning and knowledge are essential prerequisites to achieve the moral virtues. Therefore, the Chinese society of all time after Confucius has a meritocratic character - the most gifted should govern. Those at the top, the leaders, should be the ones who have the most knowledge, and therefore, believed to be the morally best. Another important aspect of Confucianism is the weight placed on specific relationships between people. The relationships include five «bands»: 1. Ruler and subject, 2. Father and son, 3. Husband and wife, 4. Older and younger and 5) Friend and friend. The last relationship is equal. The first four relationships have a superior-subordinate relationship. The interpretations of how these relationships really function vary a great deal. For example, there is an intense discussion, not least among Chinese feminists, about how the relationship man-wife really function. What most interpreters emphasize is that common to all the five relationships is that they are reciprocal. Even if the starting point is that the subordinate shall respect the superior, this principle is conditional. The respect is conditional upon the superior providing well for the subordinate, including material conditions and development for the subordinate to become a good human being. If the superior does not meet this obligation, the subordinate has the right to revolt.

Confucius' starting point was precisely the criticism of incompetent leaders in both his own state and neighbouring states. They misused power over their subjects. The two most important of Confucius' followers were Xun Zi and Mencius. Both lived several hundred years after the master's death. The two continued Confucianism in fundamentally different ways. Mencius clearly continued the humanistic legacy. He emphasizes man's innate ability to do well, like an ethical intuition to develop the virtues: rén/human fellowship, yi/justice, and 🗆/rules for proper behaviour. Therefore, people would inevitably develop themselves and the community for the better. Xun Zi, on the other hand, underlined the realistic and materialistic aspects of Confucianism. He stressed that morality should be instilled in the society through traditions and in individuals through training. In retrospect, Lynyi (Analects) and the comments to it from Xun Zi and Mencius formed the key written source of Confucianism as a philosophy.

Their vastly different interpretations of the master's thoughts had great importance through the influence of another thought orientation in contemporary time - *Legalism*. This was a strictly benefit-oriented philosophy, which primarily emphasized on what to do to secure the emperor's power. The authorities used harsh measures, if necessary. The legalists were, therefore, not positive to Confucius' emphasis on the self-realization of the individual human being, but supported the weight on respect for the superior. The legalists won an important victory when China's first emperor, Qin, took power over the whole country in 223 BC. Important for the further development of Confucianism was the touch points between legalism and Xun Zi's more materialist interpretation of Confucius (as distinct from Mencius' humanistic orientation). This led to Confucianism, strongly influenced by legalism, becoming state ideology, with the main task to ensure the emperor's power. A crucial instrument for the maintenance of the state ideology, as political control instrument, was the education of key civil servants – the mandarins. The key point of this education was a particular form of examination – *The Imperial Examination*. It continued until 1905.

Mao opposed Confucianism, seeing it as a reactionary cultural heritage. However, after Deng Xiaoping's change of ideological direction in the 1980s, Confucius became increasingly accepted, and is today embraced by the Communist Party. Many believe that marxism with its distinct Western ideas did not take particular cultural root in the Chinese masses. In addition, a number of negative events associated with this ideology, not least the missteps that were committed in the Mao era, further weakened marxism's ideological position. Even the ruling Communist Party gives constantly signals that distances itself from classical marxism. Expressions like «Socialism and democracy with Chinese characteristics» are consistent rhetoric. After the weakening of marxism, many claim that there is a moral vacuum in China. Religious sects like Falungong and extreme forms of nationalism now, partly, fill this vacuum. The government fears such tendencies. They might help to undermine the ongoing positive social development of the country, which is a result of several generations' hard toil and sacrifice. As a strategic move to counter such forces, the government and the Communist Party now precisely encourage positive attention to Confucianism.

The previous president, Hu Jintao, was explicit in his encouragement to study the old master, and to follow his principles. In particular, he highlighted the goal of social harmony to create a harmonious society. In common with Confucius, the president held that China should put emphasis on honesty and unity, and see the importance of a close relationship between the people and the government. The previous prime minister, Wen Jiabao, reinforced the government's new ideological course by stressing the long lines of Chinese political philosophy, from Confucius via Sun Yat-Sen, the creator of the Republic of China in 1911, until the People's Republic in 1949. He pointed to issues like view upon man and democracy. From the old master and until this day, values such as love, humanity, communities and harmony through the acceptance of different views are valid. His thoughts are hailed as essential part of «democracy with Chinese characteristics». Moreover, the government actively uses his legacy in China's exports of Chinese language and culture. Communist China now establishes Confucius institutes all over the world.

As a teacher, Confucius was a role model. By his own conscious self-development and by the values and principles he tried to transmit to his students, and by the way he taught, he was himself an example of what he meant the students ought to see as destination for their own learning and development. The content he conveyed, and the way he did it, are two main categories in all forms of curriculum, namely *content* and *method*. From his example, 2500 years ago, Chinese educators have designed the curriculum, which I label the Confucian curriculum for social harmony. Next chapter explains.

5

Curriculum for Social Harmony

The definition of pedagogy as a subject varies a lot among different countries and cultural spheres. For me, pedagogy is knowledge about the connection between teaching's *why*, *what*, *how* and *examination*. Put otherwise, 'why' concerns justification for 'what' shall be learned (content) and 'how' is about teaching method. Examination/test is control of the student's achievement of content.

Various curriculum traditions, design practical pedagogy differently. Confucius himself did not design any practical pedagogy. That happened long time after him. During history, Chinese educators organized his thoughts into a cohesive curriculum. In order to understand Chinese curriculum in our time, it is necessary to familiarize with his moral philosophy, and see how thoughts on education are part of the philosophy as a whole. I do not command Chinese, and I found no texts in English presenting a Confucian curriculum and practical pedagogy. I decided, therefore, firstly to go directly to the source – Confucius' book, *Lynuy* (Analects) to find evidence of attention to curriculum and practical pedagogy. The book appears in many languages, and is often equipped with detailed comments on the text. Secondly, I had in-depth discussions with Chinese professors, who were specialists on education, about how they thought Confucius' ideas were influencing practical pedagogy even today.

Lynuy is the source for understanding Confucius' way of thinking in general, and, in particular, why the Chinese have such great respect for knowledge and strong motivation for learning. With China as a global superpower, *Lynuy* will increasingly be important reading also for the rest of the world, if you want to understand China better, or, if you would like to learn from Chinese educational philosophy, in order to apply useful ideas in your home country. *Lynuy* is a modest book in scope. In a translation into Norwegian, the book includes 20 short chapters with 499 paragraphs, some so brief that they just make up a line or two. If you exclude the translator's comments, the book covers barely a hundred regular book pages. Most readers will experience the book as a sympathetic and appealing account of talks between a respected and admired teacher and his mature, interested students. It is a beautiful book where the general tone is of mutual respect and care for each other. The importance of emotions comes clearly forward, not least through the weight on poetry and music. There is force in the mutual relationships between the teacher and individual students. Confucius mourned for several years when his favourite student died.

Lynuy is the Chinese's cultural Bible. During the 2500 years after the talks between the master and his students took place, Chinese interpretations of the book differ, depending on China's changing political context, such as Empire, Liberal Republic and the People's Republic. Nevertheless, in 2016, in Communist China, the old master is as present as ever. Not least has his thinking constantly modified Western educational influence when it appeared in China. The book as a whole is a content component (syllabus) of a curriculum with the purpose of creating good people in a good society. Within the book as a whole, I thought it useful to identify the paragraphs where there is explicit reference to the importance of knowledge and learning. Lynuy has a double significance for understanding the evolution of curriculum and teaching in China during history. First, the book provides *goals* and *content* of the schools' curriculum. Every child in China learn to know about Confucius' thoughts, about how to become a good person, his moral philosophy. Second, there are statements from the master, which gives signals about how to teach, about *teaching method*.

In 15 of the book's 499 paragraphs, there are specific statements indicating clear roots of what later became a Confucian curriculum tradition. In chapter II, paragraph 4, he says that when he was 15 years old, he was determined to learn. In paragraph 11, he stresses the necessity of learning about the past to understand both the present and the future. He says, "The person who learns, but does not think, is on the wrong track, and, the one who thinks, but do not learn, is in danger". These are clear messages that learning and thinking are important values. At the same time, he reminds us that not all people have equal ability to learn and to think. People who can learn and think well are attributed particularly value. This is a meritocratic view of people's ability to learn. Meritocracy means that people's talents and skills decide which power and authority they shall have. Confucius' meritocratic attitude is visible in VI. 19. He says, «The person, who is over medium, can talk about the highest. The person, who is below average, cannot talk about the highest». His view of how efforts can enhance learning in a person that is not born clever, comes forward in VII. 19, where he says, «I am not among those who are born with knowledge. I am one who loves and eagerly strive after knowledge about antiquity». This statement is one key to understand why East Asians think they will succeed in the end, if they work hard.

Confucius himself taught four specific topics: cultural heritage, behaviour, devotion and to be reliable (VII. 24). Knowledge is essential to create something - in VII. 27, he says, "Maybe there are someone without knowledge who can create something, but I am not among them". People should learn throughout their whole life, «Be firm in your faith to follow the right (moral) way, and love learning to your death» (VIII. 13). Further, he underscores the importance of learning by the following words, «Learn as if you could not reach it, as if you were afraid to lose it» (VIII. 17). He believes that it is particularly important that the rich shall learn, «When people have become rich, what should then be added? Give them learning» (XIII. 9). This means that the rich then will manage their power in relation to other people with more wisdom.

For Confucius, *teacher* is a title of honour. However, there are circumstances where something takes precedence over respect for the teacher, namely when there is a need for human compassion, «When you stand in front of the compassionate, you do not need to give precedence to the teacher» (XV. 35). One of the most quoted statements in Lynuy, is one that applies to equal right to education, «Where there is training, there are no classes» (XV. 38). This statement is ambiguous; there are many ways to interpret it. Ambiguity and multiple interpretation opportunities is something that applies to *Analects* in its entirety. Various interpreters have understood the master's words within their own particular frame of reference. This is a reminder to anyone reading a key philosophical text. You ought to be conscious of which "glasses" you apply, when you interpret the text.

In XVI. 9, he has a statement that is considered especially important to explain the meritocratic attitude among people in the countries that are affected by Confucius «Those who are born with knowledge are the top. Those who have gained knowledge through studies are the next. Then follows those who have learned with much (practical) effort. Those who have been struggling, but not learned, are the lowest». Education makes people different: "People are by nature close to each other. By training far from each other" (XVII. 2). From the outset, all people are equal. Education makes them different, for good or bad. In XVII. 3, his meritocratic attitude is reinforced, «Only the wise at the top, and the lowest, the stupid, don't change». This means that you cannot force the wisest to do any harm, and the lowest, the stupid; you cannot force to be good. A core point in Confucius' thinking, is his perception of scholarly knowledge (= «digested information») as a basic condition for reaching the six moral virtues. In XVII. 8, he says about the relationship between virtue and learning:

1. To love the compassionate, without loving learning, is leading to stupidity
2. To love knowledge, without loving learning, is leading to immorality

3. To love truth, without loving learning, is leading to crime
4. To love honesty, without loving learning, is leading to narrowness
5. To love courage, without loving learning, is leading to rebellion
6. To love firmness, without loving learning, is leading to unruliness

These theses indicate that it is not knowledge in the simple sense, as information about facts, but scholarly knowledge, that is essential to reach the virtues. Besides learning and knowledge, Confucius puts very strong emphasis on music and singing as subjects in humanistic personality development.

My discoveries of particular statements on education, in the Analects, and the book as a whole, is one part of my backdrop understanding of Confucianism, as a moral philosophy and a philosophy of education. The other part is the discussions I had with students and colleagues in China, Taiwan and Hong Kong. From these combined insights, I try to design key dimensions of the curriculum framework that has shaped understanding of what education is all about in China and the neighbouring "Confucian" countries.

Many equate Confucianism and the Chinese civilization. Confucianism has for 2500 years summarized and included in it everything that is valuable in the Chinese cultural heritage. In the course of history, Confucianism also assimilated and absorbed valuable elements from outside. For Confucius, the overall purpose of education was to create social reforms through training of individual members of society. By cultivating ideal ways of living and achieving as complete development of the individual's personality as possible – you will get the ideal social order. He believed in the importance of the individual to ensure progress and reform of society. Through his own teaching, he demonstrated his ideas in practice. The ideal life is to learn all your life in a society without social divisions.

Taking the Analects as starting point and Confucianism as perceived by Chinese students and educators today, it is possible to construct an «ideal type Confucian curriculum». In this curriculum, there are two main *goals* – individual goals and social goals. The individual goals include a subjective and an objective dimension. The subjective dimension is all about self-cultivation. Here are included, firstly, an objective of morality; respect for the traditions and to do what is right to your fellow human beings. Then, there are objectives for the intellectual and for the physical parts of education. Under the objective dimension, we first find individual objectives - to give peace to others. Second, there are social objectives, comprising two stages of societal development. At the first stage, the goal is to create "peace and quiet" at social micro level, in the closer human connections and, then, at the second stage, to create the ideal society - «the great harmony».

The content students need to learn in order to reach these goals has two main categories: the moral and the intellectual. The content of morality teaching includes love, which is the greatest of all virtues. The rules for proper behaviour is a next important content component. The rules for proper behaviour are both expressions of social regulations and expressions of personal feelings and desires. Then, the content includes respect for parents, the basic force of all virtues. The last bit of content regarding morality is to follow the golden mean, or to avoid exaggerations. The intellectual content category includes poetry, history, music and the rules for proper behaviour. We see that knowledge about proper behaviour is both a moral and an intellectually content component.

Confucius' teaching *method* we can learn about from his own practice. He seemed to have an intuitive grasp of the principles that today are fundamental for effective learning. Many Chinese teachers think that in a perspective of pedagogical practice, his teaching method is his most important legacy. They see the method's efficiency as unsurpassed. Overarching, he seems to have a democracy ideal, in the sense that teaching should work well for all.

There are four overriding principles of the teaching method: Explain practically, activity, individualization and motivation. Moreover, it is important that the teacher himself practices what he teaches – he must show love, good conduct, respect for the parents and moderation. Confucius emphasized strongly that everyone should have the opportunity to learn. In terms of students' way of working, he recommended five steps: study widely, examine exactly, think carefully, discriminate clearly, and practice seriously. Two essential overarching norms for the student was perseverance and humility. There is no shame in failing an examination, but it is a shame to give in. Confucius also emphasizes certain external conditions that the teacher should be aware of: What is going on in class should be in a harmonious relationship with authorities, family, religion, rituals, ethics and arts.

There is no doubt that Confucius' ideas and his own teaching have had a fundamental effect on Chinese civilization. His ideas and his example continue to have effect on identity formation among people in East Asia. An important educational point he was not explicit about, was evaluations and examinations, or *control of the learning results*. For him, it seemed that evaluation of the student was a natural part of the teacher's task. Through daily contact and conversation, the teacher informally knows what the students have learned. Even if he has not mentioned examination, he has expressed a thought about «lifting the talent - after having acquired results from the study that should make him a civil servant». This expression may indicate awareness about the necessity of examinations, and have contributed later to legitimate The Imperial Examination. Its purpose was to select the most learned candidates to key positions in the imperial state administration (mandarins). The earliest traces of this examination is from the West Han dynasty, 206 BC.-8 AD. It was, however, under the Sui dynasty, 605 AD that the examination became an important part of the state administration.

Confucius was clearly a humanist. Of his two, most important disciples (Mencius and Xun Zi), the first carried on the humanistic tradition. The other was more system/state-oriented, and probably he contributed most, along with the legalists, to make the Confucian curriculum and The Imperial Examination important instruments of the state administration. This examination system continued until 1905. Many hated it. Nevertheless, it was, undoubtedly, pivotal in the formation of identity not only in China, but also in Japan, Taiwan, Korea, Hong Kong and Singapore. The examination modernized over time, but its nature and the high respect for it remained. Common to the East Asian countries today is that they all rank at the top in international comparisons of education quality. Perhaps it is not coincidental that they also are among the world's strongest economies.

The examination system as an institution still has a very strong position in East Asian culture and educational tradition. Also today, *Gaokao* in June is a serious reality for Chinese students that graduate from secondary school. This is the examination day across the country. The result of this examination is crucial for further opportunities in higher education. Over thousands of years, people in the Confucian cultural area acquired an identity where education, and respect for education, is one of the most important elements in life, both regarding your self-image and for social mobility. The imperial examination has played a very special role both for the development of attitudes to education, and for how a particular element of curriculum, the examination, is a tool for political control of an empire. This qualification system is the theme of the next chapter.

6

The Imperial Examination

The Imperial Examination has long historical roots. Even before the first dynasty (Qin, from 220 BC), there were different tests for those who should work in the country's central state administration. Eventually, these tests developed into The Imperial Examination. It became an institution with crucial political and educational significance. The purpose of the examination was to make a selection of the potentially best candidates with the intent of employing them in that state apparatus at all levels. The design of the tests aimed at making optimally objective measuring devices for evaluating the candidates' level of knowledge. The testing amounted to a lengthy process of increasingly stronger screening of the candidates. Candidates, who passed, got a degree and appointment to a particular department. There was a ladder of degrees, from lower to higher, where the higher would lead to a higher position in the civil service. In 605 AD under the Sui dynasty, the examination was formally established. Towards the end of the imperial period, in the 1800's, people increasingly hated the system. In 1905, the government abolished it. However, in revised forms, its basic logic has lived on, and continues to characterize both recruitment to the public administration and educational thinking in general in East Asia.

The purpose of the examination was to find the very best qualified to govern the country, under the emperor's leadership. The tests intended to measure the candidates' level of knowledge, in two categories of content: the six arts and military skills. The arts to be tested were music, mathematics, writing, and knowledge of the rituals and ceremonies of both public and private life. The military skills included archery and cavalry (warfare on horse). The content or curriculum later expanded to include *The Five Studies*: military strategy, civil law, taxation, agriculture and geography, and, in addition, *The Confucian Classics*. The latter included, among others, The Four Books: 1) The great learning, 2) The principle of the golden mean, 3) The Analects and 4) a book by Confucius' disciple, Mencius, with anecdotes and conversations.

The actual examination consisted of a test battery, conducted at municipality, county and central levels. Quotas for admission were very small. This limited the number of candidates that got through the eye of a needle. For example, there was an annual limit of three hundred examination candidates for positions in the central administration. The candidates often took the examination a number of times before they finally could achieve a degree, and thus obtain a position. The first-stage examinations were The Child Examination, taking place annually and open to everybody from early adolescence age. The county level examination, called The City Examination, took place every three years. The central level examination, called The Conference Examination, occurred every three years in the capital. The top level was The Imperial Court Examination, held every three years, under the supervision of the emperor himself. Only one of a thousand candidates managed to reach the highest level.

The examination took place under very austere material conditions. Each student could only bring essentials like water bottle, night pot, bedding, food, inkstand, ink and brushes. Examination officials carefully checked that the students did not bring with them hidden, written materials. The student got three days and two nights to write The Eight Task - a literary composition with eight distinct paragraphs. This happened in a tiny room, with a makeshift bed, writing desk and a bench. The student had no disruptions during these three days. There was no communication with others. If a student died during the examination, the guards wrapped the body in a straw mat, and threw it over the wall surrounding the building.

The examination had enormous significance for the candidate. Everything was at stake. Parents and student had invested everything they had, in order to give their hopeful the chance to win the jackpot – permanently employed civil servant with great privileges. It was a tremendous stress. Therefore, it is no wonder that there occurred several attempts at cheating and corruption. In order to avoid "snout factor-effect" (meaning that the sensor recognized the student's handwriting), a public person copied each paper. The written assignment required that the student had one hundred percent accurate quotes from the classics in the curriculum. Only one character designed wrongly, the consequence was fatal – complete failure. No examination. Thus, students turned very inventive in finding ways to bring with them a secret copy. Sometimes they had written the texts on their underwear.

Those taken in complicity of cheating, whether it were students or examiners, could count on severe punishment. At the county level examination in Beijing in 1658, unsuccessful students rioted. They complained about corruption in connection with the examination. The penalty was harsh for those involved. Several government officials and students got death penalty. Personal property was confiscated and many sent into exile for many years. Still, the examination system worked well over many years. This was because it reflected a basic value perception in large parts of the population. Through the centuries, Chinese families, clans, communities and even counties devoted their resources to educate young promising men, with the one purpose that they should be able to successful social climbing with the help of examination.

For some of those who had invested everything to reach "the promised land", refusal became fatal. Suicide was the solution. Overall, the Confucius-inspired examination still had positive significance for China. The arrangement meant initiation of the same values for the local elites and ambitious elite candidates in the whole of China. It was only 5% of those who passed the examination, and even fewer who actually became mandarin. Nevertheless, the scheme in itself all the time entailed a hope of being the one who might finally succeeded. This maintained motivation and belief in the system. Usually, also those who failed the examination did well. They did not lose social status. It was not shameful to lose, but it was shameful not to try. Actually, «the losers» were very well educated in Confucianism. They got jobs outside the public sphere, as teachers, culture worker, managers of local projects, managers of private schools and charity work.

The Imperial Examination had great influence on the culture and society of imperial China. The scheme has responsibility for the power shifts in several of the imperial dynasties. The examination significantly influenced the social structure throughout imperial times, until 1905. The power that earlier just a few noble families around the emperor had was through the examination transferred to an educated class of people from the countryside. They became a clan of scholar bureaucrats in the state administration, with increasingly greater power.

Neighbouring countries such as Vietnam, Korea and Japan introduced a similar examination system, to get the cream of the national intellectual talent into the state administration. Also in India and the United Kingdom, the Chinese examination system had influence for recruitment to public service, by affecting similar examinations. Not least was it important for the state leadership to keep a solid grasp on this talent-elite's time, resources and ideological goals. It was triple important. They secured the emperor's power, they were kept away from business that otherwise could have threatened the imperial power and they constituted the most convincing example of how important and profitable it was to pursue literature studies and education. The examination was a continuous reminder for the whole population of how important education was.

The examination system expanded constantly. During the Song dynasty (960-1279), a particularly strong expansion took place, in order to counter the influence of a group of military aristocrats that had begun to stir. The emperor felt his power threatened. The number of examination candidates increased fivefold compared to earlier. This solidified the learned bureaucrats as a separate power class in society. The actual recruitment procedures for examination candidates were, thus, important for the balance of power in society. For example, the introduction of quotas for certain groups was particularly important for the emperor's grip on power. One concrete case was the eunuchs. They were especially loyal to the emperor. During the Ming dynasty (1368-1644), there were more than 70000 eunuchs in the emperor's service. China's most famous eunuch, Zheng He, lived at this time. He was a court-eunuch, and famous for his merits. He was navigator, discoverer, diplomat and fleet admiral. In retrospect, especially admired for his naval expedition to South-East Asia, South Asia, the Middle East and East Africa between 1405 and 1433.

In the last period of the empire, in the 1800's, the examination system was the central government's main strategy for holding on to the loyalty of the elite groups at local level. Their loyalty secured in return that the government remained integrated in a time where it appeared ever more tendencies to increase regional independence and attempts to break with the imperial power. The examination system distributed its privileges (employment in the public sector) based on quotas of the candidates at the county and municipal levels. It meant that the central state administration recruited from around the country in a quantity that roughly were in relation to the size of the population in the various counties. Exceptionally academically strong people from around the country, even those in remote areas, had a chance to succeed on the examination, and thus achieve the privileges that were associated with the position. The examination-based state administration affected simultaneously political stability and social mobility.

The class of scholars, selected by The Imperial Examination, came to dominate the social development, also in negative terms. During the last two dynasties, the Ming and Qing (1368-1911), the scholars were the cause of a rather constricted view of knowledge and learning. They were primarily humanists, and not concerned with the nature of science and technology. This could impede the economic development, in particular. They also strengthened the emperor's wilful power in a way that made China greatly delay its political modernization. This had disastrous consequences for the country in 19th and the 20th centuries. The country was about to be completely colonized by the Western powers and Japan. Although criticism of the examination system was growing stronger, it was only in 1905 that the government formally abolished the system. This is the time, when the very empire disintegrates. It is hardly a coincidence. The examinations had been important for the maintenance of the empire in China for 1300 years. At the same time, it is worth noting that, although abolishment of the old system in 1905, the following modern examination system designed to recruit government officials, in significant ways, reflected the old system.

The Imperial Examination is triple interesting as an educational phenomenon. Firstly, it has been a crucial factor in making China earlier than any other country establish a strong and effective state administration. It has been essential in order to manage such a large and complex country. Second, when the West and Japan modernized and turned militarily strong, the lack of modernization of the curriculum of The Imperial Examination became fatal. The old curriculum entailed the maintenance of a state administration that was no longer qualified to master modern challenges. This was a main cause of China's dramatic weakening in the 1800's. Third, today it looks like the Confucian examination legacy constitutes a competitive advantage educationally, for East Asia in the meeting with the West in the global knowledge market. After including Western natural sciences and technology in their curriculum, the Chinese have achieved greater mastery. Simultaneously, the heritage of The Imperial Examination with humanities' subjects have maintained their Chinese identity. Thus, today it looks as if the synthesis of classical Chinese knowledge and Western science and technology is the winning card in the global power competition.

In the next chapter, however, attention is, first, on conditions that can be attached to the negative effects of the Imperial Examination - China's international humiliation, and, then how the examination's distinctiveness also has contributed to strong identity, effective learning and the country's revival to great power.

7

China's Humiliation and Revival

To understand China's strength and national psyche today, it is necessary to take a retrospective glance. Today's China has to relate both to a glorious and tragic history. Both histories nourish the pride of the country and motivation for again making it financially and politically strong. The country's *education culture*, with historical roots in Confucianism and The Imperial Examination, is a central nerve in country's development. This chapter outlines the country's political and economic development in recent times.

The name China is in the West written in different ways, e.g. in English: *China*, or in French: *Chine*. Both pronounced with pretty much the same sound. The name has its origins in the name of the first emperor who ruled over the whole of China, Qin (221-206 BC.). The pronunciation of Qin becomes Kina, China and Chine, in respectively Norwegian, English and French. Another explanation of the meaning of the name comes from the word Cina in Sanskrit. In Chinese, however, the country's name is Zhōngguó, which means Kingdom of the Middle. Those who lived outside the realm were barbarians, non-civilized people. For thousands of years, the Chinese considered their country the centre of civilization. The system of education and examinations consolidated their identity. In the 1600's the outside (barbarian) world was of no interest for China's rulers.

The Chinese are very conscious of their history. The *Han Chinese* was, and is the completely dominant ethnic group in China. They make up

92% of the population. The rest includes 55 ethnic minorities. The first emperor, Qin, was in power for just 15 years. Then, the Han dynasty (202 BC-220 AD) took over, which gave rise to the term Han Chinese people. With two important exceptions, the Han Chinese always ruled China. The first exceptions were the Mongols, under Genghis Khan and his grandson Kublai Khan. They conquered China and became *The Yuan Dynasty*, who ruled China between 1271 and 1368. They tried to discontinue The Imperial Examination. They were not successful. *The Ming Dynasty*, who took power from 1368, further developed the examination as a tool for political integration and control. Ming lost power to another foreign ruler, *The Qing Dynasty*, in 1644. They were Manchurians, and ruled China until the fall of the empire in 1911. They first reinforced the use of The Imperial Examination, but then, in the end, had to abolish it, in 1905.

The first accounts of China in the West appear in the 1300's. Marco Polo claimed to have visited China while the Mongol Yuan dynasty ruled the country. Through the Marco Polo accounts, the West got the very first reports about the impressive level of development in China. The Yuan dynasty was the first to rule all of China from Beijing, as capital. With their conquests to the West all the way to Europe, the Yuan created the world's largest empire ever. This fact is popular in Chinese history teaching, and underscores Chinese national pride. The Han Chinese came back, when the Ming dynasty beat the Mongols in 1368. The Ming took over an empire that had already been in strong development, not least through trade, increasingly also with countries outside China. The emergence of large population centres like Beijing and Nanjing led to growth in the private industry. Especially, there were specializations in different forms of small industry based on paper, silk, cotton, porcelain and ceramics.

In the nearly three hundred years, Ming ruled China, economic and social development continued, but though with some isolationist features, which may contribute to explain the slump that hit the country in the 1800's. The Ming Period represents a high point of aversion against non-Chinese people; those outside the country's borders were uncivilized. This was also the time for the emergence of Neo-Confucianism.

It contributed to the Chinese introversion. The emergence of Neo-Confucianism started already in the late 700's. It was an attempt to create a more rational and secular form of the classic Confucianism, which had been influenced by mysticism from Daoism and Buddhism.

Nevertheless, China was not isolated in the Ming Period. Foreign trade and contact with other countries increased significantly, in particular, with Japan. Still, there were claims that the government in this time was less interested in revenue from trading, and would rather strengthen agriculture. This orientation may be because the founder of the dynasty himself was a farmer. The Ming emperors made several reforms for the population as a whole. While previous dynasties extended feudalism, Ming rulers went the opposite way. They tried to reduce the power of the feudal lords. The government confiscated land properties, divided them and rented them to small farmers. At this time, private slavery became illegal. The government significantly reduced poverty.

Like previous rulers, the Ming had a strong central government that united and controlled the huge empire. The emperor's position was growing stronger, although the central administration was still the emperor's primary instrument to keep track of a huge bureaucracy. The central administration selected through The Imperial Examination, carried on values and instrumental thinking from Confucianism. Simultaneously, the very same central administration eventually prevented the Ming ruler from being able to adapt to changes in society. This led in turn to the fall of the dynasty.

In its view of itself as the world's centre, Ming tried to expand China's interests outside its borders. This happened by requiring that neighbouring rulers were to send their ambassadors to China in order to pay a tax, that symbolized their subordination to the Chinese emperor. Indication of Ming China's growth and development is the fact that it produced 100,000 tons of iron per year. Book printing technology developed. The Imperial Palace, in Beijing's Forbidden City, reached the height of glory in this time. In the Ming-era, the development in South China speeded up.

The production of new food-crops in the sub tropical climate increased. In addition, porcelain and textile industries grew powerful.

A very sad event in this period was the worst earthquake disaster ever. Under the Shaanxi earthquake of 1556, 830.000 people died. It was in the Ming-era that the great Chinese Wall was completed. The weight put on this work and, not least, the major investments show how important this project was, to defend the empire against external enemies in the West, North and East. The two non-Chinese conqueror dynasties had both come from the North.

In 1644, the Ming still had to give in for a conqueror from the outside, the Qing dynasty in Manchuria, North of China. The capture cost China dearly. 25 million human lives were lost, and the country's economy slumped drastically. Culturally however, the Manchurians accepted Confucianism as ruling ideology. Culturally, the dynasty became Chinese, while ethnically it was Non-Han. The Qing also reinforced Chinese culture significantly by making the Kangzi Dictionary. This is the most comprehensive dictionary of Chinese characters ever made. A Qing-initiative to strengthen the country's military organization was the creation of the Eight-banner system. The structure reflected eight ethnic groups, with Han, Manchurians and Mongols as the most important ones. Eventually, Han became dominant. The Qing increased China's geographical area significantly. Xinjiang, Tibet, and Mongolia became parts of China. For today's China, these are important historical facts, when it comes to legitimacy of its control of Tibet and Xinjiang.

In 1683, a Ming-admiral, from his base on Taiwan, made a last attempt at reclaiming China for the Ming dynasty. It was unsuccessful. However, the admiral, the Han Chinese Koxinga, who led the rebellion, became a major Chinese hero, both in China and Taiwan. In the coastal city of Xiamen on the Mainland, opposite Taiwan, a huge statue of him overlooking the Taiwan Straits, remembers him. On Taiwan, there are several temples in his honour and a university has his name. Koxinga also received great honour for having thrown out the Dutch, who tried to colonize Taiwan (Formosa).

At the end of the 1700's, during the Qing dynasty, China was at the height of its power ever. The emperor reigned over more than a third of the world's population, and the country had the world's largest economy. In the 1800's, decline began. The inner development of the empire stagnated, and from the outside, Western imperialism threatened. The 19th and 20th centuries implied a series of humiliations for China. *The Kingdom of the Middle,* for many centuries the world's most powerful nation, was continually humbled, and feared at times complete colonization by foreign powers. In 1840, Great Britain militarily beat China in the first Opium War, and forced China to accept the Nanjing Agreement. The Agreement implied forced import of opium to the country, which had dramatically devastating effects for the health of the population. In addition, China had to cede Hong Kong to Great Britain. These events, however, were only the beginning of a series of humiliating deals with a number of imperialist powers. Humiliations continued also after the fall of the Qing dynasty in 1911.

The foreign policy defeats spurred a series of domestic attempts of rebellion against the government. In 1864, the government turned down the Taiping rebellion, a particularly dangerous one. The rebellion cost 20 million lives. Although the imperial power managed to knock down all rebel attempts, the material and human costs were enormous. It was, however, worse that the imperial authority was severely impaired. The government army acted poorly, and the emperor therefore attempted to get support from local military forces. However, the government lost control of them. They turned local warlords and contributed effectively to fragmenting the power of the central government, and to a comprehensive civil war.

After the military defeat to Great Britain, there appeared various movements during the second part of the 1800's, which aimed to modernize China, in order to defend the country against foreign imperialism. In particular, it was important to strengthen the military. These attempts failed due to internal contradictions. A new humiliation was waiting. In 1895, Japan beat the Chinese fleet. China had to cede Taiwan to Japan.

The defeat led to a new attempt at comprehensive reforms in the country - The Hundred Days' Reform. The Widow Empress, Cixi, effectively stopped the attempt. At the start of the 1900, the Boxer Rebellion began. It was a violent reaction against the foreign imperialists, but actually harmed Chinese Christians and missionaries. The Widow Empress supported the rebels. The reactions from the great foreign powers were fierce. A so-called relief expedition of eight nations (Great Britain, Japan, Russia, Italy, Germany, France, United States and Austria) invaded China. They pounced the Boxer rebellion, and forced the Qing government to make a series of concessions. These humiliations from outside, reinforced civil unrest across the country. In 1911, however, a big change occurred. The Xinhai revolution ended the Qing dynasty, and instituted the Republic of China. This event is the beginning of modern China. However, problems and humiliations had not ended.

A major force behind the 1911 Revolution was Doctor Sun Yat-sen. His revolutionary ideas inspired young people in the central administration, officers and students to demand the end of the empire and the establishing of a republic. The elections in 1912 made him China's first president. An important continuation from imperial times was his development of procedures for the recruitment of government officials through an institution called *The Examination Yuan*, clearly inspired by old The Imperial Examination. The new examination institution was so important that it became one of the five ministries of the new government. Confucianism and the basic ideas of The Imperial Examination thus continued in the Republic of China.

Sun quickly had to resign in favour of Yuan Shikai. He had previously been prime minister under the emperor. In the next few years, he worked hard to abolish the democratic institutions established after the revolution. Not only that. In 1915, he appointed himself Emperor of China. This initiated a political wildfire. He met fierce resistance. Faced with a likely rebellion he chose to abdicate in March 1916, and died in June the same year. Thus, there was a power vacuum. The republican government was very weak, and numerous local warlords were able to pursue their interests in a way that turned China into a prolonged civil war.

While these events were going on in China, another drama unfolded in the West - the First World War (1914-1918). Germany lost. At the peace negotiations in Versailles, the victorious powers profoundly redesigned the world map. The winners of the war took over German colonies, including those in China. The Versailles Peace Congress "gave" these former German colonies in China to Japan. The Chinese reaction was *The May 4 Movement*. It was a sharp protest against the way the great powers treated China. Especially humiliating was the transfer of former German possessions to Japan. The protest succeeded. China refused to sign the Versailles Agreement. With the help of the United States, China in 1922 got the areas back. The May 4 Movement was the start of a comprehensive cultural movement in China in the 1920s and 1930s. The movement had some clear goals, and some distinct enemies. The goals were nationalism, patriotism, progress, science, democracy and freedom. The enemies were imperialism, feudalism, local warlords, autocracy, patriarchal relationships and blind adherence to traditions. The last point affected Confucianism. These intellectuals' dilemma was their double ambition. They wanted to make China technologically and economically modern and strong, and simultaneously, safeguard a strong Chinese identity. In this dilemma lies the seed of why Confucianism has maintained and increased its importance. The intellectuals' overall goal was to strengthen China as a nation with both a strong identity and competitiveness among the world's nations.

In the 1920's, Sun Yat-sen attempted to unite the various rebel groups to create national unity. The Soviet Union, who had just succeeded with a communist revolution in Russia, supported him. He was also in alliance with a modest Chinese Communist Party. Sun died of cancer in 1925. His brother-in-law, Chiang Kai-shek, carried on Sun's mission. Chiang managed to gain control of the nationalist party, Kuomintang. Militarily, he succeeded in gaining control of South and Central China. He tried to establish tactical alliances with warlords in the North. In 1927, he found the time ripe for attempting a final settlement with them. He failed. At the same time, the communists, under Mao's leadership, managed to establish an effective guerrilla army in North-West China. Eventually, there was a hard struggle between nationalists and communists. Even if the two parties in 1937 were able to enter into a formal alliance with the common aim of throwing out the Japanese, there was still fighting all the time between them during the time Japan occupied the greater part of Eastern China (1931-1935).

In 1937, the Chinese-Japanese war formally started. It eventually, became part the Second World War. The Japanese committed widespread war crimes in China, including biological warfare. Most known is maybe the Nanjing massacre in 1937. The city was the part of China that most cruelly felt the effect of Japan's «all three policies», which meant, «Kill all, burn all, loot all». During the Nanjing massacre, the Japanese buried civilians alive. The massacre is known as the rape of Nanjing. There occurred mass murder and mass rape, and between 250 000 and 300 000 people killed.

In 1945, American atom bombs meant complete Japanese defeat in World War II. In China, the civil war between the nationalists and the communists flared up. In 1949, the communists, in practice, controlled Mainland China. Taiwan, which Japan had had to return to the nationalist government in 1945, remained under the nationalists' control. When the nationalists and Chiang Kai-shek lost the civil war on the Mainland, they fled to Taiwan. He brought with him the entire Nationalist Party's leadership, many supporters and key people from the central administration, among them his own son, Chiang Ching-kuo, who later succeeded his father as dictator president, and became a very important person for Taiwan's economic and political development in the direction of democracy. The bureaucratic top competence that Chiang Kai-shek brought with him from Beijing turned out to be very important for Taiwan's own development, especially after Chiang had to realize that there was hardly any quick return to Beijing, with the Americans' help.

An interesting point in the educational context is that the nationalist government in 1947 restored the reformed imperial examination that Sun Yat-sen had introduced immediately after he became president in 1912.

The system has since continued in Taiwan up to this day. In Taiwan, I myself learnt about how my master and doctoral students were preparing for this examination. Those who passed would receive a coveted position in the public sector.

From 1949, foreign humiliations of China were over. Since then the country has increasingly, and especially from the 1980s, been on successful march forward, with the exception of the Mao period. With Mao's victory in 1949, the Chinese again became masters of their own house. The positive psychological impact of this fact can hardly be overstated. Mao himself symbolizes the end of humiliations. His military leadership gave the Chinese back national pride and self-esteem. Economically and culturally, Mao was a disaster. He failed in his attempt to eradicate the ancient Chinese culture, with Confucianism as the core and an examination system to recruit the best to the central administration. All the time, from the fall of the empire in 1911, there had been broad agreement among key stakeholders that the country needed modernization. That was the opinion of the nationalists, the communists, and, in particular, Deng Xiaoping (1904-1997). They all favoured heavy investments in science, technology and education. At the same time, *the identity* that was rooted in Confucianism and the institutional successors of The Imperial Examination were vital to China's recovery of power, and international position in the second half of the 20th Century. It is reasonable to regard the political pragmatic, Deng, as the great political architect for both the strengthening of Chinese identity and financial successes.

While China as a nation experienced foreign imperialism, civil war and revolution, there were also impressive individuals who made great efforts to maintain national pride and educational optimism in the Confucian spirit. In the next chapters, follow stories about the efforts of some exceptional individuals. They illustrate the power of Chinese educational culture expressed as educational patriotism.

8

Rich Emigrants Building Knowledge at Home

As the preceding historical sketch shows, the 1920s was an extremely turbulent time in China. Many Chinese believed that frail higher education and research was a particularly important reason why the country was about to be eaten up by foreign imperialist powers. Therefore, many individuals felt it a patriotic duty to support projects that contributed to the knowledge-defence of the fatherland. In the course of the 1800s, and the first part of the 20th Century, many Chinese in southern China emigrated, not least, to South Asia. Many did very well financially. Singapore, which later became a successful city-state, is a lasting expression of business talent and ability to work hard among Chinese emigrants. There was a flow of funds from successful Chinese emigrants, back to the fatherland, where they had their cultural roots. Emigrants from many countries are sending money back home. That is normal, but it is unusual to earmark the money for education projects as a common good.

When I first time came to Xiamen University in 2002, and strolled around the campus, the first thing that struck me was that this was the most beautiful campus I had ever seen, Stanford and Wuhan included. On the eastern side, on the slope down towards the South China Sea and the Taiwan Straits, you can see the old, original buildings made from wood. They are revered and very well maintained, and still in use. They are all in traditional Chinese building style with the characteristic «hat» on top of the building. Westwards, you see the shiny, modern campus, with a dominant 23-story building of concrete and glass, but also this one with the «hat» on top, and surrounded by several slightly lower buildings, all very modern. In the angle between the old and the new is a huge marble covered plaza. Steps from the square leads down to a small lake, surrounded by weeping willows. Opposite the lake, there is a stage, and in the slope above, natural amphitheatre seats. A bridge leads over to a beautiful small island. There you see several statues, symbolizing the older teacher with devoted students around him. You can feel a presence of Confucius and his disciples. Later, I, myself would enjoy having discussion groups with my students on the island. Under the same first stroll on campus, I became aware of the statue of a man, neatly dressed with a hat and vest, in Western style. The statue was very centrally located, yet the person himself seemed modest. It was Tan Kah Kee, the founder of Xiamen University. He and his family emmigrated to Singapore early in the 20th Century.

Xiamen University is today among the twenty best in China. Not least, did it get a powerful boost after the central government decided that Xiamen City was supposed to be a "special economic zone". The city is one of a handful of port cities given especially favourable conditions to be spearheads in accelerating the economic development in the country as a whole, after 1987. Others are e.g. Shanghai and Shenzhen, close to Hong Kong. A funny point to ponder is that all the special economic zones have roots as seaports for the imperialist powers, when they occupied parts of the East China coast in the early 1900s. On Gualangju Island, which is located a five-minute ferry ride from Xiamen; you clearly see traces of French architecture.

The businessperson, Tan Kah Kee founded and funded not only Xiamen University, but also Jimei University, located on the other side of the bridge connecting Xiamen Island with the Mainland. Throughout China, people know about Tan and admire him for his efforts, but naturally, mostly in the province where we find the universities he established. On Xiamen Campus, there is a separate Tan Kah Kee museum.

His financial gifts to establish universities in his home country was much more than passive charity. In the end, he gave his entire fortune to the operation of the two universities. The cause of his commitment was just his concerns for how poor and weak his country was in the early 20th Century. He spent all his own finances to strengthen the homeland. He envisioned two main strategies to achieve strength for China. One was industrial development and the other was education. Education was a prerequisite for industrial development. Quality education, he believed, would save and develop China.

In the first place, neither his family nor he himself were rich. The reason he went to Singapore was that his father had a business there. His father wished his son to take over the business. In Singapore, he joined the group of Chinese people who had a common interest in supporting China. Tan's business went very well. The profits he first used to invest in schools for Chinese people in Singapore. As wealth increased, he started the transfer of substantial sums of money to his home country, to build primary and secondary schools, as well as different types of vocational schools. After having established all these schools, he saw a special challenge. There was a great need for good teachers. This was one concern that made him decide to create a university in Xiamen. When the university came into operation in 1921, it had the two subjects. It offered studies in commercial subjects, in order to stimulate business talents, and teacher training for those who would work in secondary schools.

The large statue of him that we today can watch on campus, erected long after his death, was an expression of gratitude from those who benefitted from his visions and investment in education. All investments were entirely his own funds. In contemporary exchange rate, the investment was about 125 000 US dollar. At the same time, he promised to contribute 350 000 dollars in the first four years. He was able to do this, because he succeeded very well in the rubber industry in Singapore, after the First World War. His intention was to provide major contributions in the years to come. What he did not envision was that business could be risky. He met difficulties, and was on the edge of bankruptcy. It turned difficult to continue the money transfers. Friends warned him, if he continued supporting Xiamen university, he could very well go bankrupt. He distinctly rejected all advice on being careful. Even after it was obvious that his financial situation was dangerous, he continued to give 40000 dollars to the university's operating expenses each year.

In 1930, the bankruptcy was a fact. The only solution he so to salvage his most important investment, was to give the university to the government. This he did without asking for any sort of compensation for himself. The private university became public in 1937. Until then, Tan ran the university at his own expense, at the expense of his own business. Privately, he lived a very simple and frugal life. His only passion was to invest in education in his home country. When I, today, ask students about how they consider the founder of the university, you clearly see their pride. He is still a great inspiration. The statue of him on campus and his museum will remind new generations of students about what is important to do for their country.

The story of Tan has exemplary value for what was, and is, a trend indicating how emigrated Chinese people relate to the fatherland. The rich in China, before 1949, were often people who had made a fortune out of the country. There is a number of examples of how the wealthy invested in educational offerings in the home country. Another famous figure at the same time as Tan was Hu Wenhu. He invested not in universities, but in primary and secondary schools. Also today, this tradition is alive. The most famous in later years, is Li Jiacheng, who founded Shantou University. He paid all costs to get it into operation. Then he gave it to the provincial government of Guangdong. Simultaneously, he continued to contribute to the operation of a number of schools.

As a guest researcher at Xiamen university in 2003, I got office space in the 23-storey modern building. This building, built after 2000, also is the result of gifts from Chinese expatriates. A well-known donor in the new millennium is Shao Yifu. His major project is to give money to the leading universities in China, so that they can be equipped with the most modern laboratories, student facilities and libraries. Buildings named after him are found throughout China. He has also favoured Xiamen, where he has funded an ultramodern international academic exchange centre.

Shao Yifu reminds us of the American tradition of naming buildings after those who have given great gifts. This tradition now also has come to China. Tan, however, was different, in another time. He clearly rejected that his name should give grace to auditoriums and buildings. While he still was alive, the university would build an auditorium named after him. Tan firmly rejected this proposal. After his death, many buildings have his name, among others, even five new buildings on the modern part of the Xiamen campus. Particularly in the southern provinces of China, as Guangdong, Fuijan and Zheijang, there are several examples of emigrated Chinese who have given large sums to educational purposes in their home areas. They staked their fortunes on building knowledge based power plants in their mother country. They inspired new generations to invest in learning science and technology from the West. Simultaneously, the curricula retained their weight on Chinese language, history and literature in order to strengthen Chinese attitudes. A great respect for teachers and examinations continued.

The strong educational patriotism among the emigrants that have become rich seems to be a particular Chinese phenomenon. A neighbouring country like India does not have anything similar. A main reason for the difference may lie in the political and cultural history of the two countries. India was a British colony for a great many years. Therefore, the Indians seem affected by colonialism in a different way than the Chinese. The Indian elite has largely taken over Western culture, and English is the administrative language. Emigrated, rich Indians do not send money to national projects at home, but to their families. In the 1800s and 1900s, China felt the bitter taste of invasion and attempts of colonization. Nevertheless, it remained all the time an independent country, with its own language, homogenous culture and a several thousand year's own civilization. This sense of a long history of independence, cultural distinctiveness and homogeneous culture can explain much of why emigrated Chinese people can develop such a strong patriotism, and make them so eager to see their country strengthened. Today, the Chinese government encourages clever students to study abroad, only to come home to contribute in the knowledge building.

The war against the Japanese (1937-1945) had tough consequences for Xiamen university. The fact that the university has had a tremendous growth and development, and today is one of China's best, is in some sense a result of what happened during the war. The war forced the university to leave Xiamen Island, and escape to the mountain areas in the western part of Fujian province. The university's president at that time was Bendong Said. He was a very special leader, particularly when it came to finding solutions that made the university able to survive under difficult war conditions. Said had worked as an engineer in the United States, before he returned and became a professor at Tsinghua University in Beijing, today China's leading university of science and technology. In 1937, the government ordered him to take over the leadership of Xiamen university, which had then become public. Everything happened quickly. In less than a week, he discontinued his duties at Tsinghua, and went south. The new job started at the same time as war with Japan broke out. It was a time of crisis for the country, and for the university.

The government had strongly advised him not to move the university to the South, because Japanese attacks might come just from that direction. Therefore, he moved to the mountains in the West. Some old temples served as teaching facilities. The best local hotel became residence for professors. He also found a house to serve as a canteen and some houses to become dormitories for students. A small temple served as his housing and office. Today you will hardly find any university where the whole management consists of one person. That is, nevertheless, how it was in Xiamen university's new campus in the mountains. Sa Bendong was the only one in the administration. He took care of everything; teaching, planning of construction works, employment of professors and, not least, he pushed the government to get money for investments. He worked day and night, and it eventually harmed his health. Colleagues and students saw a bowed-head president of 39 years, who got increasing problems with his walking.

Bendong was very strict with the students, both when it came to their professional work and their daily behaviour. Tough academic tests occurred all the time, as something normal. In addition, there were often knowledge competitions between universities, something very common at the time. Xiamen university always won. This was the reason why the university already in the war years, earned the honorary title «The Academic Power Station of the South». Bendong was president for seven years. In 1943, he turned seriously ill, and had to go to the United States for medical treatment. When he came back, however, the health problems continued. Nevertheless, he accepted the job as head of the State Research Institute in Beijing. He died in 1949, 47 years old.

After liberation, the university moved back to Xiamen. Wang Yanan became president. He was a famous marxist economist. As leader of the university, he had a different focus than Bendong. While Bendong had to prioritize practical survival in a difficult time, as well as strategic measures to ensure the university's position, Wang went more directly on the students' work discipline and stimulation of talents in order to achieve top quality. He appreciated especially the research-based studies. In his opinion, to raise the quality of research-based studies was the main task of a university president. He frequently conducted measures aiming to stimulate the students' independent research-orientation. Even though he was very busy, he always found time to talk with students who wanted to consult with him.

The emigrated businessperson, Tan, founded what became the success story of Xiamen university. He established it, and provided for the operation of it with his own funds until he went bankrupt. Then he succeeded in making the government willing to take over. He received no compensation. In his understanding of a meaningful life, it was reward enough to create an academic power station in his hometown on the South China coast. The university survived not only the brutal Japanese invasion war, but just used a difficult time, evacuated to the mountains, to consolidate its academic and organizational power. In recent years, the university has extra stimulus, after the Xiamen City became a special economic zone (SEZ). That has given a sudden jump in the demand for labour with higher education. More than half of the students said that they were motivated to apply for studies at Xiamen university, because the increased opportunities they expected to have in a SEZ, after finishing their education. The SEZ status has contributed strongly to a very solid economy in Xiamen. It has also made it possible for the city to provide significant financial support to the university. The university is now a joint project between the state and the municipality, due to the mutual interests in creating top academic quality in an economic zone in dramatic growth.

The educational patriotism of a diligent businessperson, Tan Kah Kee, was the start of Xiamen university's success story. Without him, Xiamen had barely been a successful SEZ today. A poor boy, a rice-cake baker, benefitted very much from the university that Mr. Tan had created. He himself became an educational entrepreneur and the founding father of higher education research in China. Next chapter is about what he told me.

9

A Rice-Cake Baker Graduating from University

My most exciting meeting with a Chinese colleague was with Professor Pan Maoyuan. When I met him, he was 85 years. When he turned 90 years in 2010, we met in Taiwan. He was then on a tour as guest lecturer on the island. He has amazing health, and the rest of his group has problems keeping pace with him, when city walking, either in Trondheim or Paris. Pan's own life reflects the most dramatic period of China's modern history. At the same time, he himself created history, as institution builder and founder of research on higher education in China. If you want to understand why the history of education, curriculum and pedagogy has a special significance in China, Pan's life story itself is the best illustration you could ever wish. When I met him during the celebration of his 95-birthday in 2015, I asked him what kept him in such a good shape, and he replied, «I have good health, because I teach».

Pan was born on August 4, 1920 in Guangdong Province in South China. His childhood was not particularly harmonious. His parents had little education and were very poor. His father barely completed primary school, the mother nothing. His older brother was very clever and academically oriented. He worked as a substitute teacher in a primary school. He was certainly an inspiring role model for his younger brother. In the course of his short life, he died 21 years old; he managed to publish a book of poetry, inspired by classical Chinese culture. Family poverty meant that Pan did not see his childhood as particularly good. However, he thinks that poverty helped him develop his ability to endurance. He was particularly keen to understand why his brother had studied so hard, while simultaneously belonging to a poor and little-educated family. The answer was the parents' attitude to education. They realized their own living situation and thought that if the children received education and cultural insights, they would understand why the family was so poor. Moreover, they hoped that education would make the children understand what they themselves could do to avoid having to survive on heavy manual labour.

Pans father supported the family by making rice-cakes, which he sold in the street. Later he opened a small shop. Pan had to do house work at an early age, and, he learned to grind rice. At the age of 95, Pan says with a wry smile, that he probably is no longer much good when it comes to work on the rice pad, but to grind rice he still can do better than most people can. The brothers Pan took obviously well care of the educational opportunity their poor parents made sure that they had. They got very good grades. Pan bluntly rejects the idea that their capability could be due to inherited genes. Both he and his brother were products of the surroundings. The reasons for good school results were firstly, that he had understood the necessity to be diligent, and, secondly, his older brother had influenced and supported him much. Even if the father was very poor, he was able to save enough to manage the school fees. His brother helped Pan with Chinese and mathematics. When Pan had finished primary school and his brother lower secondary school, their father could not support them anymore. His brother got a job as a primary school teacher, and Pan helped his father baking rice-cakes. When Pan recollects his early school days, he remembers that he had to walk to and from school each day, a distance of 2.5 kilometres. He liked to walk, also because that gave him possibility to take exciting side trips from the main road. At home, he had time to read a great deal outside the textbooks, mostly short stories. He remembers two books he read - novels about *The Three Kingdoms*, and *The Outlaws in the Wilderness*. He also got hold of some foreign books, translated into Chinese,

Even if Pan was poor, he was able to find money to buy books. Since he was at school in lunchtime, his father gave him one cent for which to buy food. He often dropped the lunch, and saved the money so that he could buy books. His daily diet could then be porridge in the morning and rice in the evening. He got stomach problems, because he was often hungry. The school was too poor to have books for lending. The City Library, however, was available free, and came to mean a tremendous value for Pan's informal learning.

The curriculum in primary school was about the same as today, Chinese language, mathematics, science, social studies, and music. Pan really liked to read outside of the curriculum. He was particularly interested in Chinese. In lower secondary school, he chose Chinese as specialization. When Pan was at the end of primary school, the lower secondary school headmaster came visiting. The purpose was to motivate the students that would soon transfer to lower secondary school. The headmaster asked each student to write a short story. At the time, Pan's brother was already a student at this lower secondary school. Pan's short story had obviously impressed the headmaster. A few days later the headmaster asked Pan's brother about what Pan was going to do after primary school. He learnt about the frail family economy, and that Pan, after primary school, was supposed to be at home and do house work. The headmaster said then that he was impressed with Pan's short story and that he thought the boy should continue his schooling. He offered to halve the tuition, which was $ 2.5 per semester. Half would then be 1.25 dollars. In addition, cost and lodging amounted to 0.25 per month. In this context, even a 2.5 dollars tuition fee, per year, would be a very heavy burden for Pan's family. Nevertheless, the father decided that Pan should continue. However, after school, he had to bake the rice-cakes.

To earn a little extra, Pan sent short stories to a newspaper and got money for them. Thus, he could afford to buy schoolbooks and stationary. At the age of 11-12, Pan submitted more short stories, but only a few reached publishing stage. Being turned down was disappointing, but, when compared to other serious incidents in life, this was easy to carry.

When Pan turned fifteen and graduated from lower secondary school, his older brother became seriously ill. Pan took care of him and looked after him until he died. Pan became very fond of the headmaster of the lower secondary school. He was caring and strict at the same time. The headmaster reminded Pan that some of the students came from rich families. For them, the school achievements did not play a big role. They could anyway enter the family business. When you are poor, as Pan was, it is different. Education was the bright future of the poor. Pan respected the headmaster a lot, but was also anxious for his criticisms. Many of the teachers were very old. They wrote with a brush, and had learned to write beautifully even while the Qing dynasty ruled the country. They based their teaching on many old books. They made Pan influenced by traditional culture and Confucian ideas.

At the age of 15, right after lower secondary school, got Pan a job as lower secondary school substitute teacher in his hometown. It was 1935 and this was the beginning of his teaching career. He was not particularly pleased with himself as a teacher, especially because he simply did not know how to teach young children. Before each lesson, he prepared meticulously, with a lot of learning materials and he made a detailed plan for the whole lesson. Nevertheless, after 15 minutes, he had done everything outlined in the plan, and he was unable to think of anything more to do. The children were noisy. When he turned to the blackboard, they threw paper planes at him. This was painful experiences for a person that had always dreamed of becoming a teacher. The problems he experienced caused him to wonder whether there exists a special method to teach young children. This was the beginning of his interest in education as a discipline in its own right. He found a book titled *Educational Overview*, written by a famous Chinese educator long time back. Pan found the book difficult, and he began to think that he probably needed to study education and pedagogy more thoroughly, if he were to learn how to achieve successful teaching. Thus, he began dreaming of a teacher training college.

A friend of his, who knew about Pan's dreams, introduced him to a newly established private teacher college. Soon after, there came a ban on private teacher colleges in China. All had to be public. Pan managed barely to get into the last class of the private school. The subjects he met were education, educational leadership, methodology and educational psychology. Pan loved these subjects. These private training colleges based on charity, had no school fees. Still, he needed some funds for living. Pan had two possible sources, continue to write short stories or to teach in a night school. He chose the latter, because it meant more money. This life lasted for two years, until 1937. Then disaster came. The Japanese invaded Shantou, the city where the school was located. The studies had to stop suddenly, and Pan fled to the interior of Guangdong Province. There he succeeded getting job as a teacher. In addition, he was involved in the work of political propaganda against the enemy. Moreover, he participated in the training of youths who would become soldiers. The training included, in particular, moral and patriotic strengthening of their character. Everything happened very quickly. It was a time of acute crisis. Eventually, he became a soldier himself, and participated in the fighting for half a year.

After active military service, Pan joined *The Association of young Comrades' Resistance against the Enemy*, affiliated to the Communist Party, and approved by the Nationalist Party (The Kuomintang). In the early stages of the war against Japan, there was cooperation between the two parties. Pan was very active in the resistance movement, first against the Japanese, and, later, when the communists and nationalists were no longer allies, he actively fought against the nationalists. As part of the propaganda work, he wrote many short stories to tell people in general about the corruption and brutality of the nationalists. Pan was a great admirer of Sun Yat-sen, who became China's first president in 1912. Even if Sun died in 1925, his thoughts continued to have great influence on patriotic young Chinese. Rooted in Sun's thoughts, it was natural that the nationalists and the communists should work together. Many with communist sympathies actually joined the Nationalist Party.

Sun's successor as leader of the Nationalist Party was Chiang Kai-shek. He opposed communist collaboration, except when it was necessary of tactical reasons, as when Japan attacked. Under Chiang Kai-shek's leadership, many young Chinese experienced that the Nationalist Party left the basic ideas of Sun Yat-sen political legacy, not least his ideas about social justice. Thus, more and more found that the Communist Party, with marxism as a guiding star was more likely to succeed in creating a more harmonious China. The fight between the two parties developed into a bloody civil war, which would last quite a long time, until 1949.

For young people in their twenties, such as Pan, life was becoming very dangerous. He was often at great risks. Particularly risky was life as underground activist in the fight against the nationalists. One day, one of his superiors, also a communist leader, advised Pan to get away, further west, for security reasons. He respected the advice, and thought simultaneously, that if he moved on, he could perhaps get a chance to continue his higher education, preferably together with some of his soldier friends, which were in a similar situation. However, in the turbulent war situation, it was not easy for them to orient themselves. Many of the universities had fled and established temporary campus further west. Pan thought of Sun Yat-sen university, but it had moved very far to the West. Another possibility could be Xiamen university, who had also moved, but not that far, just to the border area between the provinces of Jiangxi and Fujian. Pan and his friends decided to try to get there, and gamble on passing the admission tests.

From the battle area in Guangdong to Xiamen university's temporary campus, Pan and his friends went by foot for a week. Pan felt ill prepared for the tests. Many of the relevant textbooks for secondary school, he had not read. He knew very little of geometry, chemistry and biology. He knew that he was good at mathematics, foreign languages and physics. Unfortunately, the admission tests concentrated on just chemistry and biology. Pan failed. What could he do now? He could not go home. The city was under occupation.

Then there appeared a new opportunity. Just then, Fujian Province established a new teacher training college. After two years of study, one could become a teacher in the lower secondary school. The curriculum included subjects like Chinese, mathematics, physics, chemistry, history, geography, and the students could choose in which subjects they would immerse themselves. Pan selected Chinese as his specialization subject. The school was located approximately in the middle of Fujian Province. The students did not have to pay anything at all. There was no tuition fee, free board and lodging, and the students even got clothes. Pan was overjoyed. He had long dreamed of studying education and pedagogy to become a teacher. Pan's plan was to use the teacher training as a springboard, for another try at the entrance examination at Xiamen university's programme for education studies, where he had already failed once. Simultaneously with the teacher training, he read thoroughly the textbooks for upper secondary school, to be well prepared for the next entrance examination at Xiamen university. In 1941, he tried for the second time. He succeeded.

For four years, he studied the subject of education. Considering the war and the country's emergency, it was quite pleasant to be a student at the improvised campus of Xiamen university. There were no school fees, and because he came from an occupied area, not only were cost and lodging free, he also got a little pocket money. The Nationalist Party was still in power in this province. During these years, he mostly had teachers educated in the United States. The dean of the Faculty of Education had studied in the United States, and had been a student under education philosopher John Dewey. It was therefore not surprising that Dewey's educational ideas had a prominent place his teaching. Many of the professors who returned from abroad did it because it was difficult to find a job there. It was particularly difficult for those who had specialized in law or education. Those who had educated as engineers often did not come back, because they were popular in foreign job markets. The most important job opportunity for those returning home was to be a teacher in higher education. Within the field of education studies, John Dewey, was very poplar among students. However, Chinese universities at the time did not work as they did in the US. It was European university traditions, not American, that influenced Chinese higher education and, therefore, the Chinese applied rather traditional teaching methods.

When Pan was in his second year at Xiamen university, he began work as a part-time teacher in a primary and lower secondary school. During his fourth academic year, he took the job as administrative head of a local secondary school. Although, the pay was modest, Pan felt privileged compared to his fellow students. As he also taught in secondary school, he found it natural to look for the connection between practice in the classroom and the theories he learned about at the university. It was not easy to see a constructive connection. The influence of Dewey's theories from American classrooms, met with another reality - the traditional Chinese system. Certainly, some small changes were possible, but it was impossible to change the whole school as an organization in a Dewey direction. Some foreign researchers assume that higher education in China before 1949 had tuition fees. That is a misconception. Both before and after 1949, higher education was a common good, and not based on school fees. The private institutions, however, often charged fees.

At Xiamen university, Pan aimed at a bachelor's degree in field of education. The main topic was curriculum studies, where there was a number of required courses. In addition to a main topic, all those who wanted to become teachers would also take a smaller course, in the subject they wanted to teach. Those who would teach Chinese had to take courses at the Department of Chinese, and the ones that would teach English had to take courses at the Department of English, etc. Put otherwise, the academic in-depth studies took place at the disciplines' mother departments. Pan was interested in marxist economics. This interest had its background in his reading some books on marxism, before he entered the university. Some of the texts were translations from Russian into Chinese. Pan envisioned that the revolution now approaching in China, would make it necessary to study marxist economic theory. In hindsight, he did not care very much about marxism at the university. He found it misunderstood. Later, he experienced teachers who conveyed marxist economics much more exciting. However, he did not take this topic to teach it.

The special motivation to study economics was firstly, that he wanted to support the approaching revolution. Secondly, he thought economy an important foundation for studying education. He thought that an educator in practice needed financial understanding. The first economics courses he came to follow applied Western economy. It was not until he heard lectures by a famous marxist economist, Wang Yanan, that Pan got a proper grip on marxist economics. However, his favourite subject to tech was humanities. As a part-time job, he already taught Chinese, history and geography. Pan considered his understanding of society and culture influenced by quite different sources. In primary school, he had read mostly the old books, and been influenced by Confucian thoughts. In the teacher college and at the university, the curriculum concentrated on Western educational theories, especially American. In addition, finally, marxist theory definitely had affected him. When Pan is looking back on his study time, he believes what is the most important for successful studies in general, is to read literature. He has continued reading literature throughout his long life. Reading of literature is also very important to understand education and pedagogy.

After graduation, Pan got married. Actually, students did not have permission to marry at this time. It was not legal. Many of his classmates had married before they came to the university. Enforcement of the ban was rather mild. In 1946, the university moved back to Xiamen. He then saw advertised an administrative position in the university's department of teaching issues. Pan applied, and got the position. The rice-cake baker was now a university administrator. The inherited motivation to learn and strong patriotism resulted in a job that would prove to be crucial, to cultivate new talents for nation building after the civil war. Pan's administrative position was a springboard to research and to the building of a new subject discipline and a new institute.

10

A New Subject and a New Institute

Pan soon was in charge of everything that had to do with teaching, for the university as a whole. He had special responsibility for in-service training all the university's professors, so that the quality of their teaching could improve. In addition, even a professor of mathematics can benefit from knowledge about the nature of teaching adult students, even those who are highly talented and top motivated students. It was exactly from his own experiences as an administrator that Pan developed such a strong interest for research on pedagogy in higher education, regardless of subject discipline. He, himself, became a researcher, in addition to being an administrator. One can hardly work in any position in a university without noticing that for scholars, research is «the meaning of life». Pan's innermost research interest was history. However, the practical experience he gained in the university administration made his academic interest shift towards the pedagogy of higher education, as a special area within the broader research field of education and pedagogy.

In his first two decades as an employee of the university, he combined administrative work, teaching and research. To be director of the university's teaching division implies hard administrative work. This position meant that he was also the vice president of the university, and therefore responsible for the long-term strategy to improve the quality of teaching and learning. When he simultaneously had a research ambition, his working days turned quite tight. Many of his colleagues claimed that administrative work would interfere negatively with their research. Pan thought the other way around. He saw his administrative experiences as an inspiration for his research. Scarcity of time was still a real problem. His research had to take place in the evenings. Moreover, he insisted on having a teaching load. Both administrative work and teaching supplied him with important data for his research on teaching quality. Pan is in doubt whether a researcher focusing on teaching practice, only can learn from reading books and articles. For him, practical administrative work and teaching experiences were unavoidable sources of inspiration for new ideas in order to improve the organizing of quality teaching.

From his own time as a student, there were three people inspiring his work as vice president of the university a lot. The first one was Tan Kah Kee, the founder of the Xiamen university. He had inspired Pan on how he could devote himself to education as an instrument for China's development, and spare no efforts to cultivate talents and improve quality. The two other persons, who inspired his work as a university leader, were two former presidents of the university, Sa and Wang. From them he had learned how he could create an academic environment that would improve research quality of the university, which was the institution's overall goal. To reach this over all goal would both increase the university's prestige and its teaching quality.

At the same time, to do research, teach and build an academic environment for the others often felt like a heavy workload. In Chinese jargon, such a work situation is to work «with two shoulders». Many professors tried to avoid such a situation. When they get an administrative position, e.g. like vice president, they prefer to stop teaching. Pan, however, insisted on continuing to teach. Teaching gave him continuously new data, and he could test out new ideas in practice. When he analysed a theory about teaching, he always thought about whether it will be applicable in practice. In the classroom, he could find answers.

Many university teachers are reluctant to take on administrative management tasks. They fear that such work may interfere negatively with both teaching and research. In Pan's opinion, however, consequences depend on whether the administrative work has a relation to your academic subject area, or not. For example, when a professor of medicine, physics or chemistry become university president, there is not much similarity between the leadership function and the professor's subject area. The two functions will not mutually strengthen each other significantly. A completely different situation occurs when the two tasks have intellectual proximity. That is the case when the university president is a professor of e.g. political science, economics, sociology or philosophy. Pan, as an education researcher had this proximity. He tried to integrate his educational research interest with the role of vice president. However, he soon discovered that existing educational theories were not of much help in his work as a university leader. This experience gave impetus to an assumption that pedagogy in higher education needed a different theoretical foundation than pedagogy and education in general.

Ideas that came up while he was teaching strengthened this assumption. Quite a few of his students aimed at becoming teachers at the university, after graduation. Pan discovered that the educational theories he himself taught students, maybe were misleading, because they reflected a different reality than the university. For example, he had taught his students that the attention span when teaching children is quite short, usually 15 minutes, and maximum 30 minutes. A practical consequence of such a theory was the advice that learning activities should be shorter than one school hour. He then became aware that when his own pedagogy-students had teaching-practice for other students at the university, they discovered that attention span could well be 120 minutes. If his students insisted on following the theory, Pan had taught them, they would in fact make mistakes. For Pan, it was clear that there was an urgent need for new theory that could guide teaching at the university. Expertise based on theories of the nature of teaching at the university is essential for administrative key positions, and for those who teach at the bachelor's level. Pan is convinced that also administrative experiences have gold's value for researchers at the university

Those who have administrative experience are more likely to consider practical application. Those who do not have such experience will more easily resort to existing theories and use them as the basis for further development of their own ideas. In general, they are little concerned with their theories' application and feasibility in real life. However, researchers with administrative experience have their own limitations. They are not always ready to accept new ideas and may be conservative, because they tend to rely on their experiences in the day-to-day business.

Essential for a research area, is its distinctive character when it comes to the feasibility and application. For example, when a researcher with administrative experience gets responsibility for making a new product in a factory, he will take into account the product's safety, costs, investment and profits. The researcher, who does not have administrative experience in similar situations, may be less concerned with expenses and possible profits. Pan takes as example building a house. An administratively experienced engineer will think carefully about how the house will function and what the expenses will be. A researcher without administrative experiences will often be more concerned about if the house looks nice, and think less about the financial side.

Pan's experiences with the limitations of general education and pedagogy, when teaching the topic to university students, implied the beginning of a work he was going to continue for the rest of his life. This work meant developing a new subject discipline within Chinese higher education – "university pedagogy". The ambition of the new subject was to benefit all universities in China. Such an ambition he could not achieve working alone. Simultaneously to running intensely his research on the pedagogy of higher education, he saw his major concrete challenge: to establish an organization where both research and teaching in university pedagogy could take place – *a research institute* at Xiamen university. His position as vice president of the university gave him great strategic opportunities. He understood well how the university worked as a system, and how he had to move forward to establish his own institute. Most importantly, for his ambition, was the full support of the university's president.

Early 1978, the decision was made that China's first research institute for university pedagogy should be established. Pan had the opportunity of picking two teacher-trained colleagues working in the university's research department, and two retired teachers to help him build the institute. The institute should perform research and teaching. Research, Pan took care of himself, while he also guided his colleagues in their projects. In terms of teaching the new subjects to students, it was not an easy task. They had to develop a curriculum, syllabus, regulations for degrees and examinations – a complete study programme for university pedagogy. Such a programme needed approval by national authorities. Pan quickly designed a proposal and submitted it to the National Academy of Education for consideration, counting on its approval. It took three years before the approval came. However, during the three years of waiting, preparations were ongoing. In addition to the group of four people from the beginning, he hired nine young researchers. The approval from Beijing meant a kick to rapid development of the new subject and institute. The research programme already designed could go ahead. The other immediate demanding task was to write textbooks for the new subject.

During the next 5-6 years, there was a tremendous development. Pan edited a foundation textbook of university pedagogy, published in 1984. It sold for more than 50 000 copies. It was required reading in universities throughout China. A national Academy of University Pedagogy appeared in 1983. After the ministry of education had decided that university pedagogy should be a separate subject at the master and PhD levels, the recruitment of students who already had a bachelor's degree started. While Pan and his colleagues rejoiced over the recognition of the new subject in China, they were worried about how they would be able to increase the internationalization of their research

First step internationally was towards Japan. Pan established contact with several universities there, and it was established cooperation on training PhD-students. It is ongoing. Professor Altbach, head of International Higher Education Center at Boston College visited the Institute in Xiamen twice. This is an important recognition of the institute's position within the international higher education research. The institute has also developed contacts with universities in a number of countries in East and South-East Asia, by the help of East Asia Department of Unesco. In its early days, the institute did not have the capacity to be very active internationally. Resources concentrated on consolidating the home base. Later, internationalization, increasingly, has high priority. The institute's researchers participate at conferences all over the world. Moreover, they do themselves organize international conferences in Xiamen. Pan is hoping that his young colleagues will prove more and more visible internationally. He is convinced of two things: the Chinese have something to learn from the West, and the West can learn from China.

It is understandable that the old professor and founder, also is concerned about his life's work having a safe future. Then the question of his successor as director of the institute turns very important. The current director, the one I met with in 2002, Liu Haifeng, was spotted by Pan right after Liu had taken his master's degree in history. Pan noted his talents and invited him to the institute to teach, and to take some administrative responsibility. Liu undertook the tasks and began simultaneously work for a PhD. His field is higher education history. Over the years, de developed this field into a specialty within the institute's research programme. The focus of his research is The Imperial Examination and the effect it had for China's political and social development.

When the modern tower block on campus was completed, the institute got the whole of floor nine at its disposal. A few years ago, the institute moved to new locations. In 2016, the institute enjoys premises in one of the venerable, older-traditional style buildings, erected by the university's founder, Tan Kah Kee, with panoramic views of the South China Sea. In clear weather, you can see Jinmen Island, controlled by Taiwan. The 95-year-old professor is obviously delighted with most things - the institute's academic achievements, the new premises and ocean view. It took «the long march» over many years to create the institute, this «engine» for the production of new knowledge about quality of learning at the university. In 2015, there was a big party including all of China's professional environments for university pedagogy. They gathered at University of Jinan, Shandong Province (birthplace of Confucius) to celebrate the 95 years' birthday of China's currently most well known teacher, Professor Pan Maoyuan. Formally, Pan retired a long time ago, but in good Chinese tradition, a founding father never really retires. Pan goes on as Honorary Director of the institute as long as he lives. He has his office and the resources he needs for his research and teaching. There is hardly taken a single important decision at the institute, without Pan's involvement. It is impossible to imagine that something done without his approval. In Confucian tradition, there is no doubt that the old teacher is the one with most knowledge and greatest prudence.

11

The Saloon

Anyone visiting Pan's institute at Xiamen university, whether they are Chinese or foreigners, are quickly aware of *Pan's Saloon*. Many see the Saloon as the very trademark of Pan's practical educational method. However, it is not a targeted measure of learning. It is an informal social gathering, having indirectly important learning effects. If organized as a voluntary evening seminar, it is uncertain if it had been just as popular. Now, virtually all master and PhD students at the institute volunteer to spend Saturday night, visiting the old professor, to chat about events of everyday life, while enjoying snacks and soft drinks. What is the point? *Tutoring*. The Saloon is a voluntary, informal learning environment, which has tutoring effects on the participants. The learning process is personal, informal and individual. The Saloon does not appear in the institute's lecture and seminar programme. The inspiration is clearly Confucian. It is about creating a good emotional relationship between teacher and students. Such a relationship is essential to facilitate genuine learning. Before presenting the Saloon more closely, I will make a glance at the educational phenomenon of *tutoring* - for students at master and doctoral levels.

For a university teacher aiming at tutoring students at the top graduate levels in China, it is not enough to have a solid academic qualification. A PhD degree is not enough. A future tutor must pass a special evaluation and get the formal approval from an academic degree committee.

Previously, a national evaluation committee had the authority to determine which universities had sufficient qualifications for assigning doctoral degrees, and to determine who could be the tutor for a doctoral student. At that time, Pan chaired the National Committee for selecting tutors for those students researching an educational topic. Since, the number of students and needs for tutors increased so much that the ministry of education in Beijing is only considering which universities should be able to award doctoral degrees. The approval of tutors is the responsibility of a committee at county level. A main criterion when evaluating a person as tutor is his academic achievements. Nevertheless, to be a professor is not necessarily sufficient. Only a few professors in some universities are qualified to be tutors. More is required than excellent academic qualifications.

In order to cultivate an outstanding master or doctor, it is not sufficient that the tutor checks that the student acquire existing knowledge in the field and the relevant research methods. The tutor must engage himself in the student's theme, through good conversations enhance the student's self-esteem and inspire him to be academically ambitious. Pan considers «academic care» as an important responsibility for a tutor. After the tutoring conversation, the student must write an assignment reflecting the discussions with the tutor. In general, extensive assignment writing is very important for the students' academic development and efforts. Pan thinks the supreme responsibility for this part of the students' learning environment working well belongs to the president of any university. To create a dynamic academic atmosphere is the main task for the top leader. It is wrong if the president primarily use his time on building matters, equipment purchase or daily administration. As a good concrete example of such academic leadership, Pan refers to Wang Yanan who became president right after the war. He was an outstanding president. When he took over, Xiamen university primarily concentrated on teaching. Not only was Wang himself an excellent researcher of economics, he also provided inspiration and atmosphere of the university as a whole. He laid the foundation for Xiamen becoming one of the very best research universities in China.

Can Norway learn from China?

The notion of «academic care» is different in different countries. Universities in China and England, emphasize such care differently. In the latter, also some non-academic activities are important. Physical education and sports have great emphasis, and play a key role in student life. A well-known example of this is the annual rowing competition on River Thames, between the universities of Cambridge and Oxford. Such events are important as inspiration for all the students, but only those that work well with the studies get the opportunity to participate. English universities also put emphasis on other measures that can help to create a strong campus culture, which will be important for the students' social life. In China, it is different. The universities put little emphasis on creating a specific campus culture. Chinese presidents trying to implement the English style are not necessarily popular. Sports achievements have no special meaning to a university's status in China. However, there are some universities that inspired by the West, try to emphasize sports. It ends up being professional training of individuals. It has nothing to do with the student environment and campus culture.

The Chinese perceived the Olympic Games in Beijing in 2008 as an international honour. The event was important for national identity and self-respect. The news about Beijing awarded the games, was greeted with great enthusiasm by all universities. Both the event itself, and that China was the world's best nation, made the games a huge success. Many thought that this would influence the students' attitude to sport. The effects have been minimal. The Chinese study culture is different. Subjects and sports are separate activities, or specialties. Some students are primarily interested in academic activities, while other concentrates on being best in a particular sport. For the vast majority, the essential meaning of being at a *university* is academic knowledge acquisition. The students attend to, listen to, and learn as much as possible from the professors. When I was a visiting professor at Xiamen university, several students offered to be unpaid research assistants. As a research assistant for a professor, they assumed they would learn more. That was payment good enough.

Pan's Saloon is his answer to «the English Challenge» - to put more emphasis on the social and emotional dimensions of students' life. Inside Xiamen campus, there is a small "village" of residential blocks for both professors and students. For students, their standard of residential facilities differ according to the students being bachelor, master or doctoral students. Comfort will increase as the student rises through the ranks. While six bachelor students have to share one room, a doctoral student has his own. The professors often have 3-bedroom apartments. The Saloon started while Pan lived on campus. He remembers well how it all began. One Saturday, a student approached him to discuss an academic question. It gave Pan the idea. He said to all the students that if they wanted to talk to him, they could come together in his apartment on Saturday night.

This was the beginning of the Saloon as a specific tradition. Every Saturday night, the students can visit the professor to chat about various things quite informally. All the students knew that they had this opportunity to air thoughts and ideas. Pan, himself could even come up with ideas or questions for discussion. The participation was definitely voluntary. Pan had no problems in understanding that some students would prefer to use the evening to read syllabus or work on an assignment. In the Saloon, there was tea, before discussions started. Later, there were fruit and cakes. Some of the students, who came from the countryside, brought local products for everybody to taste. To drink tea, eat together and discuss was the fixed habit. The Saloon is still working well (2016).

After Pan formally retired, he moved to an apartment about a 20-minute bus ride from campus. Saturday night, the students in large numbers continue to come to him, whatever the weather. Chinese and foreign guests who visit the institute, and who really want to sense its "inner academic life", are all eager to spend Saturday night in the Saloon. The guests then can get access to the institute's «academic secrets». Among foreigners, especially the Japanese have been inspired to bring the idea home. Unfortunately, reports tell that their attempts have not succeed in creating the special atmosphere that they experienced in Xiamen.

Probably Pan's particular teacher personality is a decisive factor. It is a personality that make adult students choose to spend Saturday night to sit tight, in a not-too-large living room, and discuss with an old man.

Despite the emphasis on the Saloon not having any formal organization, some preparation procedures developed. It has become common for Pan before every Saturday night to prepare two questions for discussion. This he has done as a hedge, in case the students should not have any questions. Not always, the discussions are about serious academic questions. Sometimes it is just chat about current events in China or in the world at large. It can be an international football match, the elections in Taiwan, or an Oscar movie. After Pan moved 15 km from campus, he considered letting the Saloon continue in the institute's premises on campus. The students flatly rejected the idea. They argued that it would not be the same good atmosphere.

Saturday nights, Pans living room is quite crowded. It worries him, because sometimes it is so crowded that there has been questions whether only doctoral students should come, and not the master students. He does not think this is a good idea. Due to the crush, the students have proposed and alternation, making it possible for as many as possible to have optimal access. When it comes to bachelor students in general, Pan today is a little concerned. He sees signs that more and more students do not quite seem to understand the nature of the study. More students give the impression that they really are not sure why they are at the university, and seems less motivated than before. His institute does not have bachelor's students, only graduate students.

What inspired Pan to establish the Saloon? Mostly, it was president Wang, who made Xiamen a research university. Wang used to talk to students in the evening, casually. Some Western colleagues wonder if the Saloon is inspired by Socrates, since Socrates is known for his «midwife role» when he guided his students to answer questions through dialogue with them. Pan does not think so. On the other hand, in his own regular teaching, he uses sometimes a Socrates-style. Socrates was a wise, knowledgeable authority who could lead the students systematically in their thinking of understanding what they in the first place had not understood. In the Saloon, Pans ideal is that there should be equality of status between students and teacher. Everyone can learn from everyone. He also learns from the students.

Foreign colleagues of Pan are sometimes curious whether the Saloon idea is du to influence of Confucian pedagogy. Pan does not think so. Confucius' method of teaching was not to ask the students to acquire what he was deliberating. Those who want to get a picture of the Confucius method should go to Qufu in Shandong province. There Confucius lived for the last years of his life and that is where his grave is. There are lots of temples and statues giving impressions of how he lived. There is a scene, in one temple, in which Confucius provides teaching. He is sitting on a large rock, and the students are around him in various positions and gestures. Some seated, others leaning against trees, some resting on the knees and other standing. This is quite obviously different from the present, where students sit on a row in a classroom. In the Analects, we can learn about Confucius' teaching methods. Pan highlights how Confucius asks the questions differently, and have to admit that there might be similarities with the dialogue pedagogy of Socrates. When you observe Pan's way to teaching in its totality, it is hard not to see similarities with Confucius' humanistic tradition. His emphasis on marxist sense of reality cannot prevent observers from seeing similarity with the old philosopher's way of communicating with his students. Maybe, it is both Mao's criticism of Confucius and Pan's modesty that make Pan careful in making this comparison.

Western guests at the institute are often very surprised by the fact that Pan is willing to spend every Saturday night at the Saloon. In the West, this is perhaps the most private time of the week. In this area, China is clearly different from other countries. In the West, it is most often not other than family and close friends who are welcome home on a Saturday night. China does not have such a tradition. When it comes to student tutoring, China has long had such a system also for bachelor students. Each student has his own tutor. However, 5-6 students share one tutor.

The tutor helps not only with knowledge learning, he takes responsibility also for the social and emotional aspects of student life on campus. Once a month, the tutor invites the group of students to his home for having a meal together and talk informally. Students experience a home.

Pan has experienced spread effects of the Saloon. His former students are now professors at many universities around China. From their positions, they keep in touch with their old professor in two ways. They invite him to be a guest lecturer. That reflects the professional relation. Then, in the evening, there will be a local saloon. Pan's former students, now professors, take their own students to the saloon to meet the person who is the founding father of higher education research in China. When Pan visited Hunan province a few years ago, professors from three universities made contact with their old teacher, and wanted to introduce their students to him. Pan noted with great satisfaction that his former students obviously had created good emotional connections between themselves and their students. In the evening, it was a large saloon. There were so many people that they had to move outdoor, and gather on the lawn under a large tree. Informal chatting went on until half past eleven in the night.

Is the success of the Saturday saloon in Xiamen dependent on Pan? Maybe it is true what the Japanese colleague suggested; that the students' motivation is dependent on Pan's personality? Perhaps. We will know when he is no longer among us. I think that Pan's Saloon has taught us something very important about teacher professionalism in China, and perhaps about quality teaching in general. Three characteristics are essential for being a professional teacher. First, he must possess natural authority based in *knowledge*. Students' perception that the teacher really knows his subject, something they as students do not know, is the core of teacher professionalism. Pan meets this characteristic to excess. Actually, he himself created a new discipline. The second feature is the quality of the teacher's *communication* with the students. It helps little if the teacher knows a lot, unless the communication has such quality that the knowledge the teacher want to convey, in fact is received by the student. Those having the opportunity of observing Pan's communication, whether it is a lecture, a seminar or a group, are in no doubt that, he reaches the students. The third characteristic is *care*. The professional teacher has a way of being, both in the educational situation and outside, that makes the student feel that the teacher cares about him. In return, the student likes to meet the teacher's expectations, e.g. work conscientiously. These three criteria of teacher professionalism are valid no matter the age level in the educational system. The teacher will just adapt to differences between students, in the span between kindergarten and university. Pan's important research contributions were to create knowledge about the nature of teacher professionalism at the university and test it in his own practice.

When foreign guest researchers now are flowing to China, it is rarely because of university pedagogy. Most people who come are concerned about the economy, technology and culture in the broad sense. The direct stimulus is the country's huge growth and development over the past 35 years. As in the case of the founder of Xiamen university, or professor Pan's creation of a new discipline and a new institute, China's recent dynamic development started by a particularly patriotic and wise individual, a person who saw what China needed to ensure its place in the world - Deng Xiaoping. Like the founder of Xiamen university, the businessman Tan, Deng understood well the connection between what we all live by - economy – and what makes us qualified - education. In the next chapter, we will look for characteristics of the Deng's education policies.

12

Deng Xiaoping's Education Policies

You do not need a long time stay in China and not many conversations with students and teachers, before it becomes clear whom China's greatest heroes are in modern times. Mao and Deng. While Mao is controversial in China, and often hated in the West, opinions of Deng are completely different, despite the fact that he was in charge of the Tiananmen massacre in 1989. Western respect for Deng is due to him being the architect of China's economic success after 1980. His achievements have earned him respect among Western capitalists. While the Chinese have critical views on Mao, it seems as if admiration for Deng is unison. Still, you face Mao everywhere in China, statues around the country, the big picture of him on the Tiananmen Square, he is on lit-de-parade inside his own mausoleum, and there is a picture of him on the banknotes. Why is Mao still a great hero, in spite of the serious mistakes he made? When I ask the Chinese, they give a two-fold answer. To understand these answers, it is necessary to remember that Chinese students are learning about the country's history, and that there is still a lot of people who remembers 1949 and Mao's role in the civil war victory.

In the 1930's, China was in a miserable political state. The country had been in real danger of complete colonization by Western powers and Japan. The Chinese Empire, which had been the world's leader for thousands of years, was coarsely humiliated. At the mental level, the Chinese's national pride was deeply violated. At the physical and tangible level, China experienced forced import of opium harmful for the health, the ceding of land, war reparations and cruel violence with the killing of hundreds of thousands of innocent people. China was a developing country in terms of technology and weapons. Civil war was raging between the various local warlords. In the end, the struggle stood between the nationalists and the communists. The former had the Americans' support. The communists had some support from the Soviet Union. The fortunes of war changed constantly. The nationalists controlled urban areas, while the communists had their strength in rural areas. The communists, eventually, had to take on *The Long March* through Western China. They reorganized and came back strongly. In 1949, the communists' victory was a fact. Their leader, Mao got the main credit. His military strategic genius had given the Chinese «their face back». In the Chinese national soul, it felt good. Again, there was a leader in Beijing able to stand up to the country's external enemies.

The second answer to why Mao ever is popular also applies to military matters and the defence of the fatherland. Although the communists won the civil war on the Chinese mainland, national security was still threatened from outside. While China still was financially and technologically on its knees, it was involved in one military confrontation after the other. In the years just after 1949, China did not have nuclear weapons like the United States and the Soviet Union. The United States had just demonstrated the effectiveness of such weapons in Hiroshima and Nagasaki. In turn, China was involved in the Korean War, fighting the United States, in a border war with India, conflicts with Soviets on the Northeast borders, and the constant confrontations with the United States over Taiwan. China did very well in all the conflicts and came out of the 1950s as a power with significant international military respect. Henry Kissinger believes that this was due to Mao's brilliant military strategic abilities and psychological insight, inspired by Chinese military thinking from several thousand years back. Mao understood the psychological part of the game between the Soviet and United States better than anyone else understood, and was able to take advantage of the contradictions between the two superpowers to secure China's interests.

Mao continues to be popular because he again made the Chinese proud of being Chinese, and because he was able to protect the country's independence in a critical time. Criticisms of him relate to his domestic political missteps, an ideological naivety - the continuous revolution, probably inspired by Lenin, who died before he had passed on the cultural part of the revolution in Russia. Mao's failed domestic policy was catastrophic for China in a double sense of the word. Many lost their lives by famine and other consequences of his policies. For the nation's survival, it was worse that his naive view of economic development was on the edge to make China so weak that it could again become a prey for foreign neo-imperialists. The rescue for China was, firstly, Mao's death, and that a new political hero appeared – Deng Xiaoping. The American political philosopher, Francis Fukujama assess Deng as one of the 20th Century's greatest political geniuses.

Deng never stopped calling himself a communist. However, he realized that there was a fundamental failure of communism's (and socialisms') understanding of human psychology. A consequence of his understanding was launching the label *socialist market economy* – an impossible logic for many Westerners. Such a construction should not be possible. Nevertheless, it has proved possible in China, from Deng's time and up to now. He understood what motivates people to make efforts. Out of this understanding, he designed policies of economy and education that enable China in a near future to have the world's strongest economy. Like the country used to have for thousands of years. Another of Deng's ideological corrections painful for socialists is the recognition that some are better than others are, and that those clever ones are necessary to create a good society also for those who are not so clever. Here we see Confucian meritocracy thinking expressed in Deng's ideological adjustment. The educational policy consequence being that China needs both elite and mass education. Mass education gives all possibilities to a good life, and the opportunity to continue to improve quality of life through more learning. The especially gifted we need for innovation and wise leadership.

I have earlier told about the emigrated businessperson, Tan who in 1921 created Xiamen university with the first two study programmes being economics and education. Because, he saw the other as a prerequisite for the first. Exactly the same mind-set applies to Deng Xiaoping's education policies, and, in particular, the policies for higher education and research. Education and economy are two sides of the same coin. During the Cultural Revolution (1966-1976) practically all research work stopped, and did not start again until Mao was gone and Deng had come to power. He designed new policies in a number of areas, such as economy with market thinking, scientific research and education. While Mao had thought that China could get efficient development only through political and ideological inspiration from the masses, Deng thought, the first condition for national prosperity development was to create an economy that worked effectively. Both Mao and Deng wanted to strengthen China's international position of power. Mao relied on political awareness-raising campaigns. Deng's strategy was to get an economic development that affected the daily lives of as many people as possible.

Deng's strategy followed two tracks. One was to change the economic system from planned economy to market economy. He assumed this would stimulate people's initiative and enthusiasm, and that productivity thus would increase. The second track was to make sure access of resources that could bring Chinese universities to a higher standard. This is in stark contrast to Mao, who saw the universities as harmful. Deng believed the production of highly specialized expertise was critically necessary to accelerate the economy. He also acknowledged the need to develop a more democratic climate. It would stimulate creativity in research, which in turn would influence positively on the education of talents needed in the market economy. One of Mao's slogan was «take full advantage of the power of the masses, because it is the strongest». However, Mao did not know how to inspire the masses over time. He thought military combat the most important. However, the inspiration from combat lasted for a limited time. Deng, on the other hand, managed to inspire the people to work hard, and to be motivated for a long time.

Deng realized that science and technology were vital to national competitiveness. Therefore, he repeated the famous theses from former Prime Minister Zhou about the Four Modernizations. Modernization is going to happen in 1) industry, 2) agriculture, 3) defence and 4) science and technology. Among these four, science and technology are the keys to increased productivity. In addition, it was Deng's opinion that it was of paramount importance to take full advantage of the intellectuals in a wider meaning. This entailed greater emphasis on the universities. It is not difficult to understand that Deng experienced strong admiration among the hard working, ambitious and well-educated young Chinese people. He made them imagine a brighter future for themselves and their country. It is not surprising that he got the honorary title *The Great Designer of China's Modernization.*

Among colleagues and students I discussed with, there are also those who are critical of Deng. They believe that his ideas are too close to capitalism, the main enemy in the Mao-era. Can we accept competition and social inequality as a normal situation in a socialist society? Most people believe, however, that it does not have to be any insoluble contradiction between equality ideals and communism based on socialist market economy. Market economy is free competition based on the laws of value creation. It exists as a social reality and is superior to the labels of capitalism and socialism. Deng regarded market economy as an objective phenomenon that has its absolute existence in a universal sense. The same applies to competition among people. It is present anyway, and politics cannot remove it. The market economy logic appeared firstly in the capitalist countries. It gave many people the erroneous perception that the market economy was identical to capitalism. It was from such a line of thought that Deng argued that market economy also applies to a socialist country. It is precisely this interpretation of the classic economic and ideological concepts, and the practical consequences of this interpretation, that has made Deng one of China's two greatest heroes of our time.

Deng's political theory involves the acceptance of «someone getting rich first». One of his famous slogan is «it is an honour to be rich». Some critics have argued that this is similar to social Darwinism - «the survival of the richest in a society». Deng supporters believe that there is a distinction between a long-term goal of equality and a more short-term strategy. When Deng says that it is okay that a few get rich first, that is a short-term strategy. Since China is a big country with a lot of poverty, it is impossible that everybody can get rich at the same time. Socialism in China is still at an immature stage. Capitalist initiatives are constructive as strategic measures. This means that some get rich. It does not mean that the others remain in poverty forever. Deng elaborated that those who first become rich will lead all the others to get rich together. While his first slogan «it is an honour to be rich» sounds like capitalism, the second «that everyone should become rich together», indicates socialism.

What matters is the result. Another famous Deng-slogan is «It does not matter if the cat is black or white, as long as it catches mice». For many Chinese people this is a core point, reflecting a solid Chinese pragmatic tradition. While Deng was alive, his ambition and dream was to let some people get rich first. They would constitute the foundation for the successful development of the country as a whole. Deng's dream has become reality. His other dream - «wealth for all», many older Chinese people think will materialize in the future, although it will take time. Examples of the government's efforts to reach the other dream is the price increase of agricultural products, reduced taxes for farmers and increased social measures for the disabled. Still, the ideal socialist society is far away.

In Deng's perspective, the main difference between socialism and capitalism is that the former has a long-term goal - fair and equal treatment of people all over the world. Capitalism has no such goal. Few Chinese people mention Western democratic liberalism as a possible ideological alternative. Simultaneously, the current strategy for more welfare for all, also create inequalities. Some want to work harder and earn more than others. It is inevitable. In China's history, there have been many peasant uprisings, with demands for equal distribution of land. This is an example of equality at micro level. Such equality is not real equality. Socialism is aiming higher. There should be equal opportunities at society level. Everyone will have the resources to realize their potential. Equality in socialism means the opportunity of everyone to get rich together. This was Deng's ideological interpretation. It has very great support in China today.

Research and education as means of important reforms in society led to a new education policy, where the universities came into focus. Great emphasis was on building top-universities. A group of universities that already had high quality, and with a clear potential for further development, got extra generous funding. After the ministry of education's evaluation of all the country's universities, the 211-project materialized. The aim of the project is to develop 100 top universities in the 21st Century.

After Deng was gone, Cheng Zhili, the former minister of education, was the architect and dynamic force to create top-universities. She also was eager to invite scientists from abroad to China, and to have Chinese professors and students go overseas. Today, such internationalization measures are stronger than ever. Many university leaders and professors in large research projects take visiting professorships in other countries. The Chinese would like to learn from others, and they think others have something to learn at Chinese universities. This is in line with Deng's visions. He was concerned that the pace of reform in higher education should increase. On two special occasions, he gave expression of this vision.

The first time was in 1983, when he visited the Eastern Zhejiang University. He learnt that the university actually had capacity to accept more students. This information made him think that probably the situation was similar at other universities – resources not fully utilized. For a long time, the universities "protected" themselves against too many students. Many professors felt that the quality was better with fewer students. Deng did not share this opinion, and opened access for many more students. The second time he expressed his higher education vision was when he visited southern China in 1992. Here he once more stated that the faster development of higher education was important for faster economic development. His visions resulted in an immediate comprehensive reform of higher education. It came to expression in an increase of student enrolment of 20% in 1992 and 1993. Deng had used his power and authority to take a great "academic leap forward" for the country. This is one particularly important reason for the fierce economic success in the years that followed.

Deng's higher education policy testament comprises three points: 1) establishing of top-universities, to provide more talents that can develop the economy, 2) internationalization, by encouraging more Chinese students to study abroad and invite foreign talents to China, and 3) increase the number of students to the universities. In terms of the last point, he stressed that absolutely everyone, regardless of family background, would become university students *if they had good results from secondary school.* Deng died in 1997. His education policies continue following a two-part strategic goal: Elite and mass education at the same time. This policy has the unmistakable Confucian meritocratic stamp. For a Scandinavian observer there remains a query: *What happened to vocational education?* The low social status for vocational education in China is a policy challenge. Still, the core of China's education policies, as an instrument of national economic development, is "the knowledge power stations" – the research universities. The academic quality of professors and students is decisive for creating good results. However, there is another factor essential for quality research and teaching to happen – *university leadership.* Such acknowledgment was my motivation for looking into whether there may be a distinctive character of university leadership, in countries with Confucian culture. That is the topic of next chapter.

13

University Leadership with Confucian Features

One of the starting points for this book was the importance of effective knowledge acquisition for countries to survive successfully in the global economic competition. Knowledge-based competence means strength for both the individual, the company and the country. The primary source of a country's production of knowledge is its research universities. With the global market economy as frame factor, there will be international competition between the universities. The best universities attract the best students, because students are counting on examinations from such a university will make them competitive for a job in the most attractive companies. In the introduction of this book, I mentioned how the sociologist Manuel Castells points out the importance of universities in the information technology age, "When knowledge is the electricity in the new international information economy, then the universities are the power stations that the economy is depending on". Leadership is the crucial factor for universities to be competitive "power stations". The quality of the leadership is essential for the performance of any organization that is located in a competitive market situation. Universities are no exception.

Over the last ten years, a dynamic and competitive economy is developing in the "Confucian" countries in general and China in particular. What is the role of the universities in this development? Moreover, if the universities are important, is there a distinctive character of their leadership that makes them particularly effective in the production of research and education? Is it significant for universities' efficiency that they find themselves in a culture where education, education policies, curricula and classroom practice for more than 2,000 years have been marked by the ideas of Confucius? More specifically, is it possible that Confucianism has contributed to a particular leadership style. If yes, is it likely that this style makes these universities more effective than those led with a Western style? Such queries resulted in a research project with the title "Change Leadership in Universities of Confucian Countries". Taiwan's Research Council found the project interesting, and provided generous funding for a two years' research professorship, to follow up my curiosity.

Higher education policies and universities in Japan, Taiwan and Hong Kong were the survey areas. I wanted to compare university leadership in these three geographical areas with international trends regarding changes in universities' organization. Contrary to my assumption that leadership is crucial in order to change a university's organization, I added an assumption that exactly because of Confucian culture's deep respect for university professors it might be difficult for leaders to make the professors accept organizational changes. The professors could prove to be a conservative force that opposed the changes. From my pre-understanding, before I did the concrete survey, I saw three dimensions of Confucian culture that could imply university leaders in East Asia being in a particularly favourable situation, to reach good achievements.

Firstly, in this part of the world there is a widespread, basic *respect for education* as a specific value. This implies a strong motivation among people in general to invest money and time in education. University leaders in East Asia are likely to have students who are motivated to greater effort than what is the case in other countries. Some facts for the lower secondary school, that supports such an assumption, is the Pisa-results for 15-year-olds in Taiwan, Japan, Hong Kong and Singapore. They are all in the world's top. China as a country is not part of the study, but when Shanghai (25 million people, equivalent to Scandinavia) participated in later years, the city's 15-year-olds came top in the world.

Secondly, *competition* is something natural. Accept of competition is a distinct feature of the tradition of the Imperial Examination. Competition is an important aspect of life under globalization. Hence, there is reason to think that students in East Asia see competition as a natural challenge. This may imply an advantage for university leaders in the sense that they have students showing great effort, and thus, contribute more to their universities' competitiveness, than is the case in other cultures.

Despite a rather dynamic democracy development in most of these countries, there is, as a third characteristic, a widespread *acceptance of hierarchy*. This is also a distinct feature of Confucianism, and it continues to be a cultural and mental reality in these countries. In addition to their own strong instrumental motivation for education, students have a general attitude that make them very set on doing what the professors expect of them. East Asian students' exceptionally strong study motivation is confirmed when they get the opportunity to study at universities in the West. Their work efforts are remarkable. Reports from Western visiting professors in East Asia confirm this impression. They find these students more motivated than their counterparts in the West are. Their respect for the professors is part of a general respect for authority figures, and the acceptance of hierarchy. Such respect may also apply to the relationship between the staff of the university and the leadership. However, there are also signs that the leadership in the Confucian culture comes to expression in a more indirect form than in the West.

In the West, particularly in Continental Europe and Scandinavia, university democracy and academic freedom for professors are core values. The professors have the key power of electing one of their peers as president. The president mainly has symbolic authority. This is now about to change in several countries in the West, due to external pressures for a more achievement-oriented leadership. The leadership must have real management power. Such a change is not popular among the professors. They fear authoritarian "business management" (New Public Management), less democracy and less individual academic freedom. In contrast to this western situation, you find the Confucian acceptance of hierarchy in East Asia. This cultural heritage may lead to the university becoming more effective as an organization, at least when it comes to learning outcomes. When it comes to research, the picture is more blurred. The traditional acceptance of hierarchy and orders from above may be able to increase the leadership's ability to implement changes that make the universities of the East ever stronger in the years ahead. Such increased regional knowledge strength is part of the analysis of the sociologist Manuel Castells, when he holds that the future global political and economic centre will move from the North-Atlantic region to the East Asian Pacific coast.

Confucianism is an important source of cultural sophistication, where intellectual and moral virtues combine. Humanism is a central dimension in this combination. Such understanding, applied concretely in an organization, means that Confucianism, thus may have a special effect when it comes to communication between leadership and employees. Interpersonal relationships are long term and mutually binding. Good communication is more important than the direct struggle for goal achievement. Related to leadership, it means that it is important for the leader to maintain good relations with the staff. Ideally, there is a sense of family, where both the leader and employees share joys and sorrows. Such an environment creates security and predictability, based on mutual trust. A relational-based leadership achieves the necessary authority, without being authoritarian. Authoritarianism, the vast majority will see as unacceptable. In the West, however, these concepts mix in a confused way – authority seen as synonymous with authoritarianism.

Summarized, Confucian based communication will be more process-oriented than in the West, where there is a more direct focus on the results. However, it does not look like there is a lack of results in "Confucian countries". They deliver financial results in the world's top. There is a humanist element to take into consideration. Welfare of a country and its people is not only dependent on economical success. Cultural values are essential in order to make life meaningful. If life just revolves around economy, people will end up in Max Weber's "Iron Cage". Essential meaning of life is lost; left is just meaninglessness. Again, fairly obviously, without a solid economic foundation, it is difficult or impossible to maintain e.g. a well functioning university where academic freedom can unfold.

To ensure the country a strong economy appears to have been the main target of the East Asian countries after World War II. Taiwan is a particularly impressive example. Before Japan conquered the island in 1895, it was, mildly expressed, underdeveloped. For 50 years, until 1945, it was a Japanese colony. Following, the island experienced a rather rough dictatorship for almost 40 years. Then, towards the end of the last century, to emerge as the Taiwan Miracle, when it came to economic, social and democratic development. I assume that Confucian culture is a significant part of the explanation.

In the survey of how university leaders in Japan, Taiwan and Hong Kong understood the notion of "change leadership", leaders' assessed six dimensions of change: 1) leadership, 2) research and teaching, 3) Information and communication technology, 4) staff policies, 5) funding and market relationships, and 6) internationalization. The latter concerned the importance of student exchange and employment of foreign professors. The findings mainly confirmed assumptions about the occurrence of the three Confucian values: strong effort to achieve results, respect for education and acceptance of social hierarchy.

There were, however, interesting differences between the three geographical areas in terms of how the Confucian values manifested themselves on two of the six dimensions. When it comes to establishing a university leadership, both Japan and Taiwan still apply a rather complex election system, while Hong Kong appoints the leaders. The university leaders of Japan and Taiwan also have less power than in Hong Kong. The second dimension implied distinct differences concerning internationalization. The three countries take different positions on a scale from slow to dynamic. Japan is implementing internationalization with gritted teeth. All the rhetoric about the importance of internationalization is in place. When it comes to practical implementation, there seems, however, to exist powerful forces trying "to protect" the universities against internationalization. For example, they have a requirement that foreign students must command Japanese to be accepted. Very few study programmes do not use Japanese as language of instruction.

Taiwan is more dynamic. This may be because a large number of professors have studied in the West, and speak good English. At the same time as internationalization is an overall strategic objective for Taiwanese universities, relevant practice is limited. Although the professors command English, and the students know English already from primary school, virtually teaching of all study programmes takes place in Chinese. Taking into account the very significant investments for good English training in primary and secondary schools, it is striking how frail language skills are among bachelor students. "Protection against internationalization" in Taiwan is more indirect than in Japan. In sharp contrast to Japan and Taiwan, Hong Kong appears to be very dynamic. At several universities, English is the primary teaching language, and students master the language very well. There are extensive student exchange with other countries, and the proportion of foreign professors is high.

Although the academic motivation is high in all three areas, it unfolds differently in practice. Both Japan and Taiwan have hard-working associate professors, eager to advance up to the position of full professor. At the same time, it does not seem like their efforts will contribute to higher achievements for the university as a whole. The university leadership seems neither strong nor motivated to lead the academic staff to higher achievements. This may be due to both overall education policies in Japan and Taiwan, and influence from the West-European university tradition. Hong Kong is the opposite. The motivation is high and results are excellent. Another possible explanation for the difference could be that Japan and Taiwan eventually is less "hungry" to perform, than Hong Kong. The two have for quite a long time enjoyed democracy and a generous welfare state. A further explanation is that Hong Kong is in complete lack of natural raw materials, and completely dependent on knowledge-based skills, to maintain welfare. It may also be that the struggle to achieve more democracy in Hong Kong contributes to more dynamic university development.

Confucianism's importance for "change leadership" is diffuse. There is no doubt that it has a great effect for motivation to take education, to work hard and to respect the superior. When it comes to changes of the university as an organization, development depends primarily on the educational policies and which restricting frames the university must deal with. These frames will vary between the two democracies Japan and Taiwan on the one hand and Hong Kong without democracy on the other. A glance towards China shows a particular frame factor for the university, absent in Japan, Taiwan and Hong Kong. At every university, at each level of the organization (department, faculty and central), there is, next to the academic leader, a representative of the Communist Party. He has the final say in important decisions, and is the one who makes sure that what happens at the university complies with national education policies.

Although Confucianism's importance for organizational change is diffuse, there is research confirming the existence of a Confucian dimension of university leadership in China. The study concerned the faculty level, that is, deans as leaders. Findings were six factors characteristic of what Chinese deans emphasize: 1) morality, 2) academic strength, 3) care, 4) communication, 5) justice and 6) the relationship between the leader and the led. The future will be exciting in terms of observing university development in "Confucian countries". Because of different ideological contexts, there may be both similarities between them and they may evolve differently over time.

In the next chapter, I will look more closely at one specific "Confucian country". Taiwan. Why is the island an economic and political miracle?

14

The Taiwan Miracle

When you live in Xiamen, you can actually see the "Other China", calling itself the Republic of China (ROC). Mainland Chinese call it the Taiwan Province of the People's Republic of China. It consists primarily of the island of Taiwan, but also of some smaller islands in the straits between the Mainland and Taiwan, some of them almost touching the Mainland's shores. One of them is Jinmen, just two km from Xiamen. Taiwan Island is located 180 kilometres from the Mainland. Friday nights, crowds of Taiwanese business people, working in the Mainland, are flowing down to Xiamen Port, to take the ferry over to Jinmen. From there they fly to Taiwan. There are very many Taiwanese working in China and a Taiwanese company is the largest privately owned in China. The economic relations between the two Chinas have become ever stronger. Living in Xiamen and actually seeing Taiwan-controlled Jinmen, at the same time as you have constant reports in the media about the strained relationship between Mainland China and "The Renegade Province", makes it impossible not to be curious about this "Other China".

Within education as an academic research field, there is a specialty called "comparative education". Its purpose is to compare education in different countries. When it originated, it meant, "to travel to other countries in order to learn about their education systems". Such interest for making comparisons brought me to Xiamen university, in China. It would also bring me to Taiwan. At an international research conference in

Can Norway learn from China?

Xiamen in 2004, a colleague from Taipei, Taiwan's capital, invited me to give lectures at several universities in the central part of the island.

Xiamen is typical of modern China, with vibrant growth, skyscrapers are shooting up over night, and before you turn around, a new four-lane highway is crossing the city. Taiwan seems different. Even if the cities in Taiwan also have a modern touch, the whole atmosphere feels quieter than on the Mainland. That also applies to people. It seems like they have more time and they are very polite and helpful. That is not always the case on the Mainland. Culturally, Taiwan is "more Chinese" than the Mainland. In terms of language, the Taiwanese have retained the old "classic and clean" design of characters, while the Mainland has simplified them, partly, to make it easier for foreigners to learn the language.

Before the island in 1895 became a Japanese colony, the population size was modest. Before the 16th Century, the population consisted of indigenous tribes, who originally came from the area between the Philippines and Indonesia. There are currently 13 different tribes, each with its own language, incomprehensible to the other tribes. They constitute today half a million of Taiwan's total barely 24 million inhabitants. In the 1700s, there was a significant migration from southern China to Taiwan. However, prior to 1900, the emperors in Beijing were not particularly concerned with neither Taiwan nor the people there. Widow Empress Cixi seemed to discover Taiwan only when the Japanese took over the island as part of the war settlement, after a lost conflict between China and Japan in 1895.

Japan made development speed up in Taiwan. The colonial power initiated the development of infrastructure such as railways and roads and established comprehensive development of the business world. Rice and sugar were two important raw materials. They established schools all over the island. Everyone had to learn Japanese. Even today, you meet old people who can speak Japanese. In the final stages of World War II, American bombing destroyed much of the island's infrastructure. The Japanese, however, had created a structural basis that made it relatively easy to rebuild the island after the war. In 1945, after Japanese defeat in the war, Taiwan reversed to China. Actually, it hardly came back to China. Four years later, in 1949, it was also the end for rule by the nationalist party, Kuomintang, on the Chinese mainland. The communists, under Mao's leadership, won the civil war, and the nationalists under the leadership of Chiang Kai-shek fled to Taiwan. Taipei became the capital of Taiwan, officially termed the Republic of China (ROC). Chiang thought that his stay on the outlying Taiwan would be short-lived. With assumed American help, he considered a quick return to Beijing.

As part of the preparations for retaking the Mainland, he continued the modernization work on Taiwan, started by the Japanese. He received extensive aid from the Americans both to enhance economic development and military build-up. The Americans were terrified of prevalence of communism and considered Taiwan as a bulwark against communist expansion in East and South Asia. This was the kick-start of the Taiwan Miracle. Economically and politically, the island developed into one of the world's strongest economies, with welfare state and democracy. How was it possible? There are probably three main reasons. Two are already mentioned, the Japan-led development of the island through 50 colonial years, and the Americans' aid from 1949. The third is leadership skills of the very best brand.

When Chiang fled from the Mainland in 1949, he brought with him two million Chinese. Most of them were soldiers. More important for understanding the successful development of the island is that he brought with him the Central Administration from Beijing. It was the bureaucrat elite, trained and cultivated in line with the spirit of the Imperial Examination. These people were descendants of the world's most effective state administration through thousands of years, according to political philosopher Francis Fukujama. This is the third main reason for the Taiwan Miracle. While critics label Chiang himself as mediocre, and maybe even less than that, there are two others, in his immediate family that was anything but mediocre. The first was his incredibly impressive last wife, Soong May-ling. Educated in the United States she was a cunning linguist and eloquent speaker. Towards the end of World War II, when Nationalist China was still fighting Japan, she managed to get the Americans to give China extensive military support. She completed a tour in the United States with a fiery speech in the United States' Congress, to a standing ovation. China got the support. On pictures from meetings between heads of state during World War II, where Chiang Kai-shek is participating along with Roosevelt, Churchill and other state leaders, there is only one woman present. Soong May-ling. She attended as an interpreter, because Chiang could not speak English. In post-war Taiwan, she was an important adviser to her dictator husband. After his death, she moved to the United States, and died there in 2003, 105 years old.

The other key person was Chiang's son, Chiang Ching-kuo. After his father's death, he took over as dictator president. He became chief architect for both the development of Taiwan's business world and for preparations for democracy. Two aspects of his background are especially relevant. Firstly, as a young boy he got a solid, traditional education, with an emphasis on the Confucian classics. Secondly, he had several years of study in Moscow, and was acquainted with both the Russian and Chinese communists, among others, Deng Xiaoping. When he came back during the Civil War, he was in political opposition to his father. However, because of loyalty to his father and the tide of war, he finally chose to follow his father to Taiwan, and went actively into efforts to develop the island. Both from communism and from Sun Yat-sen, the Republic of China's first president, Chiang Ching-kuo was greatly inspired to create social justice. Together with the efforts from stepmother Soong May-ling, American aid and the Japanese preparations during colonial times, he stands as one of the main architects behind the Taiwan Miracle.

During the past ten years, Taiwan several times ranked as the world's tenth strongest economy. In particular, its computer industry is at the world's top. This industry started from the idea of the "Silicon Shield Project". As part of Taiwan's attempts at creating a "Knowledge Defence", the government sent a small group of Taiwanese students to the United States to study the production of computer screens. Silicone is an important raw material in such production. Back in Taiwan, these students became pioneers of the computer industry, a dominant part of the island's "Knowledge Economy Defence", hence the nickname of "Silicone Shield", a shield against not least the Mainland. In parallel with the successful economic development, the Island has gone from many decades of dictatorship and martial laws to democracy, strong economy and social cohesion. There has been a massive investment in education for all, with startling high quality. In Pisa evaluations, Taiwan is always among the best. The country has about 150 universities and colleges. There is an ongoing debate about whether there are too many, and if their quality can increase by mergers. There is also a concern about "over qualification" or too much "academising" of education. Simultaneously, the educational authorities are aware of the value of having a highly educated population. It is a national competence preparedness for necessary changing needs in the labour market. In a global future perspective, lifelong learning is necessary to meet changing needs for skills. A high level of education for the entire population is then an important advantage. Highly educated people is likely to be better prepared to learn new skills, or to "learn to learn". It is easier for a highly educated person to be "a teacher of his own learning".

Different from many other countries, Taiwan managed to implement the economic development with retention of a very equitable social structure. This was the case also under the dictatorship. Income differences between different groups are modest and unemployment is among the lowest in the most developed part of the world. Taiwan's development is remarkable compared to others who have been colonies. Former colonies in Africa have constantly had major problems with economic development after the colonial masters left. When comparing Taiwan with other countries, there are five distinct elements explaining the success: 1) a Confucian tradition that emphasizes learning and hard work, 2) savings, 3) social harmony, 4) small-and medium-sized businesses and 5) emphasis on export-oriented industry.

In addition to Confucianism's emphasis on hard work and learning, social harmony is important. The latter may be a reason why Taiwanese leaders have staked so much on social equality. It is tempting to agree with those who argue that Confucianism has been important for successful transformation processes to modernize society. In the economic sphere, this cultural element has two specific effects. Both financial capital and capital for infrastructure greatly increase, because people are eager to save. Saving consistently leads to prosperity for people. The other trick is to create "human capital", which is another expression for education. Statistics over a number of years confirm strong motivation for saving and for education in Taiwan. This phenomenon also applies to the other "Confucian countries".

In summary, the Taiwan Miracle is a result of policies designed by wise leaders influenced by Confucian values. The policies have resulted in an unusually harmonious social development towards a welfare society, characterized by small social differences. Disturbance of the harmony is primarily by political clashes between the descendants of the 1949 refugees north of the island, and the descendants of immigrants from southern China in the 1600s, south of the island. The main conflict point applies to Taiwan's political relationship with Mainland China. The first group is in favour of the ever-closer ties to China, while the other wants full political independence. Aside from this controversy, the overarching political goal of creating social harmony manifests in three areas: small income differences, extraordinary low unemployment and democracy. Such a political goal achievement is for sure a miracle. The emphasis on school quality was at a time so strong that the government exempted teachers from paying tax. There was stiff competition to become a teacher. Assessment of school quality is an unavoidable theme when people, because of job change, temporarily move to other parts of the world. How a Norwegian family experienced an international elite school in Confucian context, is the topic of next chapter.

15

Norwegians Facing an Elite School in China

Among the many privileges Norwegian university professors enjoy, one is to have a "sabbatical year", every sixth year. A sabbatical means exemption from all teaching and administrative duties. For a whole year, you can fully concentrate on your favourite research topic. You keep your full salary, and often you have extra financial support from Norway's Research Council. There are no restrictions on where in the world you can reside during the sabbatical year. When I was going to enjoy this research privilege for the last time in my career, I chose China, to look into the development of higher education there. That is why I arrived in Xiamen on the South China coast in 2003. Xiamen is a recent big city. It is one of the five economic growth zones established, because of Deng Xiaoping's new internationally oriented economic policies. The city has had an adventurous economic development over the last thirty years. Western, Japanese and Korean high technology firms have flocked to Xiamen.

Since I was going to stay for a year, my family would also live in Xiamen. That meant need for a school opportunity for an 11-year-old. Actually, finding an acceptable school for the boy was an absolute condition for implementing the sabbatical research project. In terms of schools, with English as language of instruction, there were only two options, The Manila International School, next to Xiamen university, and Xiamen International School (XIS), located at quite some distance from our apartment on campus. To XIS, it would be a bus journey of 45 minutes each way. An 11-year-old is precious. We did very thorough comparisons of the two schools. We talked with the headmaster in both places, and some teachers and students. Moreover, we observed keenly how the schools looked like, both inside and outside. The conclusion was soon ready. Despite the big minus of the long journey, XIS was the choice.

After testing, the boy joined 7th grade of the "middle school", that is the three years' stage between primary school and upper secondary level. Classes started already on August 9. What we first experienced as unusual was that the parents' role would prove to be very demanding. From day one, a series of meetings took place. We, as parents, not only perceived that we had an obligation to participate, but quickly got the feeling of being "trained" to understand what was the school's goals and methods. The school leadership made it clear that they expected a positive and active attitude from the parents' side, and expected their involvement in leisure activities at the school, and their help with the student's homework.

In the early meetings, we were well acquainted with all the teachers the boy should have, as well as the parents of the other students in the class, the headmaster, the deputy headmaster and the inspector. The class comprised 17 students who came from South Korea, Japan, Taiwan, Australia, the United States, Sweden and Norway. Native Mainland Chinese students did not have access to XIS. Language of instruction was English. The subjects included mathematics, science, social studies, physical education, art and design technology, plus English as a separate subject. In addition, the students had to choose either Chinese or French as a second foreign language.

After less than two months, we witnessed a class with very high academic level and much well-being. In social studies and science, there were already during the two first months several project works. Simultaneously, the students had to engage in systematic reading of quite demanding textbooks. After each chapter, there was a test. Projects were both individual and group-based. They followed the same template as a research project. With some guiding from the teacher, the students determined a topic, formulated research questions and set up hypotheses. Then followed information gathering by means of experiments or by observation of something that was going on in the real world, or by reporting about something that had happened in the past. Internet use was extensive, in order to get the most current information. Finally, the student wrote a project report, explaining all activities carried out, before drawing a conclusion. The report explained about the information found, and the discussion of it in relation to the project's guiding research question and in relation to relevant conditions in reality, like health, environment, economy or work life. When the report was finished, the subject teacher had to approve it, before oral presentation in class, and all the students had to take part in the discussion. Then the teacher gave the project work a grade.

11-year-olds often learn a new language easily. They have not yet had time to become shy and anxious to say the wrong words or have a strange pronunciation. They are like sponges, and learn not at least in informal situations such as games and sport. In Xiamen, at that time, there were few natives speaking any other language than Chinese. Non-Chinese speakers did not have much choice. If they would get what they wanted whether it was in the shops, in traffic or at restaurants, they simply had to try to express themselves in Chinese. While such a situation might be a tough experience for mature adult foreigners, for our 11-year-old it almost seemed an exciting game. At XIS, most students had chosen Chinese as their second language. Even students with no previous experience in Chinese, quickly became linguistically self-sufficient. The learning curve was steep, although to remember and write several hundred Chinese characters is no simple matter.

As parents, we experienced the biggest positive surprise in the subject of English. We witnessed children who had never written a word of English before seventh grade, already at Christmas time had learnt to analyse book reviews and discuss reviews of art exhibitions published in *The New York Times*. The students had to interpret sonnets by Shakespeare, as well as even to write sonnets themselves. After Christmas, they had to write a short story where inspiration from heroes in Greek mythology connected to heroes of modern time. On top of it all, these projects in the subject of English, the students perceived as challenging, exciting and fun.

The next and almost too exciting surprise came in science. The students had to conduct an empirical study on their own. There had been discussions in the class in advance both about different themes and ways of examining them. Still, the students themselves had to find a theme that they thought possible to examine. They also had to formulate a main question that would guide the gathering of information. Finally, there had to be a conclusion, giving an answer to the research question. The students had to give a thorough account for the procedure, and they had to give reasons why their teacher should accept the conclusion as credible. The project would finish within three weeks.

Our boy thought the project exciting. He was thinking hard about choice of topic. Already next day, when we were walking in the market, he discovered someone selling small turtles. "Why are they moving so slowly?" he asked, "and, what can make them move faster?" he continued. That was the beginning of *The Turtle Project*. At school, the day after, he asked for the teacher's approval of his turtle idea. The teacher seemed a bit sceptical, but gave his "go". However, simultaneously he reminded the boy, "Remember that you need to do a thorough account for the procedure of the project". The boy's idea was that if the turtles turned very hungry, they might move faster, when they observed food. Thus, the Turtle Project started. He purchased three small turtles and kept them in a cage on the balcony.

Now, what do turtles eat? Moreover, do different types of turtles eat different food? Internet was a good opportunity to find out about turtles. He wrote down the information found, especially about food. Food available, the experiment could start. The three turtles were "starved" for varying length of time. Then, the idea was to measure whether there was difference in the time the three used to reach the food. Fair enough, so far. However, how should observations be explained in a way that the teacher perceived as reliable. Photography. He took pictures of the turtles by a time scale, hoping to show whether someone was moving faster than the others were. Sounded fine. Then something happened that was not okay at all. The turtles did not seem to care about the food, at least not during the time he could see them. Alternatively, maybe the food was not correct. One day, one of them was dead. The boy was very unhappy. This project would not amount to anything, he said. We recommended him to talk to the teacher. The teacher was responsive, and said it would be okay if he just finished the report, with the photos he had, and explained in the best possible what he had done, and not least, why he thought it had failed.

Thus, the report writing began. First, there was an introduction explaining the selection of the theme "turtles' movement speed". Chapter 2 had five pages about turtles as a species, based on information from the Internet. In Chapter 3, the project contained a description of the project, day by day, with the photos posted. In Chapter 4, he tried to think of reasons why the project was a failure, while he tried to apply the knowledge he had found on the Internet to help explain. At the end, he knew there should be a conclusion, an answer to the project question: why do turtles move so slowly, and, is there anything that can make them move faster? He gave one short answer to both questions, taken together: "I don't know".

Last step was to write down the final report, in as good English as possible. At the very end there was a list containing all the sources used for the project, like Internet-sources, as well as where in the science textbook he had found something useful. The teacher (Mr. Constable!) stressed that an exact list of sources was a particular important requirement. Receiving the submitted report, the teacher seemed pleased. However, one day, he asked, "Have you had any help with English in your report?" The boy admitted shamefacedly that his father had checked the language, and made some corrections. "Yes, I can understand that," the teacher said, "because there are some really old fashioned words and phrases". When the boy had the report returned, with the teacher's handwritten assessment, the teacher wrote the report was very good. For even if the results had not been as expected, the work was done in a reassuring way. "However, Mr. Constable commented at the very end, "If I ever discover that you have your father correct your English, I will "burn-mark" you!"

Physical education was a main subject; covering five hours per week. There were different activities to be studied and practiced in periods: football, rugby, basketball, gymnastics, volley, wrestling, football and frisbee. In addition, there was a voluntary option of four hours per week for those who wanted to qualify for the school team. There were organized regular tour-trips to other international schools in China. In mathematics, the teacher required seven grade students to master calculus as we remembered it from Norwegian upper secondary school, when we were seventeen. The Scandinavian students found schoolwork taking much more time than what they were accustomed to from home. Nevertheless, it was all right, since they generally found the schoolwork a meaningful experience. The fact that the students were foreigners in a completely alien world, in terms of culture and language, made school and classmates the very nicest social meeting point.

From a Norwegian point of view, it was impossible not to wonder what could be the formula for such good academic achievements, great work satisfaction and wellbeing, zero discipline problems and zero bullying. As parents, we turned curious about the background to this most pleasant school experience. Being a comparative education researcher, I sensed something interesting in terms of curriculum traditions – it seemed like four traditions working simultaneously. There were the Continental European encyclopaedism (many subjects), the English essentialism (positive teacher authority) and American progressivism (project work) in a Confucian cultural everyday context. I had to find out why such a school had been set up in Xiamen.

XIS came into being in 1997, as part Xiamen city's efforts to encourage and support foreign investments. To be able to offer a quality-school, the city government saw as a main pillar in its strategy to attract foreign business people with families to want to stay in Xiamen. Families with children will only come if they find a reasonably good school offer. The first funding for XIS came from two sources, 75% came from a private investor, Ms. Yang Ying. She already owned a local private school, Yingcai School, located right next to XIS. The remaining 25% of the investment, Xiamen City provided. From 2002, Yang Ying's own *Education Investment Company* took entire responsibility for running XIS. The company covered all running costs, until the school fees would bring balance. A board of seven members is the overall leadership of the school. Two are representatives of the parents. Yang Ying is chairperson of the board. There is also a representative of Xiamen City. The other members are education specialists, including a professor from Xiamen University.

XIS was the first international school in Fujian Province approved by the ministry of education in Beijing. Chinese students do not have access, only foreigners. The school's funding is fees paid by parents, or their employer. The fees are quite high and sufficient for the school's operation. There is no public support for running the school. From its inception, the curriculum was the K-12, an American curriculum for the course of education from kindergarten, primary school, middle school and secondary school. In 2001, there began a transition to the International Baccalaureate curriculum (IB), with primary years' programme, middle years' programme and the IB diploma programme, which includes the last two years of upper secondary education.

During XIS first five years, the school was located in a three-story building next door to Yingcai School, and could use all amenities at this school. In 2002, XIS moved into its own campus, very modern and with all conceivable facilities, e.g. its own swimming pool. The school could accept as much as 500 students. At its start on the new campus, the school had 110 students. The following year, XIS admitted 224 students from 22 countries. The largest group is from South Korea (28%), followed by Taiwan (27%) and the United States (19%). Most of the parents were business people who worked in the major foreign companies in Xiamen. The school leadership consisted of the headmaster (American), a deputy headmaster (Chinese) and an inspector (Canadian). The teachers came from United States, Canada, United Kingdom, Russia and 10 locally trained Chinese teachers. The latter primarily taught Chinese (mandarin). For various support functions, the school had a staff of 60. In particular, there were plenty of administrative personnel.

To discover and get to know such a school, both in terms of curriculum and the school as an organization, located in Communist China, made further curiosity irresistible. What sort of person is the school owner, Ms. Yang Ying? What made her initiate an "Education Investment Company"? Was profit tempting her? Alternatively, is there a connection to Chinese culture and Confucianism? The next chapter tries to give answers.

16

A Waitress Building Elite Schools

Who was Yang Ying? The first information I got from the XIS-parents, having already lived for several years in Xiamen, was that Yang Ying as a 17-year-old had come to Xiamen and got job as a waitress. Soon after, she went into the property business and became very rich. The wealth she used in highly patriotic ways, in terms of both Xiamen and China. The common denominator of how her patriotism expressed itself was the need for quality schools in Xiamen. Firstly, she thought the country needed a school of high quality for the future Chinese leaders. Therefore, Yingcai School. Secondly, Xiamen needed an international school of high quality, to encourage foreign business people to go to Xiamen, and make them stay there over time. Therefore, XIS.

In the years following my sabbatical year, I maintained contact with Xiamen University. That made it possible to keep up a dream about meeting this special woman, Yang Ying. She accepted my request for an informal interview. The meeting with her in itself was a great inspiration. The former waitress served the lunch herself, in her spacious house in the slope above the South China Sea. The way she expressed herself made it clear that this was a woman with a strong personality and great commitment. Even if the language stood as a Chinese wall between us, the way she expressed herself indicated a person with strong will to get important things done. The interpreter did a good job. However, I have never ever so strongly desired that I could speak Chinese, and get immediate understanding of what she expressed.

Can Norway learn from China?

Yang Ying grew up in a very poor family with many children in a village outside Xiamen. Boys had first right to schooling. The whole village worked in a farming cooperative. Thus, there was a need for someone to register the various contributions, so that there could be a total accounting of the results of the harvest. Accidentally, little Ying was to take care of this work. This was the background for her, even a girl, getting access to schooling. The pathway to the school was long, and she often had to carry her little brother on her back, when he was too tired.

One teacher became crucial for Ying's life. Even though tuition fees were only 2 US cents per semester, her family found they could no longer afford it, and reported to the school that she had to quit. Teacher Cai became her rescue. He convinced the parents that the girl had to continue. Ying still remembers him with deep thanks. At school, she found two subjects particularly important: Mandarin (Chinese) and mathematics. She liked mathematics best. What she learned at school, she actively applied in the work of accounting the village's harvest results. Here, perhaps we find the seed of the business talent that later found expression.

15 years old, she began working in a brick factory. The pay was 15 US cents per day. She even covered the cost of food. However, the factory provided free housing. Here the young girl did not have much space for exciting future dreams. All thought was concentrated on survival from one day to another. The most important lesson she remembers from those years was the necessity to learn to work hard. Another important experience from adolescence was that she and the others learned how to take care of each other. They learnt how to understand pain, suffering and sacrifices.

In 1987, when Deng Xiaoping introduced socialist market economy in China, Ying got a job as waitress at a restaurant in Xiamen. The butcher who supplied meat to the restaurant was a likeable person. Ying and he fell in love. They married. He was already wealthy. Together they made the butcher shop increasingly profitable. They turned rich. Yang used the capital and her talent in the real estate market in Beijing, and became very rich. How would she spend all the money? Ying opted for schools as business. She invested in elite schools. The market was wealthy "nouveau riches" Chinese and the multinational employees of a growing tribe of foreigners temporarily residing in China. The local authorities of her hometown Xiamen cheered her investment in schools, inspired by local patriotism, and hailed in a country with some thousand years of respect for knowledge.

Deng Xiaoping established five economic free zones along the coast. They were going to be spearheads in China's economic development. Xiamen was one of them, but Yang Ying worried that the foreigners might hesitate to establish themselves in Xiamen. She assumed hesitance was due to the lack of a satisfactory school offer for their children. In addition, she was concerned that the Chinese did not yet have schools of international quality standard. Yang got in touch with the local authorities in Xiamen, the local communist party and the local Association of Foreign Entrepreneurs. She wanted these key stakeholders' support for two school initiatives: to establish an international elite school for foreign students, plus an elite school just for Chinese people. She offered to pay 75% of the spending of establishing the schools, as well as guaranteeing the operating expenses, until the schools could balance their budgets based on tuition fees. She immediately got permission to proceed.

In 2001, both schools were ready. They had top material standard in terms of classrooms, laboratories and sports facilities, even a swimming pool. For the Chinese school, she recruited the headmaster and teachers from among those ranked highest in the Fujian province's evaluation of its teachers and leaders. For the international school, she recruited the headmaster and teachers from the international market for personnel in elite schools. Since being privately financed both were independent schools. Yang handpicked boards for both schools. On the board of the international school, there were representatives from the local government, Xiamen university, the International Entrepreneurs' Association and the parents. Yang was and still is the chairperson of both boards. Her thinking was instrumental and economical. To be able to offer an international quality-school would be a stimulus for Sony, Dell, and Microsoft, to establish themselves in Xiamen. To provide the local Chinese with a quality school of international standard was just the other side of the same coin. In the long term, both schools would contribute to greater economic independence in China's relationship with foreign countries.

In hindsight, Yang does not now see economic investments in themselves as the most important. When she has been fortunate enough to get access to as much money as she has, she believes that it is more important to think about how her wealth can be for the benefit of the whole society. Simultaneously as everyone must have access to good education, the society also is in need of education for an elite, people who have the very best possible conditions to lead the society in wisest possible way. These need the very best education, not least to understand their responsibilities for the society. Her main value now, is to care about others, and to create trust. Buddha has meant a lot to her. At the same time as there in China, in her time, has become ever more opportunities for many to earn a lot of money, she believes that basic trust and consideration for others all the time must be present. Otherwise, economic success will not contribute to a better society.

As a primary school student, and from her parents, she learned about Confucius. According to him, it is never too late to learn. Learning is a lifelong process. That she has experienced herself. To become ethically conscious of your own actions in relation to others is a core part of Confucius' educational philosophy. In relation to school, those students who are struggling and failing shall constantly have help to learn as much as they can. As chairperson of the board of Yingcai elite school, Yang is trying to put herself in both parents' and students' place, in order to understand how they think. She sees that parents and students perceive the efforts at school as essential to be able to experience a good life in the future.

Yang is very concerned about the teachers' needs. As chairperson of the board, she feels the responsibility to inspire the teachers. It is important for her to make sure that each teacher gets the feeling of appreciation. She is committed to creating a family feeling among the staff. She has introduced an award system. It acts as a pension scheme for teachers, and shows the close relationship between effort and reward. She wants significant pressure on teachers to make efforts towards their students, but without negative stress. As a school leader, she is concerned about indirect leadership and moral leadership. If she succeeds in making the individual teacher feel that he has an important job to do, there is no need of much leadership from her side. Motivated teachers manage themselves. Yang deplores bossy management at any level.

Even if Xiamen International School and Yingcai School are quite different in many ways, Yang takes initiatives to make the schools learn from each other. A main difference between them is that Yingcai continues a thousand years' tradition with respect for education and teachers. Tough admission tests and many examinations are normal. In the Chinese tradition, it is important to work hard. Simultaneously, many Chinese people think they might be less creative than in the West. Yang wants to combine Western and Eastern educational thinking, and bring the best from both. Yang is not a communist, but is aware that communism is trying to contribute to a better society for all. This it has in common with Confucianism and Buddhism. In all three ways of thinking there is an expectation that you shall practice what you learn, and try yourself to be a good example of an ethical right way of living.

Her greatest joys have been to see students at her two schools, at the same time, doing well academically, and showing social responsibility towards other students and the school community. Both schools celebrated ten years' anniversary in 2006. She is clearly proud that one of the graduates from XIS is now at Harvard. A fact she takes as a clear indication that XIS really is of international standard. When she extends her visionary thinking about her school successes so far, she envisages that from her elite schools there shall graduate clever, morally conscious and strong leaders, who in the future will be in charge of both politics and business. Her joy of Yingcai and XIS has inspired her to establish two similar schools in Beijing.

In recent years, she spent, in parallel with creating elite schools, significant amounts to help poor children in Western China to better schools, as well as to do something for those who are struggling with serious diseases. For the rest of her life, she has three dreams: 1) Establish a larger number of centres for voluntary blood donation around China, to help people who have blood cancer, 2) Establish 1000 schools for those who lack access to school – The Hope Project, 3) Support blood cancer research. She has already spent one billion Chinese yuan on these projects. That is far from enough. Therefore, she challenges the authorities and other wealthy to contribute. Above these three dreams, however, lies her love of schools and education. Highest possible school quality for most Chinese is what Yang sees as the best guarantee of a harmonious development of society - inspired by Buddha, Confucius and Communism.

Yang wants others to get more of what she barely got a taste of – quality schooling. When she established XIS, she assumed that also highly educated foreign parents think like that. The successful waitress, Yang Ying, is part of a long and extensive tradition of poor Chinese who went to Singapore or the United States, became rich, and then sent money home to build schools and universities. Education with quality is the main agent to create economic development, ethical awareness and a good society for all. It may prove difficult, for even the richest countries in the world to make their education system have the same quality as international elite schools. However, it may be instructive also for the education authorities of rich Western countries to familiarize with such schools. Maybe, insights about such schools could inspire new ways of spending education budgets. In the next chapter, we will look at two aspects of an international elite school: curriculum and resources.

17

An Elite School's Curriculum, Grades and Resources

The foundation for any ambitious school is a *curriculum*, understood and taken seriously by teachers and school leadership. The curriculum is the academic contract between parents and school. Parents who familiarize with the school curriculum, want to know what sort of learning results, the school aims to achieve for the students. Where there are alternative school offers, parents can compare curricula and pick the one they think best respond to their expectations. In the international schools, such as the XIS, the most direct expression of what will be the result of schoolwork is - grades. They are simple and clear indications of how far students have reached in their learning. Behind each letter grade is a number of points. Taking the grade as a starting point, the teacher provides supplementary feedback to the parents. Then follows discussion between student, parent and teacher about how the grade can improve. While the curriculum is the formal and principal framework for how concretely to organize learning, the material resources are key prerequisites for successful learning in practice.

A professional school leadership is constantly working to improve consistency between curriculum and learning practices for the school as a whole. XIS is an accredited school, meaning that the school's owner has signed a contract with an international firm whose specialty is to make overall reviews of schools. The firm assesses school leadership, teachers, curriculum, and material conditions. If the school "pass", it gets a certificate that applies for five years. Frequently, the school does not get the certificate right away, but must first correct the weaknesses found. To retain the status as an accredited school, it must constantly make efforts for improvement. For a private, commercially based school, accreditation is a key factor in the marketing. Therefore, leadership and teachers are in a continuous improvement process.

Two types of compliance criteria apply. Firstly, there shall be an obvious logical connection vertically, about how well subjects and ways of working upwards the class ladder connect over time. Thus, chances increase for the student having a natural progression between the different class levels. The second criteria is on horizontal connection. The ambition is optimal connection between the subjects and ways of working within a specific class level. There is, not least, a challenge to get to the best possible integration between different subjects. The entire process is as open and simple as possible; making it easy also for students and parents to get involved in it. In order to facilitate such transparency, links to content and topics are on the school's intranet. Information about good vertical and horizontal connection between topics, subjects and ways of working are visual on big posters outside the classrooms.

XIS started out with curriculum of American K-12 type. Eventually, the complete educational programme turned towards curriculum principles and learning materials from the international IB Organization (International Baccalaureate Organization - IBO) with three stages: 1) from the kindergarten to fifth grade level primary, 2) from lower secondary sixth grade level to tenth grade level, and 3) diploma programme at eleventh and twelfth levels. The school's board clearly wishes the headmaster to see increased quality of the educational programme as the highest priority. Expectations of increased quality was behind the board's decision to change from American style curriculum to IB, and it involved itself with strong support to implement the IB curriculum. The board requires regular reporting from the headmaster and teacher representatives of the students' learning and about the curriculum implementation. Selected teachers come to the board meetings to give oral information about how they implement the IB programme. Observed from outside, there seems to be a very good relationship between the content of the curriculum (syllabus), teachers' plans for individual hours, students' learning activities and testing system. Such a consistent relationship is essential for school quality. According to the headmaster, this important relationship increased significantly by the allocation of considerable time for teachers' planning. Proper time for planning is a key part of the teachers' overall work plan.

Testing and grading are according to strict procedures. When it comes to the percentage of correct answers needed to achieve a particular grade, a strict scale applies. To achieve an A+, requires between 98% and 100% correct answers. Having between 93 and 97% correct answers, makes an A. Less than 60% correct answers means fail. The admission procedures of the universities and colleges in countries where XIS-students want to continue studies, requires such a precise scale of grading. However, the total assessment of the students' achievements is a summary of more than just a letter grade at the end. IB rules for testing has a distinct set of indicators that control the student's learning outcome on various aspects of the individual subjects. In addition, there are grades for project works.

Simply expressed, two main factors explain the high quality of learning observed at XIS: curriculum and school organization. XIS began its operations applying a curriculum of the American progressivist tradition ("learning by discovery"), and then gradually changed to IB, which is influenced primarily by Continental European encyclopaedism, but also by American progressivism. Overall, the IB curriculum is in harmony with the accreditation standards for international schools. One reason for the popularity of IB is the fact that a growing number of parents are on the move between different countries. Such changes in the international labour market, led to a need for coordination of standards between international schools, no matter which country they are in.

The practical teaching at XIS is strongly subject-centred. Simultaneously, the teachers relate and integrate subjects and topics to challenging problems of real life. This ambition of making learning relevant is obvious in the many projects the students have to carry out. Learning in the project is problem-centred. Students learn by solving problems. What they learn, they relate to the reality they have around them. In this way, students learn to be conscious and responsible in relation to the society. Normally, the teacher is in charge of organizing projects. The project's problem statement has its starting point in a subject, e.g. science. At each class level, teachers meet to discuss and to observe the projects in relation to each other, to ensure that projects based on different subjects, together produces a coherent totality and to avoid fragmentation. The subjects are the central nerve of the project works. Students learn the contents of the textbooks at the same time as the project goes on. When the project work is completed, the students must give an account on how the problem solving results of the project matches the content of the textbooks. The textbooks reflect the disciplines. The subjects keep track of the knowledge learned in the project.

Seen in a comparative curriculum perspective, XIS integrates in their teaching American (progressivist) student-centred learning with English (essentialist) emphasis on moral awareness, and the European tradition with a strong emphasis on a variety of subjects (encyclopaedic). Solid and up-to-date expert knowledge is the key condition for creative problem solving, for active learning and ethical awareness raising about the responsibility for the society and the environment. The teachers stress that the subjects come first and last. The project work is only a relevant remedy as long as it clearly contributes to the learning outcomes documented on the knowledge tests. The tests are frequent, and with less than 60% correct answers, it is fail. To get an A, there must be 96% correct answers. XIS has a mock examination every quarter and examinations before Christmas and the end of the year. Parents and students get a manual from the school, which thoroughly explains what is required in each subject for A, B, C, etc. Failing on tests occur frequently. Standards must maintain. However, students have plenty of new opportunities to try again. Students who struggle receive extra help.

The second main factor explaining XIS' success is the school's *organization*. The label 'organization' includes the school's owner, board of directors, leadership team, teachers, other staff and the parents. Material resources come in addition, and they are in abundance. However, foremost there is one particular aspect of the organization that demonstrates its quality: leadership quality and teacher quality in interaction with parents and owner/board of directors. This interaction makes possible an implementation of curriculum leading to students achieving a high professional competence. This makes all stakeholders happy. The board has decided that the school's quality be considered every six year by an accreditation company, which either gives approval, or inform about what needs to be improved within a certain time limit, for the school to continue as accredited. This stamp, the school needs to make itself visible in the international school market. It is in this market business people from for example, Sony, Siemens, Dell or Ikea, also being parents, will orient themselves before they decide about taking a job in Xiamen.

The headmaster is on contract, after being headhunted in the international education market. He has an excellent education background and previous highly relevant practice. His way of integrating theory and practice at XIS is a clear success. He is one of the main reasons why XIS delivers quality. He has complete freedom to hire and dismiss teachers. He can decide on the redeployment of resources and educational programmes, if he sees it as necessary to reach the school's goals and to keep the board and parents happy.

Hiring of teachers comes after a painstaking selection process. There is stiff competition for a position at XIS. The headmaster interviews each teacher before employment on contract. Renewal of the contract beyond the first year only happens if the headmaster, after an overall review, believes that the teacher in his practice shows academic weight, enthusiasm, and care for the students, as well as the ability of constructive cooperation with colleagues. While the headmaster is the primary condition to create school quality, the teachers are his essential instruments to make the students stretch, work hard and perform, and therefore thrive and enjoy the school environment.

According to parents' expectations, XIS is an excellent school. This is because there is a successful interaction between three factors:

1) a creative, innovative and visionary Chinese business woman, 2) a truly international curriculum that creatively integrates elements from the English, European and American curriculum traditions — in a culture area characterized by Confucian philosophy and 3) a school organization with very professional staff, on an aesthetically pleasing campus, with the most modern equipment for both academic and sporting activities. The very first condition to reach good learning achievements is a school leadership, who simultaneously understands what parents want and how to organize the available resources so that the parents get what they want, and for which they are willing to pay high school fees. Thus, it will be exciting to get an idea of how precisely *the leadership* of an international elite school is composed, and how it perceives its job.

18

Elite Shool Leadership

The school's board of directors has the overall responsibility for running the school. The daily leadership group at XIS consists of headmaster, deputy headmaster and an inspector. The deputy chairperson of the board has a central role, when it comes to recruiting the three daily leaders. Ms. Yang Ying is chairperson. XIS is her own business, but she is not a professional educator. Therefore, she made sure the board has a deputy chairperson with extensive background from the education sector, one who is actually the academic chairperson. He is retired, however, more active than ever. His basic education is marine biology from Xiamen university. The university is the leading research institution in marine biology in China. Upon completion of university education, he was a teacher and headmaster of a primary school, before he became the president of a teacher education college in Xiamen. Next step was appointment as inspector at the department of education and culture in the Xiamen City Government. The department is responsible for thousands of local schools. In retirement, he still conducts countless professional tasks in the field of education, research and non-governmental organizations at national and local levels. Ying Yang saw him as a significant academic capacity and invited him to be deputy chairperson of the board.

His vision for the XIS is that school should be a showcase to the international business community. The school's curriculum shall make sure that the students become world citizens with an international and multicultural way of thinking, at the same time as they become responsible, caring, creative and hard working. For the school to be able to work in the direction of this vision, the first condition is to hire an outstanding headmaster. The headmaster must be a capacity on knowing what schooling is all about, meaning thorough practical experiences, great work capacity and good at communication. In order for the school to be excellent, the board, the staff and the parents are involved. Some leadership tasks are only for the board. These include the hiring and termination of headmaster and deputy headmaster, the approval of the school's overall strategy, budget and student admission regulations. The board takes the big decisions, and the headmaster determines their implementation.

The best way to find a good headmaster is to use a professional recruitment company, which ensures a good process to find the best. While in service, the headmaster must pass an evaluation each year. Evaluation is by a questionnaire, made by the recruitment firm that parents, teachers and other employees fill in. The board also offers parents and staff the opportunity to meet with the board of directors, in the course of the evaluation period, so that they may verbally elaborate on their assessment of the headmaster. The headmaster also has to make a written self-evaluation.

XIS's headmaster is from the United States. His education background is a bachelor's degree in English literature and education, followed by a master's degree in educational administration and a Ph.D. in educational law. Practice background includes six years as an English teacher in secondary school, followed by one year as inspector in secondary school. Then came five years as inspector at the middle school and ten years as a school superintendent. All these practices, he has from the United States. Then, his international career began with, first, two years as a primary school headmaster at an international school in Peru, then three years as an assistant inspector of The American School in Shanghai. Next stop was Beijing, where he worked for one year as headmaster. Before his placement in Xiamen, he was for two years headmaster of the American International School in Sydney.

The selection of a headmaster begins with a recruitment firm receiving and considering applications. The firm forwards to the board applications from those it thinks are best suited for the position. The board will shortlist the two or three supposed best candidates, and invite them to Xiamen for an interview. The chosen one has a three-year contract of employment. The present headmaster is convinced that it is critically important for a school leader to have been a teacher before he becomes school leader. He believes that there is a big difference between being good enough, and being talented. Teachers will more naturally accept leadership by a talented headmaster. It is very important for a headmaster to have strong and genuine understanding of ethics. As headmaster, he has undertaken a very large responsibility to reach the board's overall goal for the XIS - to lead the school so that it has an international reputation as excellent.

When it comes to the headmaster's role as human resources leader, it is important to show care for the teachers. Simultaneously, over all most important for him is to have high expectations of teachers' professional work. Teachers must either already be excellent, or prepared to work to become excellent. It is important to be a visible headmaster, meaning always having an open door for the teachers if they like to discuss with him. However, simultaneously, it is important not to be so visible that the headmaster is overshadowing the other in the leadership team. A headmaster of an excellent international school should only keep the position for three to five years. Shifts in the leadership position creates dynamism in both one's own personal development and in the school as an organization. A "stable school does not exist". A school is either in progress or in decline. The board has the responsibility of finding the headmaster that creates progress.

The headmaster must follow up the teachers so that they develop a sense of being leaders of learning in their subject fields. Such follow up happens by involving the teachers in the goal setting processes, decision-making processes and communication processes. This will give them a feeling of ownership towards the school. Hiring and dismissal of teachers are perhaps the headmaster's most important tasks. What he looks for when he will be hiring a new teacher is enthusiasm, intelligence and proven ability to succeed. When he considers the applicants, he looks especially after their knowledge base, previous academic achievements and if they are good at communication. He sees it as crucial to be able to have face-to-face interview with the applicants. When it comes to dismissal of a teacher who does not deliver, there is a series of steps to take before the resignation is a fact. The headmaster must get involved in the teacher's problems and try to find out how he can help him to get on, before there is any talk about a termination process.

The deputy headmaster position at XIS is not just an ordinary deputy position. Even though the position ranks below the headmaster in terms of regular decision-making, the deputy headmaster at XIS has special duties, which the headmaster does not have. Like the headmaster, the board hires him. That is not the case for the third member of the leadership team, the inspector. The headmaster picks him out. The deputy headmaster is a local Chinese, and is in charge of controlling that the school's business is in accordance with the interests of Xiamen City and Chinese interests in general. Therefore, the board has granted him permanent employment. A glance at his qualifications shows that he barely is some random choice from the board. His professional career began with teacher examination from Fujian County's Pedagogical University. After graduating, he taught for seven years in a local secondary school, rated "very successful teacher". His students participated in many knowledge contests, and many of his students took first place. He then moved on to the Xiamen foreign language school, where one of his roles was to act as "model teacher" for headmasters and other professionals who visited the school.

This was at the time when Deng Xiaoping opened China to the world. The model teacher's headmaster recommended participation in a competition to join an international exchange programme for teachers. He was one of sixteen teachers who went to Australia. There he got the opportunity to familiarize with advanced teaching methodology, techniques for classroom leadership and to gain better insight into Western educational philosophies. When he came back, he became a member of Xiamen City's education commission, with particular responsibility for in-service training of teachers at the local teacher education college. In the course of the ten years in this job, he earned a master's degree by taking evening classes. At his college, he became department manager, with half of the time for teaching and half for administration. In 2000, the Xiamen City Council's minister for education asked him if a position as deputy headmaster at XIS was of interest. The minister was aware of his strong interests in Western-dominated education. It was important for the city government to have a local Chinese in this position, in order to ensure long-term stability in the leadership of the school, as well as local Chinese control. From his "Chinese position", as deputy headmaster at XIS, he sees a two-fold challenge for the school: firstly, to ensure that students achieve a high level in English and the other subjects. Secondly, the international students shall gain an understanding of the cultural variety in the world, including teaching them to respect Chinese culture.

The third member of XIS' leadership team, the inspector, is an important administrative support player for both headmaster and deputy headmaster. The headmaster selected him for the position. His qualifications consist of two bachelor's degrees. The first is in humanities, with history, specializing on ancient times. The other is in teaching methodology for English as a foreign language. In addition, he has a master's in school administration. His leadership practices began, while he was teacher, by taking care of some administrative tasks. The international career began as an administrator at an international school in the United Arab Emirates for one year. Back in Canada, he was for three years headmaster of a middle school, followed by two years as inspector of an upper secondary school. Back on the international arena, he worked one year at the Canadian International School of Hong Kong in a position with both teaching and administration. Then came XIS. He is convinced that the excellent school leadership is above all, powered by enthusiasm, passion and belief in what you do, and that you make such spirit visible in the school environment. School leaders need to have the talent of asking the right questions, and most importantly, a lot of patience.

The overall educational leadership expertise at XIS, and how it came into place, is overwhelming when you inevitably compare with the Norwegian public school. Firstly, at XIS there exists an abundance of knowledge and skills, when it comes to the academic part of the leadership. From the headmaster's doctorate and downwards, there is great breadth and dept. Together they understand what the purpose of school is, what students should learn, how to teach effectively and how to control that they actually have learned. Both the deputy chairperson of the board and all three members of the leadership team stress the importance of good communication, between leadership and teachers, between teachers and with parents and students. The attitudes of the three in the leadership team express clearly a caring culture. The teachers shall have care. The leadership keeps an eye on teachers showing care for the students, beyond their "academic care" for their learning. If some students are struggling, they shall have additional learning support and guidance to get on as far as possible.

The leadership trio, as a whole, covers three primary sub functions of school leadership. Firstly, they implement *learning leadership*, guidance of the teachers in their efforts to make students reach learning goals stated in the curriculum. The way the leadership stimulates and support teachers on other life areas than the professional, shows a conscious *human resource leadership*. When you notice how the school looks like – and observe that classrooms, special rooms and outdoor sports facilities are aesthetically pleasing, then you see the result of a professional *financial-administrative management*.

The leadership's vision is to make XIS an excellent school in academic terms, providing graduates to excellent universities in different countries. When excellence makes the school visible in the international school market, it will help to motivate foreign business people to seek positions in companies in Xiamen. Thus, the school helps to strengthen China and Xiamen, which was the motivation for Yang Ying to invest money in establishing it, and to pay operating expenses until school fees balanced the accounts. High quality of the leadership as a whole, owner, board of directors, headmasters and inspector is essential to find good teachers. However, ultimately the teachers' professional weight and creativity is crucial for the results students achieve, and that it is what the parents as customers demand. Elite teachers is the topic of the next chapter.

19

Elite Teachers

It is the teachers that make the crucial job - to get the individual student himself to wish to learn. What sort of people is it, who have chosen to work on a 1-year contract at an international school in China? How do they perceive the teacher role? Are they just the leadership's instrument to transmit the contents of textbooks, or do their perception of their role include more? Everybody has an opinion about what is a good school. Perceptions vary about most aspects, but one thing all agree on - the teacher is crucial. There were many occasions at XIS where teachers and parents met. That gave me the opportunity to become better acquainted with several of the teachers, and the possibility of airing the questions I have just asked.

The science teacher in grade seven was from Canada. His education consisted of a bachelor's degree in science with an emphasis on mechanical engineering and educational seminars with an emphasis on the teaching of science and math. In his job as a teacher, he kept himself professionally updated by attending the courses of Global Education, as well as participating in in-service-training courses on curriculum development. After XIS changed to the IB curriculum, he took courses in IB education for science, math and technology. He began his professional career with three years as teacher at a public school in Malawi, followed by four years as teacher in a secondary school, in Canada. He was then facilitator in a development programme for youth - Youth for Social Justice. The time in Malawi gave him a lasting stimulus to want work outside America. He began to think in the direction of an international school, and certainly in China. Through a colleague, he learned about the position advertised at XIS. He applied for the position. The headmaster at XIS interviewed and, then, hired him. When I met him, he had taught for four years at the XIS, in science, mathematics and technology from seventh to twelfth class.

He stresses that when you are going to teach students from different countries, it is necessary to be aware of what kind of educational tradition, the students have been in before they come to XIS. At XIS, something he appreciates very much is that the curriculum is process-based. Thus, the subjects are more relevant to the students. It also makes it possible to set up measurable indicators. Then, students can more clearly see which knowledge areas that they master satisfactorily, and which needs more working. Students who do not have English, as native language is a big challenge. When he is planning the teaching, he keeps a particular view on making the teaching perceived as meaningful by the students. When the class consists of both students with English as their mother tongue and a group where the degree of being able to command English can vary significantly, it is really demanding to create meaningful teaching. The teacher, therefore, must find activities that reinforce learning. He does that by creating realistic exercises. What is feasible in practice will increase the students' understanding and the possibility that there will be genuine knowledge acquisition by the student. Effective evaluation is critically important. Both the learning process and the knowledge achievements need proper evaluation. Assessment of the process is by observing the students, when they are working in the lab, and when they present their written work. Tests, quiz and students' written summary of the laboratory work control the knowledge acquisition.

The results of the evaluation is also a feedback to the teacher. If the students are not performing well enough, the teacher must consider what he can do for the students to become better. This science teacher sees three strategies to keep himself professionally updated as a teacher: 1) observing colleagues and let colleagues observe himself, 2) attend courses and conferences on themes that apply to his subjects and 3) access to academic journals of his subject interests. He stresses that the reading of peer-reviewed journals is an important hallmark of being a profession, or not. The use of the internet in teaching is useful, if the teacher has good control of how students actually use it. In his science classes, there is active internet use when students conduct supervised research. It is also useful for downloading work-examples that are difficult to practice in the classroom. In his classes at the middle school level, the students use about 15% of the time on computer-based activities. This increases to 20-25% in upper secondary school.

In our discussions, the science teacher often return to what he thinks are particularly important elements of a teacher's professional competence. He believes that the teacher must be aware of, in all his behaviour, that he is an effective role model for his students. Moreover, the professional teacher have a good understanding of gender differences and their importance for the learning situation. This is particularly important when the class has students from different cultures. At last, he stressed that the teacher must be good at conflict resolution and able to communicate clearly with both verbal and non-verbal means.

The mathematics teacher in grade 7 is a native Chinese man with a bachelor's degree in science and math, including teaching methods in science. The post at XIS is his second after graduation. He saw the announcement on the Internet. He applied for the position. He got it, and is now in its fourth year in Xiamen. He has had renewal of the contract three times. The specific motivation to apply for the post was to get to know students and teachers from other cultures. He is convinced that he has learned a lot from the foreigners. In teaching, he thinks it is demanding to become familiar with the background of the various students, especially when both his own and many of the students' level of English can cause misunderstandings.

Something that fascinated him greatly, when he acquainted with XIS was his colleagues concern about process orientation in teaching. The concept was highly unfamiliar in relation to what he had experienced as a student in the Chinese system. He is excited about the principle of student centred teaching, and believe teaching then is more efficient, and giving the students a more holistic understanding of the subject, compared to what happens in traditional teacher centred teaching. Simultaneously, he thinks that a successful process orientation in teaching is dependent on the fact that he knows his subject very well, and that the students have high respect for the teacher. Otherwise, the work of learning may slip into a waste of time. Something else that was an unfamiliar and very exciting experience was to learn that teachers at the school's math department themselves designed the syllabus and selected the textbooks. Such freedom for the teachers must still result in a curriculum matching the requirements of American and European universities and colleges. In China, teacher do not have the freedom to select the textbooks.

He is excited about the IB programme for the lower secondary level. The manual is a useful tool when he wants to show how the various themes intertwine, and what the intersection between different subjects is. This helps him to make students understand the purpose of what he wants to convey. In the evaluation of what students have learned, he emphasises on techniques that shows that students can apply concretely what they have learned. By analysing the students performance in tests, quiz and projects, he can see where they have their weak points, and insert additional teaching exactly where it is needed.

The English teacher in grade seven is from the United States. She is 22 years old and in her first year at XIS. She has a humanities bachelor, with two main topics, literature and pedagogy. Before Xiamen, she was a teacher in a school for disadvantaged children in inner city Newark. She is quite critical of the American school system. Compared to XIS, she thinks the public school system in the United States is far too controlling of the teacher, when it comes to what resources the teacher can use and how she teaches. Coming to Xiamen was coming to educational freedom. She experiences that she has all kinds of opportunities to be innovative and creative in her teaching. There is also much more cooperation with the other teachers, than is the case in the United States. Before applying for the position in Xiamen, she got hold of all information about the school that was available. XIS seemed exciting and she wanted to travel. That was her two motives for applying.

When she explains her way of teaching, we notice American curriculum progressivism. She thinks a well-organized group is a superior method for knowledge acquisition in a multicultural classroom. She needs research-based knowledge in her teaching, and the easiest way to find it is on the Internet. Ethnic News Watch is her favourite place on the Internet. Something particularly pleasing with the curriculum at the XIS is that it is good to show the connection between the subjects. In her planning of teaching, she sees two key skills: Foresight and afterthought. The teacher should be aware of the direction in which the teaching goes - what is the purpose. By afterthought, she means awareness on what is already learned. In other words, there must be a long time relationship in teaching. Creativity is also an important element of teacher planning. She emphasized that a good plan for the learning session must be challenging and emerge in an interesting and original form.

The two most important skills in actual teaching is flexibility and natural curiosity. A plan for the teaching must never be a straitjacket. A good plan may turn in different directions, because the practical situation does not always appear as you thought when planning. With "naturally curious", she means the teacher shall push students to be curious, to go further in their thought processes, even further than dictated by the planned activities. In addition, when it comes to the importance of evaluation, she stresses that the teacher must be creative and flexible. By flexible, she thinks that the teacher must be able to assess in several different ways, and be prepared to consider all types of learning, also the one that occurs unintentionally. The latter may be relevant or irrelevant, but the teacher must be open to see it. Creativity in assessment means finding different test methods. You should not just rely on one alone. Regardless of the test programme chosen, it must be possible to compare the results with a given standard.

How can one work to become a better teacher? She thinks that improvement occurs through conversations; discussions with colleagues, inner conversation with herself, as well as trying to pick up some of the mass of written material available for teachers. She thinks the Internet will continue to be an important aid for teachers, primarily because it allows teachers to keep in touch with each other globally. When she summarizes what she means by claiming that a teacher is excellent, she thinks of a person that above all communicates well and loves her subjects. More specifically, she thinks that the good teacher can demonstrate the application of knowledge in the real world. The good teacher tumbles all the time with curious questions, e.g. how will thorough understanding of literature make me a better person?

This young teacher is perhaps the most professional one I have ever met in my life. It was she that already during the first two months of the school year, inspired 11-year-olds, with not very good English, to consider book reviews in the New York Times. She made them write sonnets on the model of Shakespeare and compose a short story where Alexander the Great and Nelson Mandela were the heroes in the same story. Even though she lost students when families moved from Xiamen, she did not simply accept the breaking of connection with students she cared far. She felt responsibility for the students' further learning; wherever on the globe they might have gone. There is Internet, email and chat capabilities, she stated.

In this chapter, I have shown the sunny side of being a teacher at XIS. I portray three elite teachers. They had all passed the eye of the needle for employment. The science and math teachers continued in their positions year after year. That means that they each year were weighed and found professionally heavy enough. The last one, the English teacher was in her first year. I know that she continued. These three are all winners in the international market for teachers. Humanly speaking, there is also a night side for teachers at XIS. That are the teachers that the headmaster does not find good enough, and that do not have renewal of contract. They can have a hard time. It is never pleasant to fail. People in the international teacher market have to take that risk. It should be obvious that the school is primarily for the students. It is an injustice to students if a school allows itself to keep lifetime incompetent teachers or school leaders. In such a case, the school has primarily become a place for the teachers and not for students. Then the school has not only become pointless. It has become dangerous. A school with poor teachers may produce stupid students, contrary to the logical purpose of schools. A stupidifying school may damage the students' self-image and it may be a violation of the human right education is determined to be. In such cases, the parents get the opposite of the best conceivable life insurance they want for their most precious. They are deceived. However, it turns out that different parents see the same school reality rather differently. Then, there may also be disagreement about what is a good teacher. In the next chapter, we will see how parents with backgrounds in various curriculum traditions consider the same reality – XIS.

20

Koreans and Swedes Do Not See the Same School

At the beginning of this travelogue, I told about a mother in Japan, who, when her daughter had to be away from school because of illness, herself went to school and got a complete list of what little Yoko should have learned while she was ill. Then, the mother got hold of a private teacher, who ensured that the absence did not make holes in her child's learning. It appears that the parents, and especially the mother, almost like a law of nature, show strong school care for their children. I have also previously told about rice-cake baker Pan Maoyuan, who later became a professor and created a new university subject and a new institute. He had such school caring parents. They wanted their children to have a better life than the poverty they themselves had endured. Fiction shows that parents all over the world think in this way. One of the founders of the encyclopaedic curriculum tradition and the unified school model, the Czech educator, Comenius, said that the mother is the child's first teacher and called the first childhood years – the mother's school.

The many arrangements for collaboration between school and home in Xiamen, gave me the opportunity to familiarize with parents from different countries and have their opinion of the school. The parents had in common a strong commitment to see their hopefuls experiencing an educational programme that would give them a good basis for coping with adult life

Can Norway learn from China?

The parents I met with came from Australia, the United States, former East Germany, South Korea and Sweden. What was their background, and what they think about XIS?

The *American* mother has two children at XIS. This is her first year in Xiamen, but the family has previously lived in Guangzhou and the children attended the international school there. She, therefore, can compare XIS to another international school in China. She finds it a bit difficult to assess the academic standard, because XIS is a young school, where perhaps important routines are not yet completely in place. For mathematics teaching, she gives the school a top mark. English teaching she sees not completely on top. She is very concerned about students' safety. That may be because her coming from New York. On safety, she gives a top mark to XIS, convinced that the school has a safe and secure environment. She is also pleased that much learning is by project work, where students must work in a group and learn from experiences. She thinks that students generally have positive attitudes and to a high degree treat each other with respect. Still, she wants to see the mentor scheme expanded. In this programme, experienced students act as helpers for newly arrived students. The mother is very satisfied that both of her children (one in grade 11 and one in 12) have had a nice maturation process during their first year at XIS.

The *German* family comes from former East Germany, and both parents graduated from there in the Communist era. Their son is a student in grade six. The family had previously lived four years in Moscow. The mother is in no doubt about the academic standard at XIS. It is higher than what the boy experienced in Germany. She gives XIS top score in all subjects, and cannot see any areas where the school could have done any better. Her son must have experienced a little bit of unpleasantness, since she emphasizes that it is a normal part of growing up that children sometimes have problems in relation to each other. She praises the teachers to be sensitive to what is going on between the students and that they all the time do their best for the students to be nice to each other. Especially she is happy with the language learning. Her son hardly spoke any English before they arrived in Xiamen. After three years at XIS, he is almost fluent in the language. She is thrilled that her son has made contact with children from so many different countries, and she thinks that he has gotten some friends for life.

During her three-year period in Xiamen, the German mother experienced a change of headmaster. She is sure that is an improvement. The previous headmaster did not have very much contact with the parents. The current one is completely different. He has a lot of contact with both parents and students. Simultaneously, he encourages a lot of contact between teachers and parents. He also pays much attention to the rest of the school's staff.

The *Australian* mother is a parents' representative on the school's board. Therefore, she is much more familiar with the school's total business than the other parents are. She has a son in grade 7 and a daughter in 11. Both the parents and the children are very pleased with both XIS and their stay in Xiamen. Because the father works for Kodak, who experiences major problems, the family fears a swift return to Australia. The family has lived for four years in Xiamen, and has experienced several changes at XIS during that time. The mother is especially pleased that the board has succeeded so well in finding a new headmaster. He is in a class of his own, compared to the previous one, and to the experiences she has from Melbourne. At the same time, she is well aware that the Chinese deputy headmaster plays a central role in the school's effective operations. As a board member, she participated in the discussions about the school's move from the US K-12 system to the International Baccalaureate (IB). She strongly supported the change.

When she compares XIS with Australian schools, she thinks that XIS has improved its quality after the transition to IB. The subjects are clearer than before. With the IB model, XIS is more similar to a school in Australia. Simultaneously, she is increasingly fascinated by experiencing how excellent teachers "like magicians make project work produce subject knowledge". The weakness of the US model appears in cases where the teacher is not academically good, or have poor classroom discipline.

Then the time spent in project work may be a waste. She finds it hard to find negative critical points about XIS, because her involvement in the school's development, and from obtaining some sort of ownership to the school. With the transition to IB, she thinks that XIS is a better school than what she remembers as a very good school in Australia, with many students that do well. There is one thing she misses a little bit. That is the diversification in the parent group's social background. At home, in Australia, among a school's parent group you find people from different social backgrounds equally respected. Although she and her family enjoy living in Xiamen, with XIS as the core of their social environment, it all feels a bit exclusive. The foreigners, business people with good salaries, but also people from the university sector, is a privileged bubble in a city of millions, where most are working people. Although she enjoys a comfortable life, she looks forward to come back to a life with "normal" people in Australia.

The *Korean* mother tells that before the family came to Xiamen, they lived in Sri Lanka for ten years. There the children attended the English international school. She has one child in grade 6, and one in 7. In addition to time spent at XIS, all Korean children spend Saturday mornings at a Korean language school. She does not think that XIS has a particularly high academic standard compared to schools she knows from before. In terms of grading, she gives XIS a C on quality in general. She has discussed the quality issue with many Korean parents in Xiamen. The vast majority agrees on seeing the academic standard at the XIS as lower than in Hong Kong and Korea. She finds the amount of homework acceptable. She stresses the importance of a good school as one that gives children such knowledge and skills that prepare for lifelong learning. In this field, she marks XIS with a C +.

She has experienced a headmaster shift during the time the family has spent in Xiamen, and believes that it clearly has resulted in changes for the better. She points out that XIS gives students a lot more freedom than at the English school in Sri Lanka. There, structure was clearer and discipline stricter. She sees the students of XIS as a bit too relaxed in relation to their teachers, and she is not sure if that is a good thing. She is critical to the quality of the teaching of English as a foreign language. The teachers should push students harder. The teaching should be more intensive and targeted. If a student does not command English well, the students should repeat the grade level, until mastery of the language has improved. She is critical of the sponsor scheme (mentor), because it means that some students, especially those who are good at English, have a demanding extra work. Since most classes have few students, some must repeatedly be a mentor. Such extra work interferes with these students' learning for their own targets.

The *Swedish* parents have a daughter in grade seven. They are pleased with the academic standard, but not quite, when they compare with Sweden, and in relations to the expectations they had in advance. Their dissatisfaction is about what they see as teachers' too high ambitions for students' learning, e.g. in science. It is almost like university level of expectations to students' learning when it comes to depth of expertise and amount of detail information. In other subjects, the Swedes think the teacher progresses too fast, by trying to cover too much material in a short time. Some of the textbooks need revision, e.g. in mathematics. The book used is not adequate to visualize the connection between math topics and their use in practice. The book seems childish. There is very much homework. Sometimes you wonder if the teachers give homework just to "bother" the students. They wonder whether so much homework really is necessary.

They are happy with the social climate at school. The students respect each other, but they think this mostly due to the school being small. They have reacted negatively to what they perceive as a much more hierarchical school than they remember from home. The Swedes are critical to how the teacher sometimes uses his power. They have experienced that teachers have threatened students to behave according to the teacher's decision, e.g. a teacher may tell a student: "If you don't do as I say, then you appear in the Inspector's Office next morning!" The parents think the school is trying to create a good environment; at least there are good intentions. In relation to their expectations, they see the school environment as average an appropriate marking would be a C. They are very satisfied with the widespread use of ICT, as well as their daughter having the opportunity to learn Chinese. She would not have that in Sweden. They think that she gets a good basis for lifelong learning by getting the opportunity to go to school in another country, along with many other nationalities.

The Swedes had clearly the impression that XIS worked hard to be the best international school in Asia, but they felt that this did not happen on the students' terms. They wondered if the school's real motive for this great ambition was to boost the school's international reputation, or if it was for the leadership's own career interests. If the headmaster was successful with XIS, he would be stronger in the international market for school leaders. What about the students? The Swedes wondered about whether the school's continuous struggle for improvement was really in the students' best interest. The father told me about which school advice he would give to a Scandinavian family who thought of moving to Xiamen. He would recommend XIS, because the school covers all grades, from kindergarten through to secondary school graduation. On the negative side, he would warn the Scandinavians that XIS-teachers gave very much homework, which made big inroads in the family's private life on the weekends. The huge amount of homework affected the whole family negatively. At XIS, he thought there was too little time for a child to be just a child. At the same time he stressed that, much homework not only concerned XIS. This evil exists in all international schools in Asia.

When I try to summarize impressions from these discussions with parents, especially two aspects appear as interesting in terms of how they consider XIS. Firstly, which country the parents come from, and, secondly, which aspects of the school they view differently. At the beginning of the book, I wrote about the five dominant curriculum traditions that affect education policies, and affect parents' perception of what is a good school. The four Western traditions are essentialism (core area: England), encyclopaedism (core area: Central and Western Europe plus Finland), polytechnicalism (core area: former Soviet Union plus Eastern Europe) and progressivism (core area: United States and Scandinavia). The fifth is Confucianism (core area: East Asia).

The American mother is very happy with XIS. Like the Australians, English is her mother tongue, which makes many things regarding international education much easier. An episode that is too tempting not to mention is that the American mother was surprised to learn that they spoke English in Australia. The main reason why she is happy is, however, that she has come "home" in terms of the curriculum tradition XIS was originally based on. Even if the school now applies the IB model, a lot of progressivism at its best remains influencing teaching practice. It merges smoothly with the IB model. She believes that learning by projects, functions the same way as organized regular research, when led by a respected and professional teacher. Then learning practice based on the progressivist tradition is the cream of the curriculum crop.

The German mother grew up in Communist East Germany. In this area, both encyclopaedism and polytechnicalism curriculum traditions influence teaching practice. The first tradition dominated for several hundred years in Germany and lives on. In East Germany, however, the old tradition had strong influence from communist polytechnicalism with great emphasis on scientific subjects and mathematics, as well as strict discipline and hierarchical control. The East German school had excellent academic results. However, it was not a very cool school. On such a background, it is easy to understand the East German mother's overwhelming excitement for a school where she found students working dedicated on the subjects, but in a more relaxed and "humanistic" way and where both leadership and teachers *see* the parents and invite them in as fellow players.

The Australian mother is a bit special, since XIS is her «baby». Still, features of XIS, like strong emphasis on sciences and teachers respected because their professionalism, are congruent with the curriculum tradition she comes from, encyclopaedism. Moreover, English essentialist and elitist tradition influence Australian schooling. This coincides with the new headmaster's ambition to make XIS the top international school in Asia. This mother is very pleased, but a little worried over the elitist side. That is understandable. The Australian school is egalitarian, and has more in common with Finland than England. Similar to the American mother, the Australian has come academically "home". After XIS' transition to the IB model, it is more similar to an Australian school.

The Korean and Swedish parents are the most interesting. They are both to some extent quite dissatisfied with XIS, however, from diametrically opposite emphasizes. While the Koreans think there is too little discipline, the Swedes have the opposite view. The Swedes think there is too much homework, which is harmful to family life, while the Koreans send their children to a Korean language school on Saturday mornings. The Koreans believe the schools in Hong Kong and the international school in Sri Lanka are better than XIS. The Swedes are in doubt about whether or not they would recommend the XIS to other Scandinavians. How can we understand such different perceptions of the same school? The Koreans come from a Confucian tradition of great teacher respect, emphasis on hard work and intense preparations for the examination. These parents also have experiences from an English international school, in the essentialist elite tradition. Here, academically skilled teachers are excellent tutors, and they gain respect by a humanistic way of behaviour. Humanism, simultaneously with respect for authority, is the common denominator for essentialism and Confucianism. Therefore, the Koreans are neither pleased with what they see as a too relaxed style at XIS, nor with much time for group work. Using the students as mentors for other students, they see as a dubious use of precious time.

The Swedes come from a progressivist curriculum tradition, where the student's interests shall guide the teaching, and the teacher is primarily to be a facilitator. Although, schooling is important, it is not so important that weekends should be for homework. Most clearly, their dissatisfaction with the school appears in their not seeing the point in XIS' having the ambition to be the best international school in Asia. They wonder whether the consequences of such an ambition may be harmful to students.

The Korean and Swedish parents' different views on the same school, show the power of the curriculum tradition they themselves have grown up within. The tradition controls what they perceive as school quality. The Koreans and the Swedes observe the XIS reality, highly different. They observe and assess the same school reality with Confucian, respectively progressivist glasses. However, the parents have two things in common. First, the families are in China, because the fathers work in large international companies. Second, they think good schooling is very important. They have the same goal. It is on strategies to reach the goal they differ fundamentally.

Curiosity as to why education has such a high status in China, and wonders whether Norway could have something to learn from China was the starting point for this book. From my own experiences in East Asia, I have tried to bring up images of how ideas of a moral philosopher from 2500 years back, have affected China's development for good and bad. I have told about how his thoughts throughout history have affected individuals at various levels of society to make determined efforts for both elite and mass education in China. In conclusion, on the China section of this book, I will show, in next chapter, how China is using its Confucian educational soft power, to strengthen the nation's cultural position internationally.

21

Modernization and Culture Export

What characterizes China's current education policies? With Confucian cultural tradition and stress on learning academic subjects as foundation, the Chinese school is modernizing at rapid pace across the country. Training in marxism is sharply down. Confucianism is clearly back after Mao's attempts to eradicate it. There is a strong focus on applying ICT in teaching. School leadership, which traditionally had high status, is increasing quality through nationwide in-service training, involving inspiration from Australian and English professors. Good examination results, especially at graduation from secondary school, pay off. Those with the best results, regardless of social background, can march right into the public higher institutions, without paying tuition, and with grants to cover other expenses. Students with less good results also have access, but have to pay more or less of the expenses. In practice, there is widespread ranking of schools and universities. For the universities, rankings also apply for specific subject areas.

Deng Xiaoping is the 20th Century person who has caused the most profound changes in China, not least through educational policies. He managed the political masterstroke to make a successful transition from planned economy to socialist market economy, and he observed a clear link between economic development and education policies. He was thinking in the same way as the businessperson Tan Kah Kee, who founded Xiamen university in 1921, with the subjects of economics education and teacher training. The latter was necessary to achieve the first. Education with quality closely connects with science and technology. Effective quality improvement of the education system was Deng's priority number one, in order to achieve the restoration of China, to the economic and political position the country normally had in its long history.

In order to optimally tapping the knowledge power of the population as a whole, focus is on broad mass education and elite education simultaneously. This is also in line with old Confucian meritocratic thinking. In contrast to the time of the socialist planned economy, there is now accept for private education solutions. Since the public system does not have sufficient capacity to meet the huge interest in higher education, a student-financed private sector is developing rapidly. The policy also encourages the creation of private elite schools for basic and secondary school, with both Chinese students and foreigners as target groups. Those who establish such institutions have the right to calculate some return on their investments. That is what Yang Ying did, when she established XIS, and the other elite schools. Commercially based schools you also find in England and Sweden.

For some Western observers, especially from the United States and Scandinavia (minus Finland), what they experience as Chinese educational fanaticism seems daunting. How much time will there be to enjoy just being a child or a youth in such a culture? What about those who do not master a school so heavily focused on learning knowledge? Parents' high educational expectations may be too much for some students. Feeling of defeat may prove fatal. Vocational education has a low status. Academic education is what primarily counts. This characterizes the parents' expectations to their children, from kindergarten until graduation from secondary school. Students' time outside school is almost entirely for school's homework. Over the years, there have been reports from Japan about suicide among those who are not getting good enough examinations from secondary school, to get into the best college. This also occurs in China.

Chinese educational researchers are well aware of the challenges that the not academically oriented students pose. In the current political climate, learning smart things from the West is welcome. Chinese researchers point at three factors, where China can learn from the West. One is to create a vocational education with more status. It will help individuals, and the workplace needs them. Another measure is to be more aware of practicing student centred teaching. Third, negative effects of competition need serious attention. The Hong Kong Synthesis, featured initially in this book, many consider as a possible model for the whole of China. However, it will not be easy to get effective help to the academically weaker students. Because, both Confucius and Plato do not attribute particular value to them. In particular, Confucius is explicit. He divides people into four groups, when it comes to the ability to learn knowledge. The forth and last group is not able to learn. Therefore, it is not even worth trying. With Confucius' strong cultural authority, it is likely to be difficult to change this view on weaker students. Nevertheless, Chinese education researchers think China should learn from the West, when it comes to these students. In that case, they must manage to get parents and teachers in China to adapt the Western, humanist position – that absolutely *all* people, no matter how small the potential for learning is, should have opportunity to develop this potential.

An unintended effect of China's economic success is a hugely increased international interest in learning Chinese. More than 30 million non-Chinese people at 2500 universities in more than hundred countries are now studying Chinese. The number is increasing rapidly. Basic and secondary schools in the United Kingdom, the United States and Norway offer Chinese programmes. In China, the number of foreigners who come to study Chinese increases with more than 40% per year. In the United States, Chinese is the second most important foreign language, after Spanish, but ahead of French and German. In China, more than 400 universities offer language training for foreigners. Chinese language learning is a lucrative industry. In the United States, already more than 500 secondary schools are offering Chinese. The policy goal is to offer Chinese as a regular programme in US schools.

Chinese authorities appreciate this development, and intend to stimulate it further. The ministry of education has a separate office with the responsibility to intensify China's efforts in culture exports. The office organizes annual international conferences to serve as marketing of Chinese as a foreign language. The clearest measure is the establishing of Confucius institutes abroad. They are set up worldwide at a rapid pace. The institutes have two main tasks - to provide training in Chinese and to disseminate Chinese culture in general. Internationally, they are a cultural strategy parallel to the German Goethe Institute and the British Council.

Why do we see this explosive interest for learning Chinese in the West? What is the driving force that causes people to attend school to learn four pronunciation tones, cram a few thousand-word pictures, and be able to write, not to say draw, just as many? To learn Chinese requires quite a different effort than when learning the western world's main languages. Therefore, there must be strong motives behind. The key words explaining the motivation are profits, job opportunities and culture.

A country of 1.4 billion people with ever more purchasing power seems like a magnet for Western firms. Individuals think that being able to command Chinese may be a crucial job qualification in Western businesses in the future. Western educational institutions with tight budgets will increase their competitiveness by collaborating with the Chinese, and get them to carry some of the training expenses. Some Western governments are already thinking long term, both in terms of their citizens' skills in Chinese, and of incorporation in China proper. Apart from interests in money and jobs, a thousand years' different civilization is intriguing many westerners. Culture is exciting, and may also cause business. Added up, these attractions make China irresistible. Simultaneously, it makes a world of difference if you come to China and are able to communicate in Chinese or not. Without being able to speak Chinese when you are in China, you will have the feeling of being completely outside. The *language* is the great Chinese cultural wall. For China, on the other hand, the language is an important defence mechanism against Western cultural invasion of China. The language is a cultural wall that protects against the modern "barbarians".

Can Norway learn from China?

Two concrete historical events a few years ago triggered special interest in Chinese language. China became a member of the WTO (The World Trade Organization), which simply means that Western capital are welcome to the Chinese honeypot of a huge marketplace. The Olympics in Beijing in 2008 seemed several years in advance as a magnet for learning Chinese. The Chinese applaud the foreigners' interest for learning the language for two main reasons. The Chinese are immensely proud of their multi-millennial culture and history. The previous "centuries of humiliation" have forced them to be more modest than they like. Now is the time to show the world what the Middle Kingdom is worth, not just in terms of economy and technology, but, perhaps more important - a culture that they consider superior to the Western.

The Chinese are pragmatically keen to make money. It suits them excellently, when wealthy westerners now leave billions of dollars in China, while trying to learn thousands of characters. Chinese is a difficult language for people who are only familiar with the alphabet. Young children learn most easily a new language. Therefore, it is important to let children start learning early. Britain's former prime minister, Gordon Brown, was forward thinking in this area. He believed that British exports to China would quadruple in the course of a ten-year period. That is why he wanted that each school, college and university in the United Kingdom should establish partnership with an equivalent institution in China over the next five years.

The Confucius institutes are China's most visible soft power measures to enhance Chinese language and culture around the world. The institutes are non profit-based, but funded by China's ministry of education, and operated in cooperation with local universities or colleges around the world. It all began with a pilot project in Tashkent, Uzbekistan in 2004. Later that year, the first regular institute was in operation in Seoul, South Korea. Around the world, now more than 100 million people are learning Chinese as a foreign language at a Confucius institute. An institute operates in a professional collaboration between a higher education institution in China and one in the relevant countries. In Norway, the Confucius

Institute works in a partnership between Beijing Sports University and Bergen University College. Representatives of these institutions are on the institute's board of directors. In Bergen, also the local university is on the board.

For the Chinese authorities, the purpose of the institutes goes beyond just language learning and culture dissemination. An overall aim is to ensure that foreigners get a much clearer picture of modern China. They are also going to be meeting points between Chinese and foreigners, in order to give the former the opportunity to learn useful things in other countries that they can take back to China. In the long historical perspective, this is nothing new. Not until during the disastrous political conditions in the first part of the last century, did Chinese leaders realize that they would have to learn from already modernized countries. The clock turned back during "the Communist Emperor", Mao. He believed, like the earlier emperors that China always would be able to fend for itself. Deng, however, continued the thinking of Sun Yat-sen and other leaders of the early Republic of China. He realized that for the country to survive, to avoid new attacks from outside and, get back to its position as the "Middle Kingdom", the country had to open up, and learn from the foreigners.

The motive why Yang Ying established Xiamen International School reflects the thinking of Deng. She preferred to have a dynamic and innovative American headmaster, on contract. However, in order to secure connection to Chinese values and interests, she employed, permanently, a Chinese deputy headmaster. This illustrates an overall way of thinking among Chinese leaders. Yes to modernization, and yes to learn what makes sense from the West, but stick to the Chinese cultural character, the identity legacy of Confucius. The Chinese want to integrate from outside what is useful into their own cultural framework. They agree with Mao that the identity is the most important of all. Without self-respect, without believing that you have value, it may be difficult to master the reality. They also agree with Deng that you have to be practical realist in terms of what actually motivates people to work efforts, whether in studies or in the workplace.

Can Norway learn from China?

A game-changing feature of the way the world has evolved in recent decades is China's economic success and international position of power. Maybe it is time to twist worldviews a little bit. Would it now be an advantage for western countries, e.g. Norway, to go to China in order to learn from the Chinese? Could Norway learn from China about how to enhance the quality of Norwegian schools? Today, many wonder if the Confucius-inspired pedagogy and current education policies in China, actually is the country's super soft power. A power the country uses both to make China a financial colossus, and a cultural exporter globally. Attention in this book shall now again be directed towards Norway, the small, sparsely populated, super wealthy, mountainous country in western Scandinavia - with terrifying low school quality objectively, and worse, relatively, when compared to amount of money used per student. The practical-patriotic purpose of this travelogue was to ask if Norwegian parents and grandparents can learn from China in order to improve quality of Norwegian schools. However, before that query can have a response, it is necessary to sketch Norwegian school development after the Second World War – from the slow weathering of the school's academic character until present time's feeble attempts at resuscitation.

Norway

22

Norway Switching Curriculum Tradition

A particular motivation to write this book was the discovery of parents' role in international school development. In most cultures, parents are profoundly honest, when they have the opportunity to choose what they see as the best education for their children. The accumulated effect of many parents' concrete perception of school quality may have vital importance for the design of school policies in a country. We saw in the case of Hong Kong how the parents slowed a reform that aimed at creating a school with more Western features. In China, we saw how parents were ready to sacrifice almost everything to make sure the children would get education. When enough parents clearly mark their opinion, politicians have to listen to them. A particularly interesting example are politicians also becoming visible as parents, through their choice of school for their children. In England, it has been quite common for leading labour party politicians to send their children to outstanding private schools. Tony Blair did it. In England, elitist private schools act as model for the public school. Politicians, who loudly and clearly advocates strengthening of the public school, choose a private school, which they consider to have better quality than the public school. Also in Norway, we see similar tendencies. Elite people earlier choosing the public school for their hopefuls, now choose private and elitist solutions. That is what the Crown Prince of Norway did in 2014.

Arild Tjeldvoll

Norway has had compulsory schooling for all from 1739, when we got the first law about schooling for the commoners. The law was an effect of the Protestant Reformation in Europe. The Church, under the King's leadership, had an interest in all children learning the history of the Bible and the Catechism. It was necessary as preparation for life after death. The control of the training reaching its goals occurred at graduation at the age of fourteen. If the students did not have sufficient knowledge to pass at graduation, they did not have the right to marry. That fact was a solid reason to show strong efforts. The king himself also perceived the commoners' school as an essential means to ensure that his subjects were obedient citizens. The economic and political development of the 1800s provided an increasing number of Norwegians the opportunity to acquire more education than the basic commoners' school. The development was particularly strong after passing the law on primary school in 1889. During the 1900s, educational opportunities for all increased steadily. From 1920, there was a 7-years common school for all Norwegian children. It was, however, especially after the Second World War that school development proceeded rapidly, in terms of both length, content and methods.

In 1933, the Norwegian Labour Party made an important ideological shift. The party switched from being a socialist class party to being a people's party. It meant that the party's views on several social institutions, e.g. sports and schooling, no longer should develop specifically for the working class. From now on, these institutions should develop for the population at large, in a popular and national unity. Even before WW II, American progressivist curriculum influenced Norwegian researchers and politicians. Many Norwegians' stay in the United States during the war, and the United States' role in Europe in the post-war period had an impact. Humanistic respect for the individual student, measures to remove class distinctions, democracy and an emphasis on science and technology had strong appeal to Norwegian socialists. This is the essential background why the Norwegian school in the first decades after World War II changed profoundly, from being an academically subject-centred "knowledge school" to primarily become a political tool for social and cultural integration. The ideal society should appear, not by the past's idea of class struggle, but by having all students, learning knowledge, values and skills together, in the same class. Student-centred teaching was favoured. The overall aim was social and cultural integration of all students from all backgrounds. There were few objections that such a school could be at the expense of academic excellence in school.

Such a school policy ambition is impressive and deserves respect, although it would eventually prove unrealistic. This unified school, with progressivist curriculum, aimed at socialization while students achieved common identity and mutual respect, simultaneously with acquisition of solid academic knowledge. The goal of solid academic knowledge, Norway had already had for a hundred years. In the 1800's, the encyclopaedist curriculum substituted the Latin School. This meant that the applicable academic subjects, e.g. modern languages and accounting came at the forefront. The country's dynamic business development and international trade needed expertise, e.g. modern languages. The ministry of education's powerful director general, Hartvig Nissen, expressed the new curriculum thinking, eloquently, "New Times require New Knowledge". During the early 20th Century, it was not only the Labour Party, who fought for better educational opportunities for all. In addition, the Liberal Party was an important driving force. Before the Second World War, Norway had, simply expressed, a two-fold system of voluntary education available, after finishing the 7 years' compulsory school for all. That was the academic secondary school, preparing for university entrance, and various shorter practical-oriented schools (e.g. a trade school).

As an interesting "education bridge" between these two main directions, there was a three years' *real school*. The first two years of this school were identical with the academic secondary school. After two years, students could choose either to continue the academic path for three more years, finishing with the *examen artium* (university entrance examination), or continue for just one year with a more practical programme. The intention of the latter was to make students more eligible for going straight into working life. However, having a three years' real school, you could after a few years in working life, choose to return to the academic track, and take the university entrance examination. Education policies in the postwar period continued to aim at having more flexibility in the choice of secondary education, in relation to changing needs in the labour market.

The policies' overall aim were, however, the ideological ambition to use the school as an effective instrument for cultural and social integration of different student groups. All students should become optimally useful members of a fair and equal society. Put otherwise, the reform policies should achieve three aspects of socialization simultaneously, a common national identity, professional skills and moral education. Compared to pre war times, this was a principally new type of school, aptly expressed in the label – *The Unified School*. The implementation of the ideologically based changes of curriculum tradition, and school structure was so strategically elegant, that few people were aware of how dramatic the changes were. Critical debate about the new ideological course was limited. The objections expressed, came mostly from people perceived as privileged academicians, defending their own favourable working conditions. The critics claimed that they defended the former school's structure and curriculum, because it had higher academic quality. The unified school would imply a decline of quality. It was not until the beginning of the 2000s, that these critiques became valid, and that a school with academic quality once more tried to become a national priority.

After the school reforms of the 1960s, the quality of Norwegian school has steadily declined. The bold ambitions of simultaneously achieving solid knowledge acquisition and social integration have been unsuccessful. A fascinating confirmation of the failure is the last ten years' almost panic-stricken measures to regain a school where academic knowledge acquisition is at the centre, illustrated by phenomena like renaming the position of Minister of Education to "Minister of Knowledge" and naming a recent curriculum reform "The Knowledge Promotion". In this section of the book, about Norwegian post war education history, I will point out what I think has failed in Norwegian school policies, why it has failed and why the remedies have been wrong. First, as a backdrop for the development of the last 30-40 years, I will provide a picture of what I see as the golden age of Norwegian schooling with quality, the 1950s. It is in contrast to this the golden age that I observe the development from then and until today (2016). After the golden age, there came a long series of reforms and projects, aiming at making the school terrain fit with the ideological map. It did not take long before signs of crises appeared.

On the lower level of secondary school (age 13-16), it is impossible simultaneously to achieve a high level of knowledge and social integration, when the class includes students reflecting the whole range of preconditions for abstract thinking. If the teacher tries to keep a high level of knowledge acquisition, the weaker ones fall out. If priority is on social integration, the level of knowledge will drop. The dreadful result may be just a "retention school" where neither knowledge nor integration occur successfully. A *school* can never remove innate, individual differences. Historically, the school's distinctive character occurred, because of its design for people with certain intellectual preconditions. That is the historical origin of 'school' as a social phenomenon. That is still how most education conscious actors worldwide consider schooling, while Norway still maintains a policy that it should be possible to achieve both goals at the simultaneously.

In the 2000s, we see attempts to dress a knowledge-rhetoric upon the unified school. The desire for a school focusing knowledge learning remains rhetoric, as long as the perception of the phenomenon of school remains pervaded in a progressivist educational culture. The ideologically based curriculum shift after the war was politically successful. Most political groups joined in. The important change was *from* a Continental European encyclopaedic curriculum tradition, focusing knowledge, *to* an American-inspired progressivist tradition focusing social integration. This shift implied the groundwork for a new, distinctive educational culture in Norway. This new culture for a long time meant hostility towards a school focusing knowledge learning. The new culture implied a built-in contradiction between acquisition of knowledge and "the school as a place just to stay" for social integration. This contradiction has caused a confused debate about what are valid measures to regain a school with knowledge at centre stage. There is little recognition of the fact that learning also takes place elsewhere than in schools. There is lack of understanding that many of those with weak academic preconditions now forced to spend two years in lower secondary school can learn better in a "protected" practical work place. It is also a fact that many people, who are not motivated for school at adolescence, are "late bloomers", and take up education later in life. Then, when motivated, they should have generous support for continuing their education.

I will now make a glance to the time when the Norwegian school primarily was for learning knowledge - the golden age. This retrospect displays the standard, or frame of reference, contrasting the evolution of the recent forty years.

23

The Golden Age of Norwegian Schooling

Norway after 1945, and the end of the Second World War, witnessed an intense development in all areas of society. Still, the school the first graders met with in 1946 had many similarities with the school of a century earlier, excellently portrayed by Norwegian Nobel winning author, Bjørnson. In his novel, *A Happy Boy*, we meet with Baard Schoolmaster, who is a teacher for the boy Øyvind, the main character of the novel. He is the best in class, and at graduation, the ecclesiastical confirmation, at age 14, he should, by a tradition of respect for knowledge stand at the forefront in the church. The priest denied Øyvind this traditional right. At that time, social class distinctions were still very strong. Øyvind's parents were crofters. Therefore, the priest felt obliged to let the rich farmer's son have the forefront position, even though he was not the best. Bjørnson's second key character in the novel is an exceptional teacher - Baard Schoolmaster. The students loved him, because he knew a lot and he was a very wise person. Simultaneously, he was a brilliant communicator, who could enthuse the students with his professional presentations. On top of that, the students felt that Baard cared about them all, even those who came from modest social backgrounds. Øyvind became a clever student, not least because Baard cared about his learning. It is reasonable to assume that Bjørnson himself had such a teacher.

In 1946, Norwegian schools had left behind such class distinctions that Øyvind experienced. Since Øyvind's time, Christianity's equality ideals had merged with corresponding socialist values. In the Norwegian school's Golden Age in the 1950s and 1960s, it became increasingly less social background that prevented the pursuit of educational dreams. It became apparent to many parents and older children that after school, there were other options than to work on the farm or on the fishing smack. School efforts could fulfil dreams for both parents and children. In the 1950s, the schools were still rather decentralized. Small schools existed everywhere, in the innermost fjord, on the smallest island or in the most remote valley. The school was there, with its national curriculum and teachers used to convey it. Because the settlements and fishing villages often were very small, undivided and bipartite schools were common. Bipartite schools only had two classes. One was "the Small School" class, including all students between age seven and nine. "The Large School" class had all students between 10 and 14 years of age. A school's total population often were not more than 20 students. Because the school had only one classroom, that the two classes had to share, students only went to school every other day. Saturday was also a day at school.

The subjects were christianity, Norwegian, math, history, geography, science, writing, woodwork/handicraft, song and gymnastics. Itinerant teachers taught woodwork/handcraft. When the itinerant teachers arrived, regular schoolwork stopped. For one or two weeks, there was full concentration on the practical subjects. Teaching style for the regular subjects was the teacher's dissemination of the subject content and the students' memorizing. Memorizing applied to all subjects. If the teacher was not satisfied with the results of the memorizing, the student had to repeat the memorizing work, and present again the next day. There was always a lot of homework. Respect for the teacher was an ancestral tradition. When the teacher came into the classroom for the first lesson, the students stood up and saluted the teacher.

The teacher was not only an important person at school. Often, he was a resource person in the local community. Because he had more knowledge than others had, he was a helper in cases that required a written contact with government agencies. In the post-war period, there was widespread teacher shortage. It led to a great many "replacement teachers" in the small schools in rural areas. These untrained teachers came quite often straight from their graduation at secondary school, having achieved their examen artium, a university entrance examination. They were already keen to become professional teachers. However, they would like to take a year actually practicing teaching, in order to test their abilities as a teacher, before attending a teacher training college. Of course, these replacement teachers varied a lot in terms of professional quality, but quite often, they were very skilled. As 19 year olds, they had already decided to become a teacher. An important reason for their choice of career was often a teacher they themselves had admired, and who had inspired them to "the calling" to be a teacher. They had all been clever at school, and rarely had problems in teaching all school subjects in these small schools.

Often these teachers initiated activities for children outside school hours. They organized football teams, led the construction of ski jumps and participated in the activities themselves. In a small, rather isolated village in the time before TV, there was hardly much else, the young teacher could do on his own free time. Participation in leisure activities strengthened the respect for him even further, among both students and parents. The teacher also had plenty of time to chat with the parents, both about life in the village, and, not least, of their sons and daughters opportunities in life. The secondary school graduate of 19 years, in his role as teacher, heavily influenced parents on how they assessed their children's future educational opportunities. In a small, remote community, where no one had more education than seven years of schooling, a youth with secondary school was a well-educated important resource for both adults and children. This youth grew in maturity himself by having responsibility as a teacher. He was a role model in the community. For both students and parents, he was a visible image of which opportunities more education might contain. In secondary school, this youth had for sure read Bjørnson's *A Happy Boy*, and familiarized with Baard Schoolmaster.

The young teacher contributed to a constructive integration between the school and the local community. However, he was not the only integrating factor. A common occupational structure in many communities along the coast was "the fisherman-farmer". This structure implied that a vast majority grew up on a small farm, where everyone had to take part in the farm work throughout the year. Fishing was also an important part of the income. While the father was out fishing, the mother led the work on the farm. The fact that students only went to school every other day eased the students' participation in farm work or assisting in fishing work. Particularly for students not particularly fond of cramming psalm verses and the Norwegian King's Row, their participation in a variety of practical work was their real good life. Those clever at school, however, often longed impatiently for the next school day. The common denominator was that all the students had to learn all school subjects, and all had to take part in seasonal work, like cleaning fishing nets, berry picking, sheep slaughter, stick turfs for winter fuel and haymaking. In general, they enjoyed very much such "child labour". Participation in working life indicated that you were important for the family. The more proficient the children were at practical work, the closer they were to be a respected adult. In a curriculum tradition perspective, there were in these communities a good mix of teacher-led subject-centred encyclopaedism and progressivist project work. The project work, however, did not occur at school. It took place on the farm or on the fishing smack. In practical work, it was hardly possible to avoid applying what they had learned at school, especially in subjects of science, arithmetic and handicraft.

The families often had four or five children. After graduation, at the age of 14, they counted as adults. Not all of them could remain on the farm. Some had to move out to make money. Opportunities were rare. For the boys, the merchant fleet was especially important. In addition to having a paid job, there was the opportunity of rising through the ranks, whether it was in the engine room, on deck, or in the galley. The vision at the distance was to become a captain, a first navigation officer, a chief engineer, or chief of the galley. The girls often worked as a maid in small children families. The picture of what happens to the young crowd of the 1950s is threefold: The oldest boy will stay on the farm, or being skipper on a fishing smack. He also takes responsibility for the parents who stay resident on the farm for the rest of their life. The one, who has proved clever at school, has support to get on, to the three years' real school or to the five years' secondary school. Financial support for more than one is not normally possible. The other boys get jobs in the merchant fleet or seasonal fisheries. The girls work as maids, while they are waiting to marry and raise their own family.

In common for all of them, however, is that they had to learn two very important things as a child. First, they have literally seen how important efforts at school are - the popular youth with secondary school who was their teacher or their fellow student, clever at school, who gets the opportunity of more education, and how what they have learned at school is useful in practical work. Second, they learned a lot from practical work on the farm. They have learned to set goals for their work. They had to solve problems. They had to think, assess and act in practical reality. A rather academic school every other day and "child labour" every other day have given them a self-image, as someone who can, one that gets things done, one that master, and which, thus get respect from others. Said differently, they have achieved an identity, a self-image that involves self-respect. They think they are something, in the best sense of the phrase. Moreover, because they know they are something, they are mentally prepared to cope with reality, the struggle throughout life.

This school of the Golden Age in the 1950s is absent in the contemporary Norwegian welfare state. Seen from 2016, the two partite seven years' primary school had impressive educational qualities. No matter how remote the village was, and no matter how modest the fish-farmers' economy was, this school, with a 19 years' old teacher, without teacher training, and lots of "child labour", gave these young people a solid motivation to master the outside world. From a two partite school, one year graduating five boys, one became a carpenter, one a radio officer in the merchant fleet, one a chief currency manager at one of the country's largest banks, one an army general and one a professor at the University of Oslo.

For the latter two, their way into the outside world was via the municipal real school, which meant three years of dorm life at the community centre. The real school and a one year continuing school with vocational character, was often the only opportunities that was economically affordable for the parents. Examination from the real school kept several possibilities open. After graduation, you could either apply to a shorter professional education, e.g. one of the state agencies, find a job or, if you could afford it, continue in the third grade of the five years secondary school. For those who enjoyed schooling, the real school was a wonderful place. It meant an end to spending half the week on farm work. In the beginning, it was strange for a 13-year old to stay away from the family for longer periods. However, all your efforts could be on the subjects. The teachers, however, were the biggest difference from the primary school. They were *lecturers*. The young replacement teachers in primary school, loved and admired, they fell, however, in comparison with the lecturers. The lecturers were not particularly young. They did not participate in leisure activities. They were subject-specialists, and very conscious about their academic discipline. The lecturers of the 1950s taught in "the higher school" (real school and secondary school). This group of academic teachers is a somewhat underappreciated resource in Norwegian nation building. During the Golden Age, they trained the people who were to become the national elites. These elites were to occupy the command posts in both public and private sectors in the second half of the 20th Century Norway.

The lecturers students met in the real school had six years' university education. They were either candidatus philologiae (languages and humanities), or candidatus realium (math and science). Before entering a teacher position, they had to take a half-year's seminar about teaching methodology. They considered themselves, however, primarily as geographers or historians, not as educators. Compared to 2016, their social status was sky high. They were civil servants, appointed by the King in Council. Friday evenings, when listening on radio to Report from the King's Council, it was announced whom the King appointed lecturers. They were civil servants, and could only loose their job after a trial.

These academics conveyed their subjects with great satisfaction. It seemed like they loved their subject, and wanted the student to love it, too. Their academic insight and authority, their confident way of communication and their clear expectations to the students, often made lessons a pleasure. However, for these teachers class discipline was a simple matter, compared to today's situation with a similar age group of students. A teacher in today's lower secondary school has to teach a class of students with wide variety in terms of academic preconditions for learning. The first class of the municipal real school consisted of the cleverest and most motivated students from primary schools around the municipality. Behind the students were motivated parents who sacrificed a lot to make their hopeful get this ticket to a supposed better life than they had had. The real school had a limited number of places; hence, there was strong competition. There was a tuition fee of $ 7 per month. Today, not even a bus ticket, but heavy enough for the fisherman-farmer who might not earn much more than $ 100 a year. Clever students from poor families could get a scholarship.

The lecturers' skilled teaching gave the students a basic self-confidence. The students respected them. Because, the lecturers had *knowledge*, the students *believed* in them, when they tutored them. The lecturer, who taught geography and history, conveyed the academic knowledge he himself had acquired through six years' studies at the university. By extension, particularly in the subject of history, he ensured that the students also received general education, or humanistic character formation. He made his students understand that knowledge is the most important power means to achieve liberation from oppression, for the individual, and for the collective. Moreover, knowledge is often a crucial prerequisite for greater ethical awareness. When I later in my professional life had the opportunity to compare schools of different countries, it was with great satisfaction I could ascertain that the lecturers of a municipal real school, on the Norwegian coast in early post-war time, had professional quality on par with private, English elite schools.

The real school examination was not only a ticket to continued secondary education or several types of shorter professional training. Additionally, it was important when the youth faced the mandatory military service at the age of 18. Having a real school examination, you were entitled to enter a one-year officer's training as part of the mandatory service. Such military education was often important either for further career in the military, or in civilian work life. Besides the military content, this officer's school was a very good leadership education, as well as training in pedagogy. At that time, virtually all young men had to do military service, and not all recruits were highly motivated. Therefore, it was important that officers had good educational understanding and pedagogical skills. For those, who while attending the officer's school, had caught a genuine interest for the Defence Forces, excellent opportunities appeared. The Defence Forces offered free upper secondary school, and even a salary. The condition was that the applicant made a commitment to continue education at the War Academy after graduating from secondary school, and commitment to serve for a certain number of years.

Most of the students at the officer's school already had a full-fledged secondary education. Those with only a real school quickly discovered that this difference in educational background also represented a difference in social status. This discovery motivated several of those with only real school to take the upper secondary school examinations, if they did not want to continue in the military. After finishing mandatory military service, it was, however, not very tempting to apply to a regular secondary school, with students who were much younger. There were several alternative solutions, especially in Oslo. At their time in the real school, they had in the subject of Norwegian literature, learnt about Heltberg's Student Factory, a private, secondary crash course school. Several of Norway's most famous authors, e.g. Ibsen, Bjørnson, Lie, and Vinje had attended this school. The school gave an intensive course for those who for various reasons had not followed the normal track of education. At the beginning of the 1960s, there was in Oslo several private schools equivalent to Heltberg's in the 1800's. One of them was The Oslo Language School, in Park Road. Here, it was possible to achieve secondary school examination by a nine months intensive evening course. The class often consisted of students with very different backgrounds. Some were "spoiled city slickers", who had been so busy celebrating graduation that they "had not had time" to take the regular examination, and, therefore wanted to finish by this intensive course. Other students were of a certain age. Most of them had work experience. Teaching was from 17 to 21. Then the class gathered at Lorry Restaurant, in the immediate vicinity, for social digestion of what the teachers had just served them, in the classroom.

The school was a private business. It managed by attracting people willing to pay tuition fees. The headmaster was an inspirational entrepreneur type and a very good mathematics teacher. The English teacher had been a fellow student of famous author Sigurd Hoel, and was even a writer himself. The history teacher was a priest. The French teacher loved the French language and culture as much as he loved to teach the subject. Most students had a job in the mornings. The evenings, both at school and at the Lorry Restaurant, created a unique learning environment, and a lot of natural collaboration. The student who was especially good at one subject helped those who were weaker in that subject. However, above all, the student himself was completely and fully responsible for his learning and passing the examination. He could shirk as much as he liked. Regardless of whether you had learned in the classroom, by reading at your lodgings, or discussions with classmates, after nine months came the test: external examinations in all subjects, both written and verbal. There were no "responsive" reference to tests or efforts during the school year. Just the final examinations in all subjects counted.

June 15th the examination results were public. Many students, but not all, had made it. Those successful, in the evening, gathered at Lorry Restaurant for a well-deserved graduation celebration. The day after was working day for most of the graduates. Those who had no job, discovered that they had a valuable document in their hands. For some, the ink had barely dried on their University Entrance Diploma issued by the Oslo Cathedral School, before a one-year's position as substitute teacher in Oslo primary school was in place. The salary was good, the job exciting, colleagues were pleasant and the headmaster was a fiction writer and a very humanistic boss. The job implied a lot of free time to be used for something sensible. Both teachers at the Oslo Language School and the discussions at Lorry had opened up new visions and ambitions. After nine months at "the student factory" and having the examen artium, the university entrance examination, only one direction seem the right one - *the University*. In September, there was the matriculation in the University Grand Hall. The ceremony was very solemn. Candidates wore dark suit, tie and a black hat with silk tassel on the right shoulder. The Rector presented the Academic Citizen Letter to each of the candidates. An exciting academic world lay wide-open. It was just to serve yourself. The young graduates thought. However, it was not. First, you would have to take preparatory tests in philosophy, including logic and psychology. It was no simple matter. Many failed. For those who had taken secondary school just by a nine months' crash course, it was often easier. They had experience in planning their own learning. For those who wanted to study history or modern, western languages, there was one more preparatory trial - in Latin. Both the two preparatory tests were three semester's studies. In practice, however, it was possible to take both in one year. The two tests were both a demanding and extremely valuable introduction to the classic academic tradition of character formation.

Gradually over the recent 30 years, these tests were simplified or discontinued, and most of the new higher education institutions do not require such preparatory tests. This destiny of an academic trademark is one of many signs that the Golden Age of Norwegian education is history. To simplify also higher education, make it more readily available for more people, by lowering the academic standard, is an indication that progressivist unified school thinking has reached to the very top of the Norwegian educational system. In the next chapter, we will see how the Norwegian school, gradually, changed from being an encyclopaedic "knowledge school" to a progressivist "unified school". Knowledge policies turned social policies. Social integration became superior to academic standard. It was more important to stay together than to learn knowledge.

24

Good Will for a Unified School

When you are going to describe and look critically at the emergence of the progressivist-unified school in Norway, it is very important not to forget that the best possible motives triggered the reforms. One strong motive was removal of old social class distinctions. In the unified school, everybody should learn to respect each other, regardless of parents' social background. Academic subjects and practical subjects would get equal status. Schooling as a good, knowledge as an instrument of social progress and happiness, should be available to all, regardless of social background and no matter where they lived in the country. Simultaneously, the unifying character of the school should make students learn together in a community of natural equality, in a way that abolished earlier nasty class distinctions. Everyone would be able to acquire a maximum of knowledge in relation to his or her own learning abilities. In the clear light of hindsight, it is easy to see that this glorious ambition was a school's Utopia, appearing as a policy agenda. In the 1950s and 1960s, most people in Norway thought it made sense to reform the school in direction of Utopia. Even in 2016, you see school-utopians defend the unified school model in leading newspapers' debate columns, often representing university circles or teachers' trade unions. Good will to do the best for others shall always have respect. Nevertheless, if utopian good will results in academic decline, profound critique of it is necessary. After the Soviet's Sputnik Shock in 1957, when the Russians came first in space, American school authorities published a report, entitled *A*

Nation at Risk. American inferior education, compared to the Soviet was the risk. From then, American education became part of the country's defence policies during the Cold War. All US presidents talk a lot about how important a good school is. However, in the United States, as in Norway, what over time has developed into a particular school culture is very difficult to change. Pious political desires for better schools and detail changes *within the same curriculum tradition,* does not change the school qualitatively.

Transition from the Golden Age to the unified school was a strategic success story. The government established a separate agency, The National Council for Innovation in Education, to conduct systematic research and development work in order to make the unified school reform successful. The Council's secretariat consisted of outstanding school administrators, recruited because they had highly relevant experiences as well as a strong faith in the reform. The Council had extensive funding and got, eventually, a huge staff of project professionals. In retrospect, you wonder if "the research and development work" was a means, to justify the solutions the government experts had already invented on their reform drawing board. From the previous school structure, the reform experts had two schools at lower secondary level as a starting point – the three years' real school and the one-year continuing school. The first was academically oriented, the latter practical.

The first important reform step was structural. The real school and the continuing school merged into a two years' mandatory school for all. In total, it would take nine years, one year longer than primary and continuing school and, one year shorter than primary and the real school. The name of the structural innovation was "The Two-Track Nine Years' School", the two last years called The Youth School. It was a lower secondary school. Here, all Norwegian youth between 14 and 16 years should stay in the same school buildings, while they went to programmes reflecting the two former school types. The second reform step was to replace the division in two distinct branches with four course programmes, of varying academic difficulty. Seeing the entire cohort as a whole, students went to different classes, based on the students' capabilities for knowledge learning. It was streaming. The overall design comprised four different course plans. Plan A was for the very weakest students, those who eventually had to have a lot of special needs education. Plan 1 was for those who were weak, but believed still to be able to manage a simpler form of examination. Plan 2 was the group between weak and strong in terms of having abilities to master academic subjects. They had a somewhat more demanding curriculum and examination. The fourth group had Plan 3, a distinct academically curriculum, reflecting to a fair degree the old real school. This class comprised academically quite strong students. The unified school's over all ambition of social integration would happen when students from the four different classes were supposed to mix with each other in their breaks and in school activities outside the classrooms. Such social mixing happened just to a limited extent. The students from the different classes experienced that they had different social status.

Some places in the country, e.g. in the schools in Oslo's West end, the system of offering different course plan, broke down all together, because a great majority of education conscious parents demanded that their loved ones must be in the plan 3-classes. The second-last structural reform step aimed at solving the problems from having four different course plans. The classes coming from primary school just continued into the lower secondary level, no more streaming. Each class would have the whole spread of academic abilities. All students would receive teaching together in the same class. The new methodological principle was "pedagogical differentiation". Moreover, this principle implied an expectation to the teacher, that he would vary his teaching in any subject so that it was relevant to all students in his class, regardless of the students' intellectual abilities. He would make all students achieve optimal learning of knowledge, and simultaneously obtain social successful integration. Another label for the new principle was "student-adapted learning". The teacher would teach in a way that fitted each individual student. That could be a rather demanding task in a class of 25 students.

The finish line for structural reforms in the compulsory unified school came with the *Law on Integration of Disabled students*. All students, regardless of intellectual condition or degree of handicap, would receive teaching along with all the others of their cohort, in the same class. The existing special schools for disabled closed down. Thus, the teacher had the challenge of teaching the subject in a manner that simultaneously would be equally valid for the intellectual star pupil, who might later be a professor of physics, and the severely mentally handicapped student. Shortly after completing reforms of the compulsory unified school, the upper secondary school had similar changes, based on the unified school principle. The underlying, but overall motive for the structural reforms was that all students would learn together, learn to respect each other, regardless of whether their abilities are primarily academic or practical, or whether they are good at abstract thinking or not. In primary school such "unified thinking" generally works well. It is when children turn youth that huge challenges appear. Then hardly any pedagogical trick can hide for the teenagers that they are quite different, in terms of having relevant abilities for the historical phenomenon - *school*. Some of the youths have their self-image strengthened. They have the preconditions for mastering the academic subjects. Other students, experience that other see them as stupid, sometimes even the teachers make remarks in that direction. In the latter cases, it can be a tough challenge for a teen ager to endure two years of forced schooling.

While the teachers in the real school were lecturers of an academic tradition, educated at the university, most teachers in the new unified school had their education from teacher training colleges, in a non-academic seminar tradition. At their first appointment, they often had only the basic teacher training aimed for teaching in the primary school. They were, however, encouraged to take further education to meet the needs of teaching academic subjects in the unified school. Their further education was a module system, where they could gradually build their education to become lecturers. The modules could be of different lengths - one-year, half-year or quarter-year. These teachers were nicknamed "folk adjuncts".

They met no requirement of taking any test in philosophy, like those educated at the university. On the contrary, the academic tradition reflected in the philosophy test at the university, many key education administrators saw as a hindrance to successful social integration in the unified school. Philosophy was a reflex of the academic class society. It was a strategic goal to reduce the academic feature inherited from the real school. In the unified school, the lecturers whom the new school had inherited from the real school were fewer and fewer, while "folk-adjuncts" and, eventually, "folk-lecturers" became the dominant group of teachers. The academic tradition in Norwegian schools had received a mortal wound.

Not only should all students regardless of learning abilities learn together in the same classroom, they should also participate in the governance of the school. School democracy should be a distinctive feature of the unified school. This was a reflex of John Dewey's progressivist reform curriculum, where democracy was a core value. Like in a theatre, the headmaster directed the implementation of elections in the class for the students' class council, and the election of a students' council for the entire school. There were established regulations for what the student councils' tasks were, how they would work, and how they could influence on all aspects of school activities. The overarching goal was to make the school's total life optimally democratic. The new regime inevitably caused a reduction of teachers' and headmaster's authority. Authority was a bad word, often seen the same as authoritarianism.

School democracy was an important trend of Norwegian education in the 1970s. Three particular experiment phenomenon serve as useful illustrations of this trend. First, there was established an "experimental secondary school" where the students' general meeting had the supreme decision making power. Second, there was the "social educational study option" at the University of Oslo. A student was the chairperson of its board, meaning he had a strong say when the board appointed professors to teach and research at this experiment study. Third, at the University of Oslo, there was a research project called "alternative leadership forms in the school". A group of schools around the country had the opportunity to try different forms school management, all different from the traditional arrangement with a headmaster. One example was "collective management". The project team at the university had good contact with the top level in the ministry of education, both the political and the administrative. The project got massive public and financial support. Its success was so great that Parliament modified the School Act to accept other forms of management than one headmaster. However, a couple of decades later, the Act changed again, back to normal; any school shall have a headmaster. The school democracy trend had somewhat weakened.

The unified school, comprising the whole scale of variety in terms of students abilities, taught in the same class, proved enormous challenges for the teacher's daily work. Lack of motivation for schoolwork was a huge problem. There were motivation problems for weak as well as clever students. The especially established National Council for Innovation in Education had an extremely difficult task of preparing textbooks and other learning materials, that would make it possible for the teacher to meet the challenges of such a wide range of students' learning abilities in the same class. Assumed to facilitate learning for the weaker students, the curriculum's content structure changed. The different science subjects (physics, chemistry, zoology and botany) and the social studies subjects (history, geography and social studies) all merged into one new subject – the orientation subject. The rationale behind the merge was that this would help students to a more holistic understanding of the social and cultural environment. The actual teaching of the new subject would have practical problems in real life as the starting point. This obvious progressivist curriculum mind-set led naturally on to the method of *project work*. The students should work together in groups to solve a specific problem. The students would search for relevant existing information, in textbooks and other books. The understanding gained by reading, they tested in relation to real life problems, much like how a professional researcher works.

To meet the motivation problems of the unified school, project work became the panacea. Students would acquire new knowledge and becoming socially integrated while conducting the project work as a team. This thinking was completely in accordance with the educational philosophy of John Dewey. In the spirit of democracy, the importance of the local community's values and interests became of paramount importance. Captivating slogans appeared, e.g. "The national school's content and urban character is alienating remote local communities". A concrete project example was "The Lofoten Islands Project", where the goal was to develop a strong local identity, which in turn would mean greater mastery and power for the development of just that local community. Soon some cautious voices suggested that the project might involve alienation from common Norwegian values and interests.

By extension of the project work as a learning method, a new important pedagogical principle appeared - *responsibility for your own learning.* The education experts thought the student would be more motivated for authentic learning, when he himself had full responsibility for what was to do. The principle had dire consequences, not least for the role of the teacher. From now, the teacher's academic authority would be less important. The new principle implied that he was to be more like a facilitator assisting the students. This change of the teacher's role, would also achieve the goal of more democratic equality between teacher and student. The traditional teacher authority was out of step with progressivism's student-centered teaching and emphasis on democracy. Since the students now themselves were to find knowledge and apply it in project work, the teachers did not need to command a lot of *knowledge* any more. Psychological skills to praise and stimulate the students turned more important than the teacher commanding subject knowledge.

Simultaneously with the Norwegian school changing principally from subject-centred to be student-centred, serious problems appeared. One was the poor motivation of all those who were not happy that school obligation extended by two years. Another was social environmental problems at school and the school's relationship with homes having very different dedication to their youths' school efforts. The problem with the less motivated students led to the emergence of a completely new profession, the special needs educators. Challenges at school, previously resolved by the teacher directly, in cooperation with the parents and, where appropriate, with the headmaster, were now the task of the special needs educators. The profession grew quickly, because the problems following from making all achieve knowledge, simultaneously with social integration, constantly increased. Like other professions, the special needs educators developed their own particular education programme, from bachelor to PhD. They succeeded in establishing a particular department at the University of Oslo, which quickly became one of the largest internationally. Inspired by Norwegian novelist, Jens Bjørneboe's book about the boy Jonas, who had a hard time at school, the department established the Jonas Prize. It is an award to whoever makes an extra effort to integrate the weak students into regular classes.

Another profession occurring because of the problems following the implementation of the unified school was the "social educators". Their responsibility was both problems in the school environment and problems in the relationship between school and home. They overlapped to some extent with special education needs educators. However, they were not as successful as the latter in establishing a full-fledged profession. Their attempt at instituting a particular social education programme at the university did not work out very well. There was, actually established a social education programme at the University of Oslo, but it discontinued after a few years.

When the map does not match the terrain, when the students do not appreciate the unified school, the main explanation given is – lack of well-being at school. If the students just thrived better, learning would happen almost by itself. Special education needs graduates at the university wore buttons stating, "Well-being promotes learning". Poor motivation among students caused conflicts and discipline problems for the teacher. This constant problem field caused a market for external helpers, the consultants. They conveyed several hyphen-pedagogies e.g. encounter-pedagogy, confluent-pedagogy and involvement-pedagogy. The consultants were highly skilled communicators. Consultant gurus were increasingly popular at a growing number of in-service training courses for teachers. Eventually, there was an entire industry of aides for teachers having difficulties trying to implement the utopian ambitions of the unified school. While it was domestic school problems triggering a need for consultants to help teachers, the direct inspiration for the hyphen-pedagogies often came from the United States, Denmark and Sweden, never from Germany, France or Finland. Their common denominator was that they originated in countries with a progressivist curriculum tradition.

Although, the unified school tried hard to implement progressivist pedagogy, some goblins from the old school had survived and caused problems. Two remnants from the former school seen as harmful to students were grading and competition. The two are often in a contextual relation. Highlighting the students' learning results have always stimulated competition between some of them, particularly for those students that have capabilities matching the character of a school. The unified school architects saw both competition and grading as serious obstacles to the well-being assumed to promote good learning. Hence, the use of grading and traditional examinations decreased steadily. Some critiques of grading went bizarre. A professor of social education suggested publicly that football matches organized at school should be in such a way that both teams got the same number of goals. Then no one would feel like losers. Another remarkable example of aversion towards grades was the so-called 2.4 case of University of Oslo's programme in social education. In a feature article in a leading daily, a professor explained why all students at a recent examination got the same grade, 2.4. At that time, the grade of 2.5 was the critical point. 2.5 or lower (honours) was good, laudable. Numbers higher than 2.5 was not very good. The reason that all the students got 2.4 was to demonstrate that the grading of students with such a meshed scale was unfortunate for authentic learning. Those who got a poorer mark than others would feel like losers. The ideal solution suggested, and in fact introduced some years later, was pass and non-pass. There was no good reason to know who the best was.

Some critics of remaining academic features in the unified school went as far as questioning whether normal schooling really was good for students. A social scientist published a book titled; *If the School Did Not Exist*. He argued that a school without social well-being is directly harmful to the students. The good school is not primarily a place to learn, but a place to stay socially. His vision of the ideal school is an institution for the mentally handicapped, where students and staff live together in a kind of village community.

It proved increasingly difficult to make all students and teachers feel wellbeing in the unified school. The reform experts introduced a number of measures to make the school work better, e.g. more in-service-training of teachers, new, assumed popular subjects, reduced use of grading, project work and to let the students have responsibility for their own learning. Despite all these efforts, anti-academic critics continued claiming that the school still was too "theoretical", that it actually did more harm than good to the students. Many thought that the unified school was still too much knowledge-centred. By many critics, "the knowledge school" was an invective, in the 1980s and 1990s.

The implementation of the unified school took place through interaction with several agencies outside the school. Some of them had arisen as a consequence of the unified school, while others were due to overall societal development. Among the first was the Pedagogical-Psychological Service (PPS) and the National Parents' Committee (NPC). The establishing of PPS was a direct response to heavy problems in the unified school. The acronym stands for educational-psychological service. The name also reflects a professional tension between academic educators and psychologists trained at the university. While the previously mentioned special education needs teachers and social education teachers worked within the individual school, PPS was a separate institution, staffed initially with a psychologist or education specialist. The service's task was to assist the schools in diagnosing students with learning and/or adjustment problems. As such problems constantly increased, the service expanded. Eventually, social workers and special education needs teachers were part of the PPS' staff. The different professions comprising the PPS primarily reflect types of problems among students, but they are also good examples of how liberal professions grow and make themselves necessary.

Immediately, you are tempted to believe that the National Parents' Committee (NPC) is an initiative by parents, precisely to safeguard the interests and expectations of parents. It is not. The government appoints the Committee. Its mandate is to involve parents constructively in efforts to reach the goals of the unified school. Socially and politically, the committee's function is to contribute to making the state's unified school policies legitimate. Seen from the outside, and by a first glance, you may think the committee is representative of the parents as stakeholders, and that parents in general support the unified school policy. That is only partly the case. A growing number of parents turned critical of the public unified school.

The implementation of the unified school principle in both lower and upper secondary school, made the teachers' trade union structure change in important ways. Actually, school policy changes mirrored a similar change of trade unions. At the start of the reform, you found the Norwegian Teachers' Union, comprising teachers in the former seven years primary school and the Norwegian Lecturers' Union, for teachers in the real school and upper secondary school, as well as a number of smaller associations, such as the Trade Schools' Teachers' Union. Alongside the structural reforms in lower and upper school, a merger process took place among the unions. The result was the Education Association. The old Lecturers' Union was to a fair degree also an academic professional organization, concerned about subjects and curriculum matters. The later merges primarily functioned as dynamic interest groups, mostly concerned about their members' wages and working conditions. Educational policy issues and concerns about which curriculum tradition would be in Norway's interest were non-issues. The Education Association, and its precursors in the merger process, have been the most loyal supporters of the authorities' efforts to implement the unified school. Thoughts about whether other curriculum traditions might be worth considering never manifested.

Motivational problems in secondary school has also increased as an effect of social development in general. The oil-based Norwegian welfare state with ever-increasing material security for all, and easy access to free higher education have made it increasingly less necessary to make an effort to get good examinations. Everyone can get into higher education. The students' celebration of completed secondary school is symptomatic. Its special name is the Russ Celebration. It is not about academic achievements, but rather, a celebration that the process in the school as a place to stay, has ended. The way these celebrations express themselves is a sign of emergency for the Norwegian school. The graduates' senseless celebrations just *before* crucial final examinations, previously seen as decisive for further education and jobs later in life, is an exemplary expression of the unique *educational culture* that has developed in Norway from about the 1970s and onwards. This culture, which permeates all parts of society, is just not a culture for learning. The school is a place to stay, often in a quasi- learning process, under the student's own responsibility for his learning, under soft guidance of de-professionalized teachers. In international comparison, the Norwegian Russ Celebration is unique. It is also a unique sign of a school in crisis.

25

Signs of Crises

From the early 1970s and up until now, the signs of crises in the unified school are increasingly more visible. Overall, they are expressions of a fundamental mismatch between the educational offers on the one hand, and, on the other, the students' minimal motive to appreciate the forced offers. Already in 1967, teachers' first organized critical reaction towards the unified school appeared. During Easter Holiday 1967, all teachers at a lower secondary school took action. The school's leadership team was away on vacation, and the teachers took the opportunity to turn the school into an action-base. They put in a huge ad in daily *Dagbladet*, one of the leading newspapers in Norway, urging teachers throughout the country to engage in a protest against too rapid introduction of the unified school. Implementation of the unified school happened at different pace in different parts of the country. The Easter Holiday Action Group worked in a municipality having introduced the school reform quite early, implying that they already had several years of experience with this school innovation. These activists compared the unified school they worked at, with the real school, they themselves had experienced as students. The differences were shocking. In particular, two observations of life in the unified school concerned them. The first was a frightening low level of knowledge among students. Second, many students obviously had a painful time at school. Especially the students placed in the less requiring programmes, the academically weakest, seemed to have a terrible time. They kept to themselves, lonely, seldom mingling with others. In the huge newspaper ad, the action teachers asked colleagues around the country to support a petition to government to stop further implementation of the school reform, until better clarifying of its shortcomings. At the time, many real schools were still in operation, in municipalities having not yet introduced the unified school reform. Four thousand teachers nationwide, many of them lecturers, strongly supported the petition and the work of the action group, also by sending financial support.

When school life was back to normal, after the Easter holidays, the activist teachers got to feel the wrath of government authorities. Not only was their own school's leadership not happy, but the county's school director attacked the activist teachers in fierce statements in the local newspaper. He expressed salty criticism of "these freshly baked radical teachers trained at the university". He claimed that these teachers obviously had no understanding of what was the idea of the new unified school. Almost fifty years later, it is not hard to see the naivety of young idealist, actionist teachers. Many of them had applied for a teacher position in the new type of school, exactly because of idealism. As students at the university, they learned that, the new unified school was the brave new world of education. They would participate in building a better society, by making all students gain more knowledge, while thriving well together. That was these young teachers' vision. The educational reality they faced was brutal. They perceived the unified school as a violation of students' human rights. Those who had abilities for learning knowledge met with diluted teaching by academic weak teachers. That was a violation of *their* human rights. The weaker students had daily reminders that they were "school-stupid»". That was a violation of *their* human rights. Right after their "Easter Uprising" in 1967, the action seemed a wasted effort. In hindsight, these teachers deserve a lot of respect, because they maintained a chime of critical assessment of the unified school, something that was going to have increasing relevance as the signs of crises became frequent and more distinct.

Norway's modest or poor achievements in the Pisa-studies are the most dramatic indication of a profound crisis in Norwegian schools.

Although many Pisa critics think that the tests should have measured something different from what they actually do, there is hardly any doubt that the tests measure in a valid and reliable manner, 15 years old students' level of knowledge in the three subjects, reading, math and science. The test comprises the OECD countries. Already on the first Pisa tests, Norway scored so poorly, that it scared the nation. Norwegian students' academic level in reading, science and math was just below medium, compared to the other countries. When you take into consideration Norway's huge spending of money per student, the results are dangerously bad. However, these poor results are only dangerous, if you really believe that academic knowledge is an overarching goal for the school. Not all Norwegians share that goal. In that very first Pisa test, Norway almost scratched bottom in another field – classroom behaviour. Only Greece had worse behaviour. There are probably few doubting, whether there is a correlation between poor academic results and bad behaviour. A later Pisa test showed a weak recovery for Norway, which was received with cheers and as a sign that Norway now was on the right path. The most recent Pisa test was back to normal. Norway did poorly. The nation mourned in disappointment. Less developed, former communist Eastern European countries did better than rich Norway.

Several years before the first Pisa test, a university professor in the field of special education needs, in full earnest, proposed that mathematics should be an optional subject in the unified school, because compulsory studies of mathematics "made many students losers". If a conception of mathematics as an elective is widespread among teachers in the unified school, then it turns more understandable that Norway scores low on Pisa.

Another disturbing sign is the shut down of offering important foreign languages. In the real school, students, in addition to English, learned German, with a requiring, strict examination. At upper secondary level, also French was included. Both of these, culturally key, European languages were obligatory in Norwegian schools, before the arrival of the unified school. A foreign language is not only a practical means when you are abroad on holiday. In addition to the language skills per se, the students gain a certain insight into the literature of these countries and their social institutions. They acquire a lot more than a linguistic communication medium. They get an understanding of other cultures than their own. They are increasing their character formation as human beings. In addition, vocational subjects in the unified school show signs of crisis. There occur reports about students at carpentry programme, complaining it is too tiring to lift planks.

Abuse of ICT is yet one more sign of crisis. There are billion investments in computer equipment in secondary school. How much documented learning does ICT affect? Little. Simultaneously, there is expressed massive dreaming that ICT is the magic wand to achieve effective learning. What happens in a class told that they are themselves responsible for their own learning, and they have easy access to the Internet? The teacher is only required when the students themselves think they need some help. How responsible is it to make students responsible for their own ignorance? ICT can definitely be an important tool for learning. However, the use of it is completely dependent on a teacher having the authority to regulate students' use of the net in a way that actually serves the learning goals. If such a teacher is not present, the student may lose triple. He does not learn what he was supposed to learn, he is wasting his time and, often, he is learning stuff that makes him more stupid. This is a supposed image of a classroom situation. When this image is true, the school is failing its students, and abusing public resources. It is neither humane nor economic.

In higher education, "the master-degree-disease" or quasi-academic twist on practical professions' training is disturbing. Does it make sense to have a master's in sore nursing? Alternatively, is the degree just a nifty way to legitimize a pay promotion? Higher education institutions in rural areas are struggling with recruitment. For some of them, publicly funded "beach studies" is a smart motivating measure. Significant parts of the study programme's implementation takes place at a resort in South Asia, e.g. Bali. There is fair reason to wonder whether this is the optimal use of public funds. There is fair reason to question both motivation, academic results and whether higher education is a relevant means for remote districts' development policies. The examination scheme within parts of higher education seems to have become rather informal, and sometimes striking in lack of valid and reliable control of the learning results. There are cases where the sensor "adjusts" grades upwards, if the student has difficult socio-cultural preconditions. A messy examination system is a serious sign of crisis. A grade may not necessarily be worth what you think. If relaxed testing becomes widespread, it means a possible undermining of professional standard, as well as injustice among students. Foreign colleagues learning about Norwegian beach-studies and "flexible" grading, wonder whether this has anything to do with corruption.

A school, or a university, as an organization is society's tool to reach certain learning objectives for the students. In any organization, its leadership is the most critical factor for which results the organization actually delivers. That is also the case in the education sector. In 1986, the Norwegian Basic School Council assigned an external evaluation of its nationwide in-service training programme *Environment and Leadership in Schools*. The formal purpose of the programme was through in-service training of teachers, and school leaders, to make them better able to implement the new curriculum for the unified school. The external research-based evaluation showed that the programme barely had any connection with curriculum content, and assumed better teaching methods, to make students learn more successfully than before. The programme was weak on relevance to reality. In practice, the programme continued focusing on social integration. Knowledge was hardly an issue. The programme's basic assumption was that if the social environment worked well, good teaching would follow automatically. The in-service training lacked any form of serious examinations. The evaluators found that the programme had virtually zero effect in terms of improving teaching. The programme cost was 10 million USD. In a chronicle in Norwegian daily *Aftenposten*, the researchers concluded that the millions were money out the window. Even if the findings were dramatic, and no one questioned the professional quality of the research-based evaluation, the reaction from the mandator, The Basic School Council, was blunt and straightforward. The council did not accept the findings. Its consultants and bureaucrats pleaded disagreement with the findings, and rejected bluntly to let them have any influence on further school development programmes. The council's school ideology map was still superior to the school terrain. Despite, the fact that the report showed a dramatic failure of the in-service training of both headmasters and teachers, the same practice continued.

A school leader with poor professional competence affects dramatic consequences for how teachers are working and how students learn. In Norway, employment safety of headmasters and teachers is total. Only in cases where they have committed a serious crime, they risk dismissal. Hence, their life-long appoints may imply life-long leadership incompetence for that school. For parents, not having any alternative to such a local school, this is a dreadful situation. It has sometimes forced parents to move to an area where the school has a better leadership. A particular challenge for Norwegian headmasters is the Teachers' Union. There are cases where the union leader at the local school has more influence among teachers than the headmaster has. This problem over time turned so severe that some headmasters initiated a specific association for only school leaders. Its number of members increases rapidly over recent years. Nevertheless, still many headmasters keep membership in the Teachers' Union, as a separate section within the union, but subject to teachers' over all understanding of what is the proper role for a school leader. This tension has become an ever-increasing problem, after the government decided to make the headmaster position directly accountable to the schools' owner, the municipal authorities.

For the teachers, the particular education culture affected by the progressivist-unified school became a dubious pleasure in their daily work. Compared to the time before the introduction of the new type of school, teachers' social status dropped like a stone, like in the United States, the home country of the progressivist school model. Bullying of teachers and violence against teachers are increasingly widespread. It is no wonder very many teachers retire early. Many display a burnout syndrome from a job that proved mission impossible. In order to make life in class bearable for the teacher, there are downscaling of the school's academic ambitions, in favour of entertaining activities that make students behave reasonably well. The progressivist school is a tough work place. The teachers perceive that they often have to play the role of an authority-scapegoat for students' practicing of democracy. It is therefore fully understandable what still make many teachers endure such a difficult job, are some important material benefits, like a fair pay and long summer vacations. When teachers quite frequently go on strike, it is not to protest against difficult working conditions, or against a questionable curriculum tradition. The strikes are about length of vacation and pay rise. They want to keep or increase what they already enjoy; significant flexibility in their working day, good pay and relatively long holidays. In a comparative study of Finnish, German, English and American teachers, the latter appeared as a group concentrating on survival from day to day, because life in classroom was so difficult. A part of the survival strategy was entering into a "deal" with the noisy students. If the students kept a promise of behaving reasonably well at the back of the classroom, the teacher would reward them with a good grade anyway. It would not be surprising if weary Norwegian teachers too, consider taking up such solutions.

Even the university has not been able to avoid effects of the education culture affected by the unified school. Especially professors of a certain age have seen with some concern how the students have changed from the time when the professor was young. The professor feels it more difficult to teach, and increasingly experiences pressures from above to be more student-centred in his teaching. It is a long time since he was part of the group of mighty professors, appointed by the king, and enjoying several privileges. The long time tradition of professors as a respected key segment in the nation's cultural life, effectively discontinued in the 1960s. A pertinent question is, however, has the proletarianization of the previously mighty professors improved the university, academically. It is certain that a professoriate with less authority, together with widespread student democracy, have improved the academic standard. In many disciplines, the professors over the last three decades faced with an increasingly diverse student population. In Norway, it has become very easy to get into the university, and most young people have economy sufficient to spend some years at the university. The increase of students coming to the university is particularly visible in periods where the labour market for young people is tight. However, a university student is no longer a university student, as many like to think.

With the massive increase of the student population, followed some of the same educational problems that you have in the unified school. The professors are not accustomed to teaching weak students. They are accustomed to receive the cream of the crop of a cohort from secondary school. Not anymore. In many subjects, you see a threefold grouping of students. The first group consists of those who come from homes with a long tradition of attending higher education, and from the parents there is strong motivation that their sons and daughters shall climb the social ladder higher than they did. These students often fit perfectly to the tradition of *the university*. Actually, these parents prepare their youngsters for the university a long time before they actually get there. These students and professors have a mutually good relationship. The second group however, is the optimal one, as seen from the professor's perspective. These students are similar to him. They profoundly love his subject, they have great work capacity and they are ambitious. Early in their studies, they ask if they can participate in the professor's research, as assistants. Not only do they think that they learn more, they assume that a written documentation from the professor, a sort of certificate, will give them the edge when they approach the world of work. The third group is often very large, and the professors are not very excited about these students. It often seems as if they really do not know why they have come to the university. They walk around seemingly waiting for a teacher to come and guide them, as was done in school.

These students are a problem for the professor, and then becomes a problem for the university, because the administration have complaints from the students about the professors' poor teaching. Complaints communicate effectively through the students' democratic governing bodies. These students are struggling to hang on to the teaching, have difficulties making progression in the subject, and not infrequently, they drop out. In the spring of 2015, there were reports that four out of ten university students dropped out. It is a serious sign of crisis in Norwegian education, when so many young people are wasting their time and money on studies they often do not have the preconditions to master.

Norwegian university professors today also have many other problems to cope with A particularly effective way to break their former mighty position, was to find, new smart ways to become a professor. Not too long ago, you became professor, after applying and competing for a professorship, a vacant position that required full professor's competence (academic production, at least, roughly equalling three PhDs). In an increasing democratic culture, this scheme was too exclusive and elitist. The scheme implied that many well-qualified candidates would never achieve the top position of a full professorship. Many perceived this as unfair and nondemocratic. The solution to the problem was the so-called individual promotion scheme. You could become a professor without actually applying for a vacant position. When you judged yourself as qualified, you could simply apply for promotion. Then, the faculty appointed an evaluation committee of persons from the particular discipline, to assess the application. Many disciplinary circles are small. Sometimes there might be close links between the applicant and members of the assessment committee. An effect of the individual promotion scheme was that the number of professors exploded. A Swedish colleague uttered, after strolling the hallways at the University of Oslo, "At this university professors are frequent as lice". Yes, they are many now, the professors, very many, and like for the teachers in the unified school, their social status decreased steadily. Just after WWII, Norwegian professors were civil servants enjoying wages equivalent to the director general in the ministry of education. Now, the professors' salary barely compete with that of a headmaster in a unified school in Oslo.

In parallel to the impossible ambition of progressivism, simultaneously to achieve solid knowledge, practical skills and social integration, you find in some subject areas of Norwegian higher education, a phenomenon called partially practice-based professors. The implication being that different types of practice can be included as valid competence for a professor. Who in academe could ever imagine that possible? Hardly anyone who places himself in the Humboldt-tradition. The story started with people working at the university as lecturers, a university lecturer. Referring to his practical experiences, he could apply for promotion to an advanced lecture position. The position was equivalent to an associate professor requiring a PhD. The two received the same salary. The lecturer could gather even more experiences and then apply for a docent position (equivalent to professor, and the same salary). At international conferences, their titles translated into English, these practitioners were as good academic professors as anyone was. Measured by its number of professors, Norway has a vast level of knowledge. Since the many regional colleges, in the name of justice, put university privileges as standard for their employees, also this section of higher education swarmed with professors.

Professors in the western world had until recently an impressive social status and a general high respect from the rest of society. Their work place, *the western university*, historically developed into cultural monuments and intellectual cornerstones. Their history began with University of Bologna in the Middle Age. In a Norwegian context, generous individual promotion schemes and practice-based competence may not have rocked the classic university. However, when you take into account a recent effort to "communize" the university, its level lowering seems near complete. At the Arctic University, a few years ago, the university appointed a local comedian "a Laughter Professor". Several older, venerable professors found the appointment – ridiculous. A piece of status jewellery remaining is the honorary title a professor can use after retirement. He can call himself *professor emeritus*, meaning, "well deserved". It sounds beautiful, after a long life of scholarly service at a bastion of culture. The question remains, however, about how great the value of this title is, with the whole country barraged with thousands of "deserved" professors at a galloping number of new universities and university colleges. Inflation leads to devaluation.

By various measures, turning a country's intellectual elite into a mass profession can both be seen as contempt for the knowledge elite, any country is dependent on, and as a not very well considered measure for democratization. When Norwegian professors over a number of years have experienced that their status has fallen, that respect from both students and the community at large have constantly decreased, it is no wonder that they are concerned when they observe political signals of a more efficient leadership of the universities. Their very last and most important privilege, their freedom to organize their working day, as they like, may be at risk. An education minister from the Socialist Left Party suggested some years ago introduction of time clocks, in order to control the professors working time. Such threats make old professors remember their own revolutionary past in 1968. Their demonstration nerve is twitching. Such interference from politicians they bluntly refuse. Like back in 1968, they see themselves at as the bastion of intellectual power, daring to speak truth to political power. Even more so, when a female minister of education follows the socialist, and the professors think she is trying to squeeze New Public Management upon them. They wonder if the minister actually sees the university as a knowledge *enterprise*. Then the professors, like when they were young, organize a torchlight procession. Unfortunately, these many and wise professors do not understand that if the university leadership does not reform and becomes more effective and professional, the future might be even bleaker for both the professors and the nation. An excellent math professor elected rector (president) may well be a lousy leader.

Back to the foundation of Norwegian education, the unified secondary school. Outside the school, in its surroundings, there are also indications of crises, as consequences of unified education policies. One of the measures that emerged as an auxiliary for the school in order to take care of students with problems was the educational-psychological service (PPS). From teachers, school leaders and parents the service received mixed assessments. Several stakeholders questioned whether the service did more wrong than good. In the middle of the 1970s, there was a study on the consequences of the PPS' business in two outlying municipalities. The findings were startling. In the municipality without PPS, the headmaster and teachers resolved all problems, and to the parents' satisfaction. No children had to the leave the local community, in order to attend special education needs schools in another part of the country. The other municipality had access to the PPS. From this community quite many children left their home to go to special schools far away. Many parents and grandparents in this municipality were desperate to see their loved-ones unhappiness when leaving. Moreover, there were occasions of bullying of the weaker ones in this community. Other children noted which ones sent to meet with the school psychologist. They teased them. They were, to some extent, stigmatized. The teachers in the municipality with PPS felt themselves professionally overrun by the PPS expert group, with higher professional status. The PPS as a help service for teachers, created from the very best intentions, turned out to have serious, negative side effects for both teachers and students.

A dramatic sign of crisis in Norwegian schools came forward in a study of 2005, where the population in a number of European countries indicated their assessments of various conditions in a society. One of the issues was education, or more precisely, how important value do you think education is? The startling discovery was that Norway is the only country in Europe where less than half of the population think education is important (48%). In Europe at large, however, the great majority see education as a key value (81%). If this attitude is representative of Norwegian parents, teachers are in the peculiar situation that more than half of parents do not think what teachers do is important. Hence, it is easy to understand that many teachers feel strong headwind in their work. If parents and teachers are not teaming up, students' successful learning is much more difficult to achieve. When parents display an attitude of non-dedication to the value of schooling, it is also easier to understand why they so easily take students out of school, to take them on weeklong vacation trips overseas, in the midst of a school year. Such actions are a clear-cut way of saying that schooling is not particularly important. By extension, such an attitude among parents, make observers understand why Norway is enjoying the particular and tragic phenomenon of Russ Celebrations. Graduation from secondary schools is in some countries seen as so important, that poor examinations cause suicide. Norwegian graduates, *before* the final, extremely important examinations, choose to jump into senseless partying, binge drinking and flamboyant sex, applauded by both parents and the media. In recent years, the Russ Celebration is interspersed with a growing number of rapes. A celebration of this kind indicates a macabre view upon women, a view that many thought history in a country that is a world champion of gender equality. The Russ Celebration is a manifestation of a macabre educational culture, that is complete impossible to understand for people from other countries, except the United States.

A red line of this book is that progressivist curriculum tradition is the main reason for the negative development of Norwegian schools, during the last forty years. Simultaneously, progressivism is only one factor among several others that need highlighting in order to understand why Norwegian education underwent a cultural revolution in the second part of the 20th Century. The revolution resulted in a new educational culture, one fundamentally different from the culture that dominated Norwegian education until 1960, and different from the vast majority of other countries. This is a destructive culture threatening the single individual's mastery, companies' productivity and the nation's survival force in an increasingly globalised world of competition, where the power of knowledge is decisive. A particularly important dimension of the unified school culture is the view upon human nature underpinning it.

26

Misunderstandings of Human Nature

So far, in this sketch about Norwegian school development, I have, starting with its Golden Age, just after World War II, tried to describe well-meant reforms carried out to create the best possible school for an equal and democratic society. In relation to what has actually happened, the reforms failed. They have neither affected a high level of knowledge-learning nor good social integration among students. In international comparisons, Norway is mediocre or an underperformer. This, I think, is due to the special educational culture that developed as an unintended consequence of the unified school model. Why the sad developments in the school occurred, was due to how certain factors outside the school influenced, firstly on the school's content – its curriculum and secondly, on the school as an organization (school leadership and teachers).

The Norwegian Labour Party carries the direct political responsibility for the implementation of reforms that has caused crises in the Norwegian school. After the Second World War, the party decided to use school policies as social policies, as a main vehicle for social cohesion and integration of different groups in the Norwegian society. The concrete shape of this vehicle was the unified school. The party took for granted that this school model would also affect solid knowledge learning. The source of inspiration for Norwegian policies, was the United States' use of the school a tool in that country's strategy of creating a social melting pot, to Americanize various groups of people arriving from all over the world. For the Labour Party, the direct pretext was the party's decision in 1933, to abandon its class struggle strategy, and, instead bet on a social democratic reform policy. It is; however, wrong to put the entire responsibility for the reform ideas on the party. Some schools of thought, researchers and other key players in society must take their share of responsibility for providing Norway with a dysfunctional school culture.

Two directions within the field of psychology, humanistic psychology and social psychology, fit very well into the social democratic ideological thinking. Psychology as an academic discipline is simultaneously old and new. Its old roots are in Plato and his Republic, with elitist categorizing of the people into three groups (philosopher kings, the guardians and the mass). Modern psychology had a rapid development in the 20th Century. While the Norwegian psychology profession is a post-war product, the United States had a rapid development from early on in the century. Humanistic psychology has elements from both humanistic philosophy and christianity. In relation to education and learning, the student's nature is good. This is usually a basic principle in humanism. From this view, thinking education, the child is a plant only needing care and fertilizers to grow and develop. The teacher as a gardener is an appropriate metaphor for the teacher role viewed from humanistic psychology. The teacher shall show belief and trust in the student, give him responsibility and positively stimulate development. Treating the student in such ways, learning is limitless. For a good number of educational researchers, humanistic psychology was a truth, on which learning activities should build. The problem is that this humanistic vision collides with the school's reality. Not all people, nor students, are always good and has a built-in motive to learn. Many need structure and clear guidance in their learning work. A sculptor is a fitting metaphor for the teacher role then needed.

A second relevant line of psychology is social psychology. One of its mantra is that cooperation in groups is a unique good. Children's learning is optimal when they see the school as an enjoyable social environment. A common slogan is "Well-being Promotes Learning". The working day for most of the graduates. Those who had no job, discovered that they had a valuable document in their hands. For some, the ink had barely dried on their University Entrance Diploma issued by the Oslo Cathedral School, before a one-year's position as substitute teacher in Oslo primary school was in place. The salary was good, the job exciting, colleagues were pleasant and the headmaster was a fiction writer and a very humanistic boss. The job implied a lot of free time to be used for something sensible. Both teachers at the Oslo Language School and the discussions at Lorry had opened up new visions and ambitions. After nine months at "the student factory" and having the examen artium, the university entrance examination, only one direction seem the right one - *the University*. In September, there was the matriculation in the University Grand Hall. The ceremony was very solemn. Candidates wore dark suit, tie and a black hat with silk tassel on the right shoulder. The Rector presented the Academic Citizen Letter to each of the candidates. An exciting academic world lay wide-open. It was just to serve yourself. The young graduates thought. However, it was not. First, you would have to take preparatory tests in philosophy, including logic and psychology. It was no simple matter. Many failed. For those who had taken secondary school just by a nine months' crash course, it was often easier. They had experience in planning their own learning. For those who wanted to study history or modern, western languages, there was one more preparatory trial - in Latin. Both the two preparatory tests were three semester's studies. In practice, however, it was possible to take both in one year. The two tests were both a demanding and extremely valuable introduction to the classic academic tradition of character formation.

Gradually over the recent 30 years, these tests were simplified or discontinued, and most of the new higher education institutions do not require such preparatory tests. This destiny of an academic trademark is one of many signs that the Golden Age of Norwegian education is history. To simplify also higher education, make it more readily available for more people, by lowering the academic standard, is an indication that progressivist unified school thinking has reached to the very top of

Arild Tjeldvoll

other reason why students come first was due to influence from Dewey's contempt for old, European knowledge, with elitist features. He did not see such knowledge as valid in the new world. In this world, people themselves would discover the knowledge they needed in a democratic community of a fundamentally different nature than the old world's class society, from which they had emigrated.

It was this distinctive, American curriculum tradition, progressivism, which the Norwegian Labour Party transplanted to Norwegian soil after the Second World War. The ministry of education and its bureaucracy had good helpers at the university. Not all the education researchers at the university, but an increasing number, were eagerly doing research with progressivism as a fixed framework for their problem statements, hypotheses and research designs. Such research got ample financial support. Many professors of education made heroic research efforts to assist the authorities in finding solutions to the problems that occurred, when trying to make the unified school successful. Sometimes, professors were speechwriters for the minister's political marketing of the school reform. Critics will probably claim that these professors actively helped to make the school terrain match with the unified school map. Simultaneously there was a striking lack of research, which questioned the universal value of the progressivist curriculum tradition.

Another factor outside of school, which greatly contributed to weaken the school, was the general economic development in Norway. The rather moderate economic situation during the first decade after the war, made many people hungry for education, as a means to improve their lives. However, this motivation steadily grew weaker. The general idea of the welfare state, the state ensuring that everybody is safe from cradle to grave and, in particular, Norway's blooming offshore industry, have resulted in significant weakening for education that requires effort and perseverance. Although many still would argue that if only people thrive, then they learn, there are many signs contradicting the well-being hypothesis. To learn something well, requires for most people serious efforts. You need to thoroughly review the matter, and document what you have learnt by a real control, an examination. Such an effort requires that something different and perhaps more comfortable is forsaken. In such a situation, most people will first sacrifice what they do not think they really need.

The welfare state makes people less hungry. The instrumental motivation to improve living conditions is deteriorating. Education is not strictly necessary any more. In recent years, *naving* has become a relevant phenomenon. The verb word comes from the name of the Norwegian social security system. Quite a number of people, especially the young, choose "to nav" for one or more years, meaning, to live on generous social welfare means, not caring to much about finding a job. The most important thing is not to work, but to thrive. A Unicef-study from 2007 illustratively confirms such an attitude. To a question about whether academic results in school are important, responses from Norwegian students put Norway as the 18th of 25 European countries, while Finland came first. On the question about how students thrived in school, Norway came first, and Finland last. The Finns obviously make efforts, even if they do not think it is fun. However, they thrive when they see their excellent examination grades, and they are proud of Finland, when they see the Pisa results. They think they *are* something, because they *know* something.

In a perspective of curriculum traditions, Norwegians are today a people of progressivists, without being aware of it. Thus, the ideological socialization of the population after the war has been one hundred per cent successful. People take progressivist understanding of the school for granted. There is no discussion about the premises of this curriculum tradition. Progressivism has become Norway's educational culture. There is widespread acceptance of seeing the school as primarily a social place to stay, and a place of formal significance. Secondary school graduates can all move on to higher education free of charge, regardless of what grades they achieved.

Over time, the particular Norwegian progressivist culture became self-reinforcing, because a number of key players in society continuously underpin the unified school. Universities' departments of educational research educated, over a number of years, the people who occupy positions in the educational bureaucracy from the central level and downwards. Thus, progressivist culture continues into administrative thinking. The same university departments have provided teacher-training colleges with lecturers, transmitting progressivist culture to the teacher students. The mighty Teachers' Union is one of the warmest defenders of the unified school model and progressivist curriculum. Most of media applaud this educational culture. As do most of the political parties, with decreasing strength of support, on a scale from left to right. Together, these players make a very strong lobby, supporting the distinct school culture that has developed in Norway. Not too many years ago, this lobby openly favoured an anti-knowledge school. These same players are in favour of student-centred teaching and school democracy. Having democracy and equality as basic values, anything with a taste of elite standards is wrong, and competition is a bad word. Sometimes it seems as if the lobby has a bad conscience, because they themselves have obviously been intellectual school winners.

The strength of the particular Norwegian educational culture, eagerly defended by the lobby, comes out particularly clear, when there occur events seen as indirect criticism of the Norwegian school. Every time there is a Pisa-report, the lobby first states that Pisa is a wrong way to consider the Norwegian school. They claim the construction of Pisa does not catch the particular character of the Norwegian school. Therefore, the tests have little worth. Moreover, the lobby finds it worrying that Pisa is organised by the OECD, which means that there may be a shady element of economy in the Pisa rationale. Complementary, the Norwegian lobby hails the Norwegian school as a world's champion of democracy training, something the OECD economists do not find particularly interesting. Economic perspectives are opposites of what is human. Something negative. The lobby seems to take for granted that Norway will always have an economy providing a high standard of living.

True enough, some times there are people voicing concerns about the quality of the education system, not least in relation to the challenges posed by the global knowledge-economy. A few parents choose private schools or, for the secondary level, to send their children to foreign countries. Some immigrants from Pakistan also do that. They think schools in Pakistan, with an English essentialist curriculum tradition, have higher quality than what they find in Norway. With Norwegian wages and welfare benefits, the Pakistanis have no problems with school fees in Pakistan. In essence, the Norwegian unified school still (2016) has solid support from a strong lobby of influential social players. In 2015, a Finnish-Norwegian politician from the Liberal Party publicly pointed out the noise problems occurring with mentally handicapped students in a regular class. The unified school supporters bullied her away from politics. Such an attempt to highlight the need for good working conditions for knowledge learning, at the cost of social integration, the unified school lobby furiously refused to accept. An actor outside the school having particularly strong significance, for what happens inside the school is the teacher training. In relation to the school's academic ambitions, the training has proven close to invalid.

27

Invalid Teacher Training

Before the introduction of the unified school, teachers for both upper and lower secondary school (the real school) were educated at the universities. Historically, the teachers of secondary schools were graduates of the universities' subject departments, e.g. history and mathematics. After the introduction of the unified school model, teachers for the lower secondary level are increasingly educated in teacher training colleges. After structural reforms in higher education, these colleges merged with other types of colleges into what today are the regional colleges. In 2016, the teacher training is a four years' study, qualifying candidates to teach all subjects in primary and lower secondary school. After the third year, the candidate will receive a bachelor's degree, and after the fourth, and last year, a teacher's certificate. These teachers generally carry less academic weight than those educated at universities.

To get a better grip on the nature of Norwegian teacher training, it is useful to make a comparative glance at corresponding Finnish education. Socially and culturally, the two neighbouring countries have many similarities. As in Finland, Norwegian teacher education is rooted in a rural, seminar tradition. The seminars eventually evolved into the teacher training colleges. These schools' curriculum and organization were a direct reflection of the very first compulsory schools in rural areas, the commoners' school. It later changed name to the people's school. Its content and organisation had a distinct rural touch, reflecting competence needs in the local communities. The supporters of these schools were negative to the traditional academic orientation, which they saw as an expression of urban middle class values and culture more generally. The purpose of the early compulsory education in Norway was to provide young people with education in christianity and morality, culturally rooted in the Norwegian countryside. The curriculum of the first teacher training colleges reflected these rural competence needs. The curriculum covered all the subjects taught in primary, and, later, in lower secondary school. The graduates should teach all subjects of the compulsory school.

Because of the overall more liberal political climate of the 1970s, the teacher training colleges got greater freedom of choice about design of their curricula. The main subjects were the pedagogical ones, including didactics (theories of teaching), educational psychology and teaching methods. In the 1990s, length of study extended to four years. As a reflection of the unified school's progressivist curriculum, also a progressivist curriculum became dominant in teacher training. It meant that also teacher training got a distinct student-centeredness in their way of organizing practical teaching. Accordingly, there was less emphasis on academic achievements. The students in teacher training increasingly had more freedom to choose themselves which issues they should concentrate on in their studies. The principle behind this freedom was the students' responsibility for their own learning. Studies by participating in project works became common practice.

In the year 2000, the teacher colleges reported a failure rate of between 30% and 50% in subjects such as mathematics, Norwegian and pedagogy. Two years later, the situation was deteriorating. It turned out that teacher students were only able to resolve 30% of mathematics tasks given to students in lower secondary school. Compared with the time before World War II, the professional quality of teacher candidates had a significant decline. It is relevant to consider this fact in relation to the criteria applied for recruitment to teacher training, as well as to compare with Finland. Recruitment criteria in the two countries are essentially different.

By 2004, the authorities were seriously worried about the low academic quality of applicants. Hence, they decided to require a minimum standard in the subjects of Norwegian and mathematics. If this requirement had applied the previous year, 31% of those who were accepted would not been eligible for teacher education. An evaluation by the Norwegian Agency for Quality Assurance in Education, in 2006 further confirmed this weak academic level of applicants to teacher training. Among the students who entered teacher training between 2001 and 2003, only 23.7% had qualified, if the stricter requirements from 2004 had applied. It means that three out of four teacher graduates were not qualified to teach according to the new requirements. Still, such poorly qualified teachers had permission to go on teaching our children. In parallel with decreasing academic standards of applicants, graduates from secondary school show declining interest for applying to teacher's training. According to the 2006 report from the national quality assurance agency, increasingly lower interest for teacher training among secondary graduates was a trend over the previous years, all the way from the 1970s. In the period between 1970 and 2004, all applicants were, in practice, accepted, because the admission requirements were very low.

Since these students were and are, so weak, especially in academic subjects like mathematics and Norwegian, several teacher training colleges found it necessary to take exceptional steps, like requiring accepted students to take an additional course before start of studies, to compensate for their lack of competence. In certain subjects there are high failure rates at the colleges' final examinations, e.g. up to 24% in mathematics. Moreover, there are reports of teacher students having developed a general attitude of indifference to academic knowledge. An at least partial explanation of the students' low academic level is their modest work efforts. Research reports tell that teacher students have an average workweek of 24 hours. About half of the time, 12 hours, is for participation in organized teaching, e.g. lectures. Teacher students have a shorter workweek than the other students have, in the regional colleges.

One reason for the low academic level of applicants to teacher training may be that better qualified graduates from secondary school find other professional studies more attractive. Therefore, there may be a connection between the fact that the applicants to teacher education have a low academic level, and that a professional career as a teacher is not attractive for graduates from secondary school in general. Overall, not only the academic standard for teachers from teacher colleges is under scrutiny, there are also doubts about their intellectual abilities and real motivation to benefit from the extensive in-service training offered to compensate for their shortcomings. In-service training is the linchpin of the current government's strategy to raise standards in the Norwegian school. Considering how similar the neighbouring countries Norway and Finland in many ways are, it is striking that Finland for several years has been the world's best nation in the Pisa tests, while the results for Norway's part make shock waves among education policymakers. Why? Maybe one important explanation of the fierce academic difference in level of knowledge between the two country's 15-year olds is – exactly, the teacher training. A comparison between the two countries show dramatic differences, in terms of admission criteria, and the organization of the training.

The first difference is the curriculum and subjects. In Finland, they study fewer subjects, and study more in depth. The studies are research-based. Students need to study research methods. A research-based master thesis is an essential part of their final teacher examination. In Norway, they study many subjects, without particularly much in depth. There is no training in research method. Finnish primary and secondary school is in the encyclopaedic, continental-European curriculum tradition. A main implication being that the teaching is subject-centred, not student-centred. In Finnish teacher training, there is also an influence from the English essentialist curriculum tradition, with fewer subjects and studies of them more in depth. The curriculum in the Norwegian teacher education reflects clearly the progressivist tradition of strong student centring in learning. It means very much of the responsibility left to the individual student. Taking into account that Norwegian student's academic level at the outset is low, it is easy to understand that the principle of students' «responsibility for own learning» can be a risky project. There are important differences between how the two countries structure the teacher training, and where they locate it. In Finland, the teacher training is a five years' master study, located in the cultural environment of research universities. Norway has a four years non-research based study, resulting in a teaching certificate, and the study takes place in a school not being part of a university's academic culture, but of a progressivist anti- knowledge culture.

It is primarily when it comes to *recruitment* to teacher training, that the two countries are essentially different. This difference understood, it becomes less remarkable that Finnish compulsory schoolteachers make the country a school world champion. Finland recruits the very best graduates from secondary school to, exactly, become teachers. The teaching profession is one of the most popular in Finland. There is fierce competition to get into the teacher training programmes at a university. Norway has the opposite situation.

Motivation for the teaching profession and teacher training has been declining in Norway over a number of years. This is a particularly unfortunate effect of the progressivist unified school culture. A country with an academically weak teaching profession in the compulsory school has a failing competence base for further education. It makes the country's mass-higher education a colossus on feet of clay. The academically weak teaching profession in the secondary school has an absolute work position assurance. It is therefore difficult to see how Norway can get out of this critical situation. Incompetent teachers have a lifetime employment. A strong union is the guarantor of lifelong incompetence. In-service training can hardly solve the problem of weak teachers in Norwegian schools.

In later years, people from around the world with an interest in successful education have flocked to Finland. Many find it instructive to study schooling in other countries, and then bring useful experiences back home. In the Norwegian context, it is also useful to compare the unified school with other types of schools in Norway. They do exist. Some are private, and some organized by other countries for their citizens in

Norway. Next chapter attempts a contrast between the Norwegian unified school and, primarily, the French school in Oslo, and, to a lesser extent, the Waldorf and Montessori schools in Oslo.

28

Norwegian School and Other Schools in Norway

How does a Norwegian family discover The French school in Oslo? It happens when it is impossible to get access to kindergarten for a three year old, and the family randomly learns that there is vacancy in the French school's kindergarten (maternelle). The only admission requirement was that the child had stopped using diapers. The family found that there were many other Norwegian three year olds there. From day one, the children could not speak Norwegian. Only French. A Norwegian girl cried for two days. While such reactions did not seem to bother the maternelle teachers very much, the Norwegian parents seemed terrified. How would kindergarten life be for a small child? Very good, it turned out. Three years in the kindergarten were, joyfully, followed by eight years in primary and secondary school at *Lycée René Cassin d'Oslo*.

The French school in Oslo is located in the buildings of the old Vestheim Gymnasium in the Frogner district. Already when you approach the schoolyard, you notice a spirit of something non-Norwegian. The playground for the smallest children have a particularly conscious aesthetic dimension in choice of shapes and colours. All the children speak French, although it is Norwegian names addressed. Why do Norwegian parents choose to have their children in the French school, instead of in their local public school, free of charge? A comparison between Norwegian and French school may give an answer. The comparison would include the following dimensions: curriculum philosophy, curriculum, methodology, evaluation and the school's organization. The differences observed between the two schools give signals about why Norwegians are not satisfied with the Norwegian public unified school. Other Norwegian parents choose Montessori or Waldorf schools. It is also of interest to compare these types of schools with the unified school.

The Norwegian and French public schools have a common curricular heritage in encyclopaedism. The French Enlightenment philosophers, together with the Czech educator Comenius, are the creators of this curriculum tradition, with an emphasis on many subjects and a strong teacher authority. French school clearly continued this curriculum tradition, while the Norwegian school after WWII, switched to American progressivist tradition. In the latter tradition, the teacher has modest authority and the students shall learn by themselves, by discovering new knowledge. Thus, French and Norwegian education policies today operate from different education philosophy roots. This is affecting different curriculum designs in the two countries. The French school has a distinct subject- and knowledge-centred curriculum, where students must largely adapt to the existing subjects. The Norwegian is, on the contrary, distinctly student-centred. Content and methods shall adapt to all students' individual preconditions, or expressed different, the teaching in class shall be "student adapted learning". Such differences in basic educational philosophy thinking reflect in the two country's curriculum, methodology, evaluation and school organization.

In terms of curriculum's *content*, the French school has stronger emphasis on early reading training and homework, than in the Norwegian school. Difference are most prominent in subjects such as math and science. In Norway, a college-trained teacher, can teach all subjects in the compulsory school. In France, there is specific training programmes for teachers in kindergarten, primary school, lower secondary and upper secondary school (lycée). Not many years ago, mathematics was an optional subject in Norwegian teacher education. This has since changed, but the case is a good indication of the different weight on mathematics in the two countries. In Norwegian teacher education, the subject of pedagogy is still important, but reduced in later reforms. In France, there hardly exists any separate subject of pedagogy. Subjects' didactics, however, has a prominent place in the programme. Subject didactic is about how to teach well the subjects you have studied at the university.

In the French education system, teaching of mathematics and language start already in the kindergarten. The students' acquisition of mathematical and linguistic concepts you see embedded in the kindergarten's usual activities, in a refined way. It is only by thorough observations and discussions with the teachers, that you become aware of how the kindergarten is a conscious preparation for an academically oriented school. The teaching of grammar is considerably stronger and emphasized earlier in French than in Norwegian school. This naturally relates to the fact that classic languages (Latin and/or Greek) still have a position also in lower secondary school. The foundation for understanding the classic languages is early systematic grammar training. In general, the requirements of academic achievements in the French school are very strict. It is quite common that some students have to re-take a grade level (one year), or that clever students can jump one level. In Norway, this does not occur at all. Such practice would breach with basic educational philosophical principles, like student-adapted learning and social integration. The way French schools organizes physical education there are fewer opportunities for optional activities, than is the case in Norwegian schools. The different emphasis on mathematics, science, and grammar is what most distinctly separates Norway and France.

Differences in teaching *methodology* are among other things expressed in the number of students per teacher, which is generally higher in the French school. French students work effectively on their own. Classroom discipline is considerably tighter, already from kindergarten. The kindergarten's math and language preparation provide a better basis for the acquisition of more knowledge on primary and secondary levels, than is the case in Norwegian school. Syllabus and teaching materials have a more clear structure, than in the Norwegian school, and the teaching is more goal-directed.

Can Norway learn from China?

In France, the teaching is distinctly teacher centred. This is different from the Norwegian school, where, since the introduction of the unified school, teaching is student centred. There are less group work and optional activities in French than in the Norwegian school. In addition, the French school has more emphasis on presentation skills, on how to write nicely and how to keep order. The integration of foreign language students are different in Norwegian and French schools. The French increases the efforts in French language for all students no matter their mother tongue. Quite differently, the Norwegian school encourages the use of foreign speakers native language, not Norwegian. When e.g. a Norwegian three year old begins in the kindergarten at a French school, there is no acceptance of Norwegian language from day one. Even if there are other Norwegian native speaking children there, they cannot speak Norwegian among them. Everyone should speak French from the first day. In sum, teaching in French schools is teacher centred, syllabus-oriented and guided by the knowledge goals. The teaching in Norwegian schools, on the other hand, has process orientation, group works, individualized orientation, and the teacher role is that of a guide for students' taking responsibility for their own learning.

Systematic *evaluation* of students' learning achievements, their classroom behaviour and order starts already at the age of three, in the French kindergarten. The parents get information by grade cards. Systematic evaluation continues throughout primary school. The scope of control and assessment is significantly larger than in Norway. The school keeps the parents constantly updated about the status of the children's learning and their behaviour. The students have to pass formal examinations in a lot more subjects, than is the case in Norway. Only examination results count. Norway is different. The final mark is not only by a final examination, but also by a number of tests in each subject during the school year. Moreover, not only academic achievements count, when the final grade is set. In addition, the student's motivation, eagerness to learn and participation carry weight when deciding on the final grade. In Norway, students only take formal examinations in a few subjects. In subjects where there is no examination, the average of tests during the preceding year will count as final grade. Teachers' assessment of students' achievements during the school year, count ultimately equally to overall examination grades.

The role of evaluation in the two countries is a particularly evident indicator of their different pedagogy and curriculum tradition. In the French school, evaluation is something natural and logical in order to control the learning achievement, and systematically report achievements to parents. In Norway, it is the other way around. Here, the emphasis is largely on a more informal assessment of students' learning, through discussions at the parent meetings and office hours. In Norway, there have been continuous efforts not only to minimize, but also to abolish traditionally important forms of formal evaluation.

In the French, knowledge-centred curriculum, structured teaching with clear objectives, will logically require a more formalized evaluation, as a convenient means for effective communication between home and school. In Norway, with a student centred curriculum and "student-adapted teaching", formal evaluation is a negative factor. Evaluation may have negative effects on the student's self-esteem and motivation, and, thus work contrary to reaching the overall goals of the curriculum. Also in Norway, however, evaluation is important constructive feedback about student's learning. Its form should strive to be more informal. Evaluation should always take the particular student's preconditions into account, and not primarily be in relation to specific academic standards. Evaluation in Norway is relative to the student's abilities. In France, evaluation is absolute in relation to given academic standards.

In terms of the school's organizing, Norway experienced an intense debate when lowering the school starring age from seven to six. The hottest issue was whether the new first class should reflect the kindergartens' or the schools' learning traditions. In the French school, children experience the school's tradition already from the age of three in kindergarten. There is an unnoticeable transition between kindergarten and first class for six year olds. The name of the first school year in France is preparatory course (course préparatoire). It is a preparation for schooling, not just "a garden". Many international education researchers claim that the French school's kindergarten (maternelle) is the "world's best kindergarten". Such an assessment is because maternelle is successful in unifying the principles of play and systematic learning. Put otherwise, the students' behaviour both inside and outside school shows them playing and thrive, while the grade card shows that they simultaneously have learned basic linguistic and math concepts and skills. The French after school programme is the «étude», which means studies. Norway is debating whether to introduce "the whole day school", including time after regular school hours, for recreational activities, under the school's supervision. The French school with two hours "etude" directly after regular school hours, already has the "the whole day school" as a normal arrangement, for those parents who want to take advantage of this offer. However, the purpose of these two hours is not recreational activities, but to do away with next day's homework.

If the students in the French school do very well, they can "jump" a grade level, which practically does not occur in Norway. In Norway, it is more important to keep the social units together, than to reach the set knowledge goals on time. The French school has as a principle that a class changes teachers every year. Norway encourages a reverse principle; the students should have the same teachers as many years as possible. While there in Norway is an emphasis on safety by continuity of teacher-student relations, the French school has as principle to train students in adapting to new conditions. Similarly, the composition of classes and student groups deliberately changes, based on reviews from the educational staff and the school's leadership. The rationale being that such changes make it easier to integrate newcomers.

While the French school in Oslo is a French public school, monitored by the ministry of education in Paris, the Montessori and Waldorf schools in Norway are private. However, by international terms, they would hardly qualify as private, since the lion share of their funding comes from the Norwegian State. Real private schools have their funding from tuition fees paid by parents. The fees are sufficient to cover the school's operation, and, eventually, dividends to an owner that has invested in the school.

In the Norwegian system, Montessori and Waldorf count as private, because they have a pedagogy so different from the standard curriculum of the unified school, that it does not fit into the framework of the public school. Thus, they qualify for support, according to a special law on private schools in Norway. The two types of schools are representatives of very special educational philosophies, quite different from the Norwegian school. Over recent years, these two alternatives have caught increased attention in line with a growing number of parents unhappy with the public unified school. The Labour Party parents of our previous prime minister preferred to put their son in a Waldorf school instead of the local unified school. This choice may reflect a similar way of thinking to that of former British prime minister, Tony Blair, when he sent his hopeful to an expensive private school in England.

Montessori's starting point was her special education needs experiences in her work as medical doctor and psychiatric nurse. Working with mentally handicapped preschool children led her to put very great emphasis on the development of intellectual skills. The development of such skills was crucial for the children's development to freedom. Simplified, her educational philosophy is that the ability of thinking and intellectual reflection are the most crucial for individual liberation. The connection to the French philosopher Descartes is inconspicuous. The framework for freedom of choice, however, was very strict. She gave no room for creative art activities. She said, "The kids are thirsting for knowledge and work, not these stupid games". She created learning materials that would cause the children to individually training sensory experiences and develop their intellectual capabilities. Language and writing should occur early in a child's learning life. Students must pronounce words clearly and correctly. It was the surprisingly good results for weak students' learning of knowledge that made Montessori's pedagogy acknowledged, and, eventually, applied in both primary and secondary school all over the world.

Rudolf Steiner is the founding father of the Waldorf School. Steiner's educational philosophy was based in his own particular philosophy, anthroposophy. In this philosophy, humanity expresses itself in the holistic human being, able to think, have emotions and a distinct will of his own. The main pedagogical implication of this view is to develop the capabilities and powers contained in each child. The curriculum is adapted, or subordinated to the age level of the individual student. This applies in both primary and secondary school. The teaching is trying to get away from an abstract curriculum, and turn to conditions that directly concern the man himself. Only when emotionally engaged, will students profit from teaching. Ideally, presentation of all subjects must be in an artistic way. According to Steiner, pedagogy is an art, not a science. Organizationally, characteristic of the Waldorf school is that it is without a headmaster. The teaching staff runs the school, and jointly makes all decisions.

In common, the Montessori and Waldorf schools have teachers with strong commitment for the individual student's learning and liberation. In this way, they are both in good accordance with the overall purpose for the Norwegian unified school. However, then their educational theory and practice separates. Actually, they are on the opposite ends of a scale. Simply expressed, Montessori would like to reach learning targets with great systematics, structured materials and exercises designed to strengthen the student's intellectual, cognitive capacity. The Waldorf schools see emotions as the most important. Students' existential «pedagogical meeting» with «the teacher as an artist» will release the students' inherent powers at the right time in their development. Contrasting Montessori and Waldorf schools to Norwegian and French schools, it fair to see a "Latin relationship" between Montessori and the French school. The common denominator is heavy weight on the intellectual dimension. Waldorf is obviously closer to the Norwegian variant of progressivism, but it has an even stronger emphasis on the emotional dimension, and puts even stronger weight on student-centred teaching. Both Waldorf and Montessori differ from the Norwegian unified school, in that they both consistently have more dedicated teachers.

Norwegian upper secondary school will inevitably be less different from the French, because the subjects play a more central role at this level. Still, the distinctive Norwegian pedagogy of the unified school in lower secondary has also influenced the upper secondary level, in line with also this level becoming a school for all, with coordination of branches, programmes and courses. When the government introduced a common curriculum for Norwegian lower and upper secondary school, the impression of curriculum differences between schools in Norway and France intensified.

The nature of the French school as a curriculum option has interesting professional and social manifestations. Graduation from French upper secondary school provides easier access to studies internationally, than the Norwegian does. Norwegian students more often must undergo special tests before admittance. This is one indication that the professional level of the French school is high. The French school in Oslo has a very multicultural student composition, without experiencing the discipline and violence problems that characterize several Norwegian inner city schools with a multicultural student mass. This social fact is interesting, even when you take into account school size and other background conditions. Probably, the different curriculum traditions is one of the reasons for the difference. As well as dedicated parents.

Parent's choice of school is an expression of their practical assessment of available school options. Among parents with children at the French school in Oslo, there were a few years ago reports that there are 40% of the students where both parents are Norwegian, and 40% where one of the parents is Norwegian. It means that 80% of parents have a choice between Norwegian and French school. Norwegian parents choose French, even if it involves school fees for them as non-French. These Norwegians are willing to pay for their loved ones having access to a school where solid knowledge is the focus. As a bonus, these Norwegian students become fluent in French, written and spoken.

Simultaneously, in the next chapter we will see that the French school, in France, has major problems to struggle with, and that many foreigners have high admiration for the Norwegian unified school.

29

A Glossy Image of Norway Seducing Foreigners

Seen from abroad, Norway is the world's best country to live in. Such an opinion is understandable for those who only know the country from the image created by international media. It is not long between each time, there is a report, putting Norway on top, out of an overall rating on a number of important conditions for life quality, e.g. health and education. Foreigners perceive most of the state's welfare benefits to be free. People live long and report high job satisfaction. Unlike almost all other countries, Norway has no debt. Getting sick represents no economic risk. The country has more real democracy than hardly any other country. It is among the world's best in terms of social equality. The American political philosopher Fukuyama tends to refer to Denmark as the ideal country, when it comes to historical development into optimal liberal democracy. Now, international observers are increasingly turning to Norway, when they look for the ideal country. It is because the country's good economy, high productivity, and that anyone who wants to, can take higher education, free of charge. A foreign younger colleague told me before she came to Oslo she thought the stairs at the university were gold-plated.

Foreigners' general glossy picture of Norway includes, almost unconsciously, the education sector. Not just poor people from developing countries would like to live in this rich and democratic welfare-paradise, with guaranteed job, housing, schooling, and social security. Also to European well-educated middle-class, the Norwegian model has appeal. In one case, a family moved from Germany to Norway. The father was Norwegian and the mother German. The children knew both German and Norwegian languages. In Norway, they could therefore choose between the Norwegian public unified school and the German school in Oslo. The mother insisted on the Norwegian school, because she thought the German had too strict discipline. After a year, I had the opportunity to learn about her assessment of her meeting with Norway. She had experienced several unpleasant surprises. It began with all the beggars she had not expected to find in one of the world's richest countries. She thought there was surprisingly much rubbish in the streets. People were not particularly polite. The biggest shock was, however, the school. The students behaved badly towards the teacher, her children reported a lot of noise in class, and it took a lot of time, before it was possible to get on with normal work in the classroom. Grading and feedback from the school about their students' academic performance were indistinct or absent. She was upset over not knowing what her children really learned. She thought the most grotesque image of Norwegian schooling was the Russ Celebration. She could not really comprehend that it was possible. Her glossy picture of Norway was cracking. As a mother, she could not risk her children's school time abused, or that her daughter at the conclusion of upper secondary school would risk rape during the Russ Celebration. The family was considering two options. Either they could try to get their children into the German school in Oslo, or the family could move back to Germany.

This German family's experiences illustrate many foreigners' perception of Norway: from the outside, they see a country that has reached the optimum level of development for justice and opportunities for life quality. In the face of the real Norway, they experience, among other problems, a daunting school standard. Some positive qualities in Norway, however, weigh so heavily that some expatriates choose a private school solution in Norway. Thus, they can still stay in a country, that when it comes to nature, probably is the best in the world. The positive keywords most often mentioned are the mountains in southern Norway, the fjords in Western Norway, as well as the coastline and mountains of the Nordland and Troms counties.

Foreigners' admiration for the assumed quality of schools in Norway and Scandinavia may even inspire their current educational reforms, as we e.g. see in France in 2016. France is a particular nation in terms of educational history. With the great French revolution of 1789, and the slogans of liberty, equality, fraternity, the country is the very source of thinking social equality and justice for all. Simultaneously, the country, from pre-revolution Enlightenment time, is the source of the encyclopaedic curriculum tradition. In the specifically French version of encyclopaedism, there should simultaneously be educational opportunities for all, and training of elite professionals, who would provide optimal administration of the country. This is equivalent of what we now see in China. There will always be a tension between mass and elite education, because the results of the education clearly can be associated with social inequalities. In France, elite education takes place at the Grandes Ecoles (university colleges). Graduates from these schools get the top positions in the French society, in the fields of business, technology, culture and politics. When France extended the compulsory school to include lower secondary level, the country decided to keep the student cohort together in the same class, without differentiation based on talents, like in Norway. The reason was both classic French equality ideals and some inspiration from approaching progressivism. As in Norway, the French assumed a unified system might give everyone more opportunities to more knowledge, as well as achieving better social integration. Already twenty years ago, French teachers were highly critical of this model. They held that unified classes resulted in lowering of academic level.

Over the last twenty years, problems at lower secondary school in France have sharply increased. It is not least due to a high number of immigrants from former French colonies in North Africa. Like other poor immigrants, they have seen the prosperous and modern France as a place where they could realize their future dreams. In contrast to immigrants in general, they also had special rights, since they came from former French colonies. For poor immigrants from countries that totally lack an educational culture like that of France, their meeting with the encyclopaedic school and its subject centred teachers were brutal. This situation reminds a little of both United States and South Africa. Many underprivileged groups think that as soon as they are within the school walls, they have a golden future secured. It may take generations before they become a part of the school culture that underlies success in school.

In France, the major immigrant groups, often concentrated in the suburbs (banlieues) around the big cities, have become a huge social problem. Very many people have not been able to take advantage of the possibilities, e.g. education, which is a precondition for the French social model. In large numbers, they become social clients, residing in areas with a concentration of social housing. These students are losers in the knowledge-oriented French school. A few years ago, social and cultural contradictions led to major riots in the suburbs. Today, we see corresponding contradictions expressed in conflicts between Muslims and French, and between Muslims and Jews. The Jews are increasingly escaping to Israel. In the lower secondary school, there are contradictions between traditional French school culture and, especially, immigrants with other cultural preconditions. A consequence is that there will be a lot of noise and all students learn less than before. This negative development has been constantly increasing.

Each year, 17% of the students leave compulsory school without a diploma. Last year, the French army undertook a survey of 17 year olds ability to read and understand basic French. One of ten 17 year olds cannot read or understand a simple French text, according to the army. The negative academic development has also meant the score average in France is falling. According to Pisa, French 15 year olds' achievement in reading and mathematics decreased since 2000. Thus, the present socialist minister of education minister observes soberly that the French lower secondary school does not guarantee that the students acquire necessary basic knowledge. Therefore, she now proposes a number of reforms for lower secondary school, in order to address the problem issues. It seems as though she has drawn inspiration from Norwegian unified school thinking.

At the lower secondary school, it has hitherto been possible to apply to special classes for bilingual teaching in French and German, and to classes, offering Greek and Latin. As many as 16% of the youth cohort choose classes with German and French. The minister of education believes that these special offers have been a disguised way for elite parents to get a very good deal for their children. The arrangement has maintained an opportunity for teaching adapted to the clever and school motivated. She wants an end to this possibility. Her proposed solution is the Scandinavian model. She will keep all the students in the same class at the lower secondary level, and she wants the teaching to be more fun. This goal she will achieve by making the subjects more multidisciplinary, with group work and project work. For Norwegians this sounds familiar. They are the magic tools of the unified school ideology. The minister may well have studied the Norwegian glossy image, and been ensnared by noting a school with great student satisfaction, and a country that is the welfare model for the rest of the world.

Reactions to the minister's proposals clearly show the cultural differences between encyclopaedic France and progressivist Norway. First, the German government reacted by asking its ambassador in France to talk seriously to the minister of education. The common language education in French and German is extremely important in relation to the political history of the two countries, as well as to the importance of mutual language understanding between the EU's two main member countries. A German-speaking member of the French parliament (from the political right) has organized a petition among parliamentarians, against the proposed reform. As of spring 2015, 230 of the 577 deputies in the parliament had signed the petition. However, also intellectuals on the left side of the political scale have protested. Among them, a former education minister from the socialists says the proposals are shocking.

The current debate in France is intense and heated. Moreover, it has gained an overarching ideological stamp, because the leader of the opposition, and a likely candidate for presidency in 2017, former president Nicolas Sarcozy, labelled the reform a disaster. The minister has received harsh critique in the press. Some critics are teasingly claiming that Islam will be a main subject after the reform, since the minister has Moroccan background and is a muslim. Other are teasing that project work will be to build children's playhouses in the schoolyard, and, in the French lessons, students will learn rap-music instead of studying Molière and Hugo. Teachers are protesting violently and threatening, in good French style, they may go on strike. They believe that project work is an attack on solid academic subject thinking. Moreover, they are afraid of all the preparation time, project work will require of teachers. The minister's concern about many students being bored in school is by some commentators termed as «grotesque indulgence». The way the debate in France has evolved, it is highly doubtful whether the school reform proposals will contribute to socialist election victory in 2017.

The young minister of education (she is 37) has put priority on social integration and supposed good motivational measures, and hoped that knowledge attainment will follow as a bonus. Like the Labour Party did in Norway. The minister has looked to Norway and believed that is where the unified school idea really worked. She has no real-world experiences with the Norwegian unified school, like the German mother obtained. The minister has seen "the pedagogical light house" - the very solution to the dangerous situation in the country's lower secondary school. That is to make the school «more enjoyable», create «well-being» and she believes, like several Norwegian special needs educators, that «well-being creates learning». However, she got tough reactions, which the Labour Party in Norway did not experience. There is a brutal response from most of French society - across the political spectrum, including some of her own socialists, and from the teachers.

This is about the opposite of what happened in Norway, where both teachers, trade unions and parents effectively were included as supporters for the unified school. Both the Teachers' Union and the Parents' Commission for the Compulsory School Education are aggressive supporters of the unified school ideology and policies. In the French educational culture, to have fun at school is not an important value. School quality is a serious issue for the majority of French citizens, for Peugeot, for Airbus and for France as a nation. Anyway, it will be exciting to observe the French case in the years ahead. Democracy is an overall framework for the Republic's ideology. It is possible there will appear a political majority deciding that the most important function of the school is that it primarily is a place to thrive, as in Norway. It is also conceivable that France get a Muslim president, and a school characterized by sharia laws, as Michel Houillebecq fantasizes about in his latest novel, *Submission*. Literature has also previously clearly influenced the education field. In a Norwegian context, *Poison*, by Alexander Kielland, and about a century later, *Jonas* by Jens Bjørneboe are relevant examples. The first contributed greatly to wind up the classic curriculum tradition in Norway (the Latin school). The key character of latter novel is the patron saint of the special needs educators.

A minister of education is an educational leader. She is headmaster of the whole country. What kind of knowledge, values and skills «the country's headmaster» has, will have consequences for the entire education system. Not least important is the minister's opinion of what is good leadership at the individual school. Logically, competent school leadership involves understanding of the national education policy goals and their relation to strategies to reach goals in practice. You can claim it the necessity to see vertical consistency of policies. The understanding of the goals and strategy contained by «the country's headmaster» must also reside with the headmasters at school level. To make upcoming school leaders attain such understanding is the overall goal of a relevant education for school leaders.

We saw earlier, in the comparison between the public school and other schools in Norway, how the perception of good school leadership varied. Both the French school and Montessori schools have a clear and distinct leadership. It has authority. In the Waldorf schools, you have collective school leadership. What about the Norwegian public unified school? Historically, most schools were small and had no headmaster. One of the teachers took care of the necessary administrative work. Still, each teacher was his own boss. The same was the case in Finland. In Norway, the introduction of a mandatory nine years' school necessarily led to centralization, in order to reach sufficient school size. Increased size caused need for professional school leadership. In the early years, the school leader's title was director. It later changed to headmaster (rector).

The profound Norwegian tradition was, however, a school with teachers not used to obeying a leader. It therefore created frustration and to some extent a conflict, when a person who himself had been a teacher got the position as headmaster, and became a superior to former colleagues. One consequence of this tension was the experiment with alternative school leadership forms, one being collective leadership. The experiment was so effective and popular that it led to a change of school laws, making it legal to choose other types of leadership than headmaster. The experiment had its roots in humanistic psychology and social psychology. The experiment leaders thought the teachers fully capable of running the school. Moreover, by participating in the leadership function they would experience a form of continuous in-service training, since they would learn from making decisions about curriculum and budget. The first few years, the commitment and enthusiasm were present in full measure. As the «honeymoon effect» weakened, so did the commitment. After some years, the law reversed, once more school leadership should only be by a headmaster.

Nevertheless, leadership problems continued within the Norwegian school. The old tension between the independent teachers used to govern themselves and a growing leadership apparatus constantly flared up. In the next chapter, we will see how the school leadership issue created a «headache» in the Norwegian educational system.

30

Headache in Norwegian School Leadership

School leadership has been a controversial topic in Norway for more than twenty years. Already in 1988, the evaluation of a nationwide in-service training programme indicated an extremely weak consistency between national educational goals on the one hand, and the content of in-service training for school leaders, on the other. This discrepancy received renewed attention when the first weak Pisa-results haunted us. Minister of education, Kristin Clemet's attempts at reintroduction of a knowledge school in Norway from 2002, meant launching an effective school leadership training as a particularly important strategy, for the full course of change in Norwegian schools. The training was slow. Among those expected to be trainers of school leaders, there were strong fears that the new training programme would be a business-inspired "new public management". That would be something most alien to the Norwegian tradition of school leadership. There were also signs of scepticism towards the new training programme's curriculum and method. This was a reflection of traditional scepticism to a concept of effectiveness, in school leadership. The ministry reacted to the sluggishness by initiating a research programme for renewal and innovation in the public sector, including education.

Within the framework of this research programme, the HEAD project appeared. The project name «HEAD» was playing on the English word for the headmaster. The purpose of the project was just to find out if those professors and lecturers who took on the responsibility to train school administrators were loyal to the ministry. One assumption was that an assumed weak connection, or even mismatch, between the education policy goals and the content of school leader training would effect «headaches» for the ministry, which is «the head» of the education sector in Norway. A main reason why the government wanted to reintroduce the knowledge school model, and, by implication needed effective school leadership, was concern for the challenges a globalized economy would face Norway with, especially after the end of the offshore oil and gas industry. In order to have international reference points, HEAD chose to compare school leader training in Norway, with similar training in four other countries: Finland, France, England and the United States. Finland, because the country's impressive Pisa-results and its similarity to Norway socially and culturally. France was interesting because the country represents the clearest and longest encyclopaedic curriculum tradition.

The inclusion of England and the United States was because of both some common and some particular reasons. A glance at the list of international research journals for school leadership shows that research on this field is almost completely and fully Anglo-American. This means that research on school leadership in these two countries set the agenda for researchers in the rest of the world. Two special reasons for including England was firstly, that the country had established a central education programme for school leadership, the National College for School Leadership, and, secondly, that the country has a distinct essentialist curriculum tradition. Particular reasons to include the United States was the country's size, importance and decentralized system of education of school leaders, and especially, because its education is clearly marked by a progressivist curriculum tradition. There is a number of fascinating special features of school leader training in the four countries, e.g. that the Pisa world champion, Finland, turned out as hardly having any programmes for school leadership education at all. Simply expressed, the Finns achieved excellent academic results, because they had professional teachers who did not really need any professional leader above them. In Norway, however, the de-professionalization of teachers had come so far, that the government saw effective school leadership as a crucial means of getting teachers to do a better job.

The two issues the HEAD study wanted answers to were: Why do there exist a possible Norwegian «headache», and how likely is it that the headache will disappear? Answers should be found by analysis of the three largest educational programmes (from two universities and a business school), as well as interviews with those professors and lecturers who were responsible for carrying out the programmes. A metaphor of the thinking behind the questions is «the education value chain». The purpose of this image is to look for level of consistency between the chain's two extremes. At one extreme you have the goals of the national school policies. The second is the Norwegian student's academic results, as expressed in international comparisons. The key link in the education value chain is *the quality of the school leader.* The headmaster's professional competence turned especially important, after the abolishment of the regular superintendent positions at municipality level, and the headmasters becoming directly accountable to municipality authorities.

The value chain rationale implies that the school's purpose, as expressed in national policy documents, shall find reflection in the headmaster's leadership of the teachers, and in the teachers' teaching of students in classrooms. Students' learning results shall match with parents' expectations and with competence needs of other important stakeholders in the municipality. Reaching national policy goals successfully at classroom level, shall in turn effect Norway's moving upwards on international rankings of school achievements. That is the end of the education value chain. In Norway after 2002, there was an obvious tension between the ministry of education and leading economists on the one hand and, on the other, representatives of the unified school culture, a progressivist lobby consisting of school researchers, bureaucrats, media and the dominant Teachers' Union.

Inertia in social change in Norway is typical of the country as a whole, according to political scientist Johan P. Olsen. He has labelled the country a "turtle country" when it comes to the pace of social changes. The country does not have to change, because there is no need for change. Norway lacks motive for change.

Hence, Norway is changing slowly, and, in terms of school issues, there exists a heavy lobby, highly sceptical to more effective school leadership. Such scepticism also proved strong among those institutions and lecturers who had taken responsibility to educate school leaders. HEAD wanted, concretely, to investigate three dimensions of the master's programme for school leaders, firstly, the content of the programme (syllabus), secondly, how lecturers and professors in the programme understood the national school policy goals, stated in the study programme and 3) what the school leader graduates actually had learned, as expressed in their final master theses.

What did HEAD find? The analysis of the national policy documents clearly showed from now on there should be focus on knowledge centred subjects, and that the school leadership (headmasters) was effectively ensuring that this happened in practice. The new policies after 2002, seem directly influenced by Norway's modest position on international rankings, e.g. Pisa. They also show a desire for system change, in terms of curriculum-tradition, a change from progressivism towards encyclopaedism. Contrary to what assumed in advance, the HEAD surveys showed that the majority of those teaching in the school leader training programme at the two universities, and all those teaching at the private business school, had full understanding of the new national school policy goals. At the two universities, however, a significant minority of lecturers had a negative opinion of national policy goals. They believed the new goals would lead to the unfortunate "bossy" school leadership (corporate-inspired management). The curriculum at one of the universities showed a lack of connection with national political goals. The lecturers had designed a curriculum focusing on the teacher role, instead of the school leadership role. This was a sign of obstruction to national policy goals. Moreover, the graduates' master theses had focus on the teacher role, more than on the school leadership role, and, hence, carried on the old tradition of seeing school leaders as something foreign to Norwegian school traditions.

Among the three higher educational institutions examined, there appeared two different adaptation strategies in relation to the national educational goals. The private business school had created an education programme perfectly reflecting the educational policy goals, that is, full loyalty to the ministry of education and the government. Moreover, the business school, when marketing the programme to school municipalities, stressed that the school wanted to contribute to a profound change of direction for Norwegian schools, e.g. in the capital city, Oslo. What the business school had barely expected was the participants' (the master students) made non-relevant choice of theme for their master theses. Their choice reflected traditional thinking about schools, that is, the emphasis was on the teacher role, and not on the leadership role. The business school therefore found itself in cross-pressures between the municipality, its customer, wanting leadership competence, and the preferences of the master students. The latter group, in line with a strong Norwegian academic tradition of academic autonomy, assumed they themselves should decide the topic of the most important element of their training, the master thesis. The municipality's school administration obviously wanted a training focusing effective leadership of the teaching staff, while the students chose topics for their theses concentrating on the teacher role, in the old tradition. Ambitious school municipalities, thus risked getting a product they had not ordered, even when buying from the government-loyal business school.

In the two public universities, adaptation to national policies occurred by lecturers loyally accepting the national policy goals and strategies, while the curriculum design of the programme and themes for master theses reflected the old tradition, with emphasis on the teacher role. It was therefore a contradiction between rhetorical acceptance of national goals and actual practices. Lip service to government policies, and loyalty to teachers' interests, expressed in the old tradition and the Teacher Union's policies. The difference between the two public universities and the business school was the latter being loyal throughout the whole study programme, while the universities were to some extent disloyal in their design of curriculum. The similarity between all three institutions was disloyalty towards the policy goals, when accepting students' choice of traditional teacher centred themes for their master theses. Defence for such disloyalty was the need to accept the academic tradition of master students' freedom to deicide on thesis theme.

Thus, it was likely that «the Norwegian headache» would continue at the two universities, with professors and lecturers split in their understanding of the idea of school leadership, and with a curriculum that had limited relevance to national policy goals. HEAD's more specific and perhaps most serious findings of «headache», seen in a future perspective, is the paradoxical situation of the private business school. The school finds itself in a logical balancing act when it, simultaneously, displays loyalty in two opposite directions. First, it is the loyal to the government's policies for school leadership education. Simultaneously, it accepts the students' knowledge production, master theses with themes that reflect the traditional teacher focus and an anti-leadership culture. The HEAD findings at the beginning of the 2000s show that there among training institutions hardly was very strong motivation for the sort of school leadership thinking, expected in national education policies. Norway thus remains at odds with international trends in the area of school leadership training.

In an international perspective, Norway is emerging as "the odd country", in terms of school leadership training. Powerful players in society seem satisfied with the traditional headmaster, one who more than being the leader, is an administrative coordinator of the school's business. Students of school leadership meet with an ambiguous message. Rhetorical adaptation to new leadership thinking, and, simultaneously, continued acceptance of the traditional understanding of school practices. The key link in the education value chain is a school leader employed for life. This key link continues to be weak with possible fatal consequences for many students in primary and secondary schools.

Headache in Norwegian school at the beginning of the 21st Century is due to a collision between new educational policies, having returned to an encyclopaedic curriculum tradition on the one hand, and on the other, a lack of motivation for the new policies among those who should implement it. The synthesis of an old equality culture, a progressivist curriculum tradition and great national wealth make for a distinctive twist on Norwegian work ethic in general, and for the school's efforts in particular. Work motivation is steadily decreasing. The dominant Teachers' Union has a difficult role to play. Naturally, it reflects the old teacher power tradition. To support teachers' interests is the Union's essence. Simultaneously, almost unconsciously, it supports a progressivist curriculum tradition, and expresses scepticism about the government's education reforms for improved school leadership and focus on knowledge subjects. The teachers' employer is the municipal authorities. They are continuously challenging the teachers to contribute to implement the reforms.

A particular feature of Norwegian trade unions is that in the case of teachers, the dominant teacher union also organizes the majority of headmasters. This makes the Teachers' Union a heavy weight player, when it comes to define the school leader's function and role, and implicitly, what a relevant school leader education is. The interests of teachers are the basic framework for the whole union, its leadership division included. A sign that things are changing is the emergence of a separate and independent association for school leaders. This association is increasingly recruiting headmasters, at the expense of the traditional recruitment to the Teachers' Union. This change of union behaviour reflects the change in expectations to the headmaster role in recent years, namely, that the headmaster is now directly accountable within the municipality's decision-making structure. This is in accordance with an international trend.

Several Norwegian school researchers seem to play a consolidating role for the status quo of the Norwegian school. In the Norwegian research on school development, there is little attention at two of the basic issues creating «headaches» in the school - the ever-influential progressivist curriculum tradition and the unified school principle. Both affect rejection of streaming students according to their abilities in the lower secondary school. Consequently, advices from several school researchers to politicians and bureaucrats continue to be progressivist. These researchers have not been able to take into account how the Norwegian school should deal with the impact from other curriculum traditions, now taking place. Such influence from abroad was last visible by the education reform policies from 2003. Not infrequently, it seems like school researchers are in the conflict between three roles: researcher, educator and ideological activist.

Research on school leadership in Norway, often seems heavily dependent on frames of reference from the Anglo American research world. This may both indicate faith in general organizational truths about school development and school leadership, regardless of local culture and curriculum tradition. A researcher risks, more or less conscious, to be trapped between his own training to a traditional teacher role with progressivist curriculum, and a research orientation inspired by class societies with elitist traditions. This may cause confusion among Norwegian researchers when analysing Norwegian school reality.

Whether a school researcher has experience as a school leader or not, also seems to make a difference, when he is going to choose issues and conceptual framework for his research. Researchers without leadership experience, primarily see teachers and students from an individual perspective. Researchers having leadership experience tend towards seeing the school as an organization, a vehicle for teachers and students' work and for the expectations of parents, businesses, and communities. Such difference of experiences influence which "school problems" the researchers will actually observe. Researchers without leadership experience will see the key link in the education value chain different from those who themselves have experienced the link as a school leader.

After 2005, the ambiguous message of Norwegian school policies and practice appeared at ministry level. After the general elections this year, there was a new minister of education. He changed the name of his post to *minister of knowledge*. This was a most clear indication that the new socialist minister had the same overall policy goal as his conservative predecessor. The difference was, however, that the school's practices continued operating by the old progressivist culture. The mighty Teachers' Union got an even stronger hand on the policy steering wheel, than in the past. Thus, the new socialist minister of education, in loud rhetoric, announced encyclopaedic knowledge orientation, while a progressivist practice continued strongly as ever. It was this persistent contradiction, a new conservative education minister met with in 2013. Before observing his situation more closely, it is natural to make a glance back at the changes of directions in Norwegian education policies from 2001.

31

The Minister of Education and the Minister of Magic

The image of the Norwegian schools in 2016 indicates that the progressivist unified school culture no longer sits as strong in Norwegians' spinal cord. From the beginning of the 2000s, there has been regular attacks on progressivism, although with vicissitudes. A starting point was concern messages from the business world. Globalization challenged the distinctive Norwegian anti-knowledge-culture. Critics suggested a connection between school quality and the country's future economic development. Simultaneously with agreeing that economic globalization is a challenge for Norway, and that knowledge-based competence is increasingly important, there was great disagreement about which measures to take. The prevailing culture of the unified school blocked for many people's ability to see the connection between the knowledge goals, and measures required to reach such goals. One that saw this context clearly, was an economist and conservative politician, Ms. Kristin Clemet.

After the 2001 general elections, she became minister of education, and began a dynamic leadership of Norwegian education policies. She implemented a series of measures that, although there were several setbacks, marked a shift of ideology and curriculum orientation, creating new frameworks for how people would think about school. Her actions came in turn to influence the thinking of her successors in the ministry of education, ministers from the Left Socialist Party. Clemet's overall analysis had as starting point exactly globalization's effects on national finances, not least after the oil era was over. Then, the country would be dependent on brainpower that made both individuals and businesses competitive internationally. With a twist of a famous sentence expressed by the ministry's mighty director general, Hartvig Nissen, in the1860's: «The post-oil era requires that people has a lot of knowledge – if a generous welfare state is to be maintained».

In the course of her four years as minister of education, Clemet kept a tremendous reform pace. New laws and legal amendments came frequent. First, she was thinking about structural changes. There had to be changed frames for how learning takes place. That is why she opened up for alternatives to the unified school. Opportunities to establish free schools would create a general dynamics in the school sector. Educational entrepreneurs would have an opportunity to test new ideas. Moreover, especially important, the public unified school could in its own development work, take advantage of the free schools' experiences. Parents and students would have a choice. Having choices would make parents more committed to their school. Clemet seemed to have turned upside down the old slogan of "well-being promotes learning" to, "learning of knowledge promotes well-being".

Clemet also saw quality improvement of higher education as a great challenge if the country would be able to assert itself internationally. Her rational basis seemed to be, the higher education sector gets huge resources from the public, but do not deliver particularly impressive results, in international comparison, neither when it comes to research nor to students' competence. When an organization manages its resources inefficiently, it is often relates to two aspects, leadership and market. Clemet worked hard to achieve a more effective university leadership. Specifically, her mission was to wind up the traditional arrangement, where the professors elected the one among their peers they liked the most as president, whether he was leader-qualified or not. So far, leadership qualifications had not really mattered, because the president of the university is not really a leader. He is only a business coordinator at the board, and an external figurehead. The real leadership is by a heavy administration, led by a director, which is often under remote control of the ministry of education's bureaucracy.

Clemet would replace such an arrangement with appointment of a leadership-qualified president. That would be a genuine leader, responsible for the institution's goal achievements, and accountable to stakeholders in society, entitled to have expectations of the university, including the ministry. In this attempt, she partly faced defeat. Even though the former mighty group of professors now weaker, they still flexed their muscles of resistance to the minster's proposal, and they proved to still enjoy considerable respect from the population at large, and among the politicians. They are very good at writing letters to newspapers' editors, and especially well qualified to argue their case, as well as to march in torchlight parades ensuring great attention. The professors bluntly claimed that a system of appointed university leadership was just first step towards making the university to a knowledge *enterprise*. Something that would be the very antithesis to the very rationale of a university, in the classic, humanistic tradition.

The fight between the minister and the professors ended with a compromise. The institutions themselves were to decide whether to elect or appoint a new president. All the research universities, except one, chose to continue the old tradition of electing the one of their peers they trusted the most as figurehead. The exception was the Norwegian University of Science and Technology (NTNU), today the country's largest university. At its crucial board meeting on the issue, the voices of the student representatives tipped the decision in favour of *appointing* the new president, after a public announcement of the position, making clear what capabilities the board expected of a university leader. In 2015, a fusion process in Norwegian higher education made NTNU the largest institution in Norway. Recently, two professors at NTNU got the Nobel Prize in medicine. Neither the successful merging process, nor the Nobel Prize winners, do necessarily link to the fact that an appointed, highly leadership-competent professor heads NTNU.

After the structural reforms, Clemet took on the inside of the education institutions. For the school system, she introduced *The Knowledge Promotion*, a curriculum reform marking a sharp course change in relation to the tradition of the unified school. The reform entailed signals of change when it came to key subjects, teaching methods, and, not least, evaluation. She introduced national tests. It caused deafening, angry reactions from the unified school lobby. On the organizational side, she took initiative to a new school leadership education, and made the headmaster an accountable leader in the municipality's administrative line of responsibility. The Norwegian Business School became an important supplier of leaders to the capital's schools. Within higher education, she introduced *The Quality Reform*. It was about the quality of teaching and the factors affecting the pace of students' study progression. This reform also provoked many professors strongly, but this time there was no torchlight parade against the reform.

The Clemet period (2001-2005), as seen from 2016, stimulates two important acknowledgements. The first is that she experienced rather brutal encounters with the chiefs of the old educational culture, whether they were in the compulsory school or in higher education, and she had to give in on some points. The second observation is that the sum of her reform initiatives created new terms for many people's thinking about Norwegian education. It is fair to state that she somewhat broke the tradition established after the Second World War, the unified school, and laid the foundation for a school development more in line with what is common internationally. The old, progressivist educational culture was, however, still strong in Norway. This was immediately visible, when she had to hand over the educational reins to her successor from the Socialist Left Party, Mr. Øystein Djupedal in 2005.

Djupedal was a cheerful and realistic minister, until he was so realistic that he had to leave his post. The cheerful part became visible by his enthusiastic embrace of Clemet's knowledge-oriented school. He turned so excited about *knowledge* that he decided to change the name of his own position, from minister of education to *"Minister of Knowledge"*. Nothing less. For all stakeholders who had perceived the Socialist Left Party as the strongest political defender of the unified school, this was surprisingly clear speech about a dramatic change of course in education policies. The socialist minister loudly announced he would make the Norwegian school into a real knowledge school. Whether the name-change would be sufficient to change the unified school culture among teachers, trade unions and bureaucrats was a more uncertain issue. When I told about the Norwegian name-change, and the reasons for it at an international conference, one of the participants commented, *"Why don't you call him the Minister of Magic?"* Norway is the only country in the world with an education minister calling himself Minister of Knowledge. It is striking. A Norwegian minister of education on visits abroad would hardly present himself as Minister of Knowledge. It might cause associations to the Minister of Magic, running Harry Potter's Wizard school, Hogwarts.

It would soon prove that the political reality of magic minister Djupedal was similar to that of other politicians. He had to pay attention to voters in the upcoming elections, not least, to all the teachers who had voted for his party. He effectively demonstrated such political attention by attacking the system of free schools introduced by Clemet. He made clear that it would be far from easy for those who established free schools to make money, and create an education market. Such a development would "deplete the public school". He reversed the law on free schools. By such measures, Djupedal proved he was a man of action. Moreover, he was a political realist. He was also a realist when it came to higher education. He and his successors expressed significant sympathy for Clemet's reforms in this area. However, when publicly known that the socialist minister was ready to introduce time clocks for professors, many university employees had problems keeping up their party loyalty.

In the Norwegian school reality, the socialist ministers of education maintained well the unified school culture. That was as expected. The Teachers' Union was a close ally. In Clemet's time, the union had to accept the knowledge boost in schools and national tests, with gritted teeth. With the socialists in charge of Norwegian education, the anticipated dangerous development, away from the unified school, could slow down. It was, however, increasingly difficult to see which measures the new enthusiasm for the knowledge school required of the socialist ministers. On a larger educational conference in 2007, the socialist deputy minister of education had a keynote speech. On a question afterwards, whether it was correct that the Socialist Left Party's school policy had turned 180 degrees during Djupedal's reign, the minister replied in the affirmative. A follow-up question asked whether the party and the government had acknowledged the measures required to realize its goals for a knowledge school. The deputy minister replied that they had not. Soon after, he was out of the ministry.

After general elections in 2013, a minister from the conservative party was once more is in charge of educational leadership of the country. Even if the premises are different from the situation encountered by Clemet, there is still fierce opposition from the unified school culture. On the one hand, you now hear an almost unison choir singing, knowledge school, knowledge school, knowledge school. That is music in the ears of the minister. However, in practice, he faces serious problems when trying to implement a solid knowledge school. The old progressivist culture is still there, in the system, and makes it hard to get changes. The crew at his disposal when trying to implement new policies is the old guard stuck in the particular progressivist culture that has developed over more than 40 years. The old guard comprises researchers, teacher training, education bureaucracy, media, and probably still more than half of Norwegian parents do not think education is an important value. Then it is not so easy to be a successful minister of education.

It is neither easy for a minister of education from the conservatives, to match with Clemet's achievements. However, the minister, Mr. Roe Isachsen, is trying his best. His main remedy, close to being his magic tool, is in-service training of teachers. Quite immediately, it makes good sense. When students in class perform poorly academically, it is appropriate to think that students will improve, if the teachers' skills improve. "All research agree" that the teacher is the most important factor for students' learning. The problem with the in-service training strategy is that Norway for many years recruited weak graduates from secondary school to teacher education. These teachers' real intellectual abilities are questionable. In addition, these teachers are in their own thinking themselves a cultural product of the unified school. It is therefore uncertain whether they have the abilities and values required to make achievements of their in-service training corresponding to the minister's expectations. The minister also makes a new thrust for free-schools. However, he moves very carefully. This minister is also a political realist, and considers thoroughly the political consequences. Next general election is not far away.

He has met with disappointments. The teachers' strike in 2014 was a success for the Teachers' Union. It meant delaying necessary modernization of the working conditions that the school owner saw necessary to solve the problems of de-professionalized teachers. The municipality, as a school owner, is now experiencing increasing pressures from parents to make the school a better tool for school policy goals. During the strike, the teachers managed to get support from the unified school lobby, not least from the media, for their argument that the teachers must have freedom in their work situation. Such freedom was quite natural for the teachers in the old days, because they, themselves then took academic and moral responsibility for students' learning. They needed no boss to control their professional work. This is still the case in Finland. Now the situation in Norway is different. Today's teachers have neither academic nor moral authority. Therefore, they need leadership to guide them. A main dysfunction of the teachers' successful strike is delay of the necessary organisational modernisation of the public school. The strike is also a reminder that the special culture caused by unified school ideology still have considerable strength. The recent Pisa report was a slap in the face for Norway, and sad reading for the minister. In spite of the Knowledge Promotion programme and eight years with «ministers of knowledge», Norway is even worse off on knowledge achievements in international comparisons.

The minister also has events to enjoy. The capital city's education, until last year run by his own party, emerges as an exiting deviant. Oslo schools made several successful rebellions against the unified school culture. The city intensified learning measures for improved knowledge attainment, in schools and by extra measures outside school. The city's headmasters take a master's degree in educational leadership at Norwegian Business School, and they become accountable as a key link of the education value chain. They are the linchpin between democratic political decisions and implementation in the classroom. The evaluation, control of students' learning, is now more valid and reliable. The last invention is that when documented that teachers are successful at getting students to improve their learning results extra well, then teachers get extra payment. This will certainly have positive effects. Quite commonly, cash-reward tends to affect the effort, even if the representatives of the unified school culture claim that such payments are non-collegial and morally reprehensible.

What has happened in Oslo schools is a powerful expression that the educational culture in Norway is changing from a progressivist unified school culture to what is reminiscent of Continental-European encyclopaedism and the golden age of the 1950s. In spite of the welfare state's limited motivation for efforts in education, this could be the beginning of a change in Norwegians' view of education as a value. Norway may be turning more similar to the rest of Europe, where 81% of the population believe education is an important value. This may further lead to a better work ethic, more endurance and acceptance of the competition as something natural. Oslo and the Oslo-area is also interesting on other aspects of education policies. In this area, there are already several international schools. A growing number of Norwegian parents tries to get their children into such schools. Not only the country's Crown Prince thinks international schools are better than the unified school. Many Christian private schools have gained greater demand, hardly because the applicants are becoming more religious than before. They are popular, because these schools deliver good knowledge learning. Some parents of students in secondary school also find opportunities to allow students to go abroad, to schools they think are better, e.g. to the Islamic Republic of Pakistan. What is happening in Oslo is an indication that the unified school culture in Norway has reached its peak, and is now facing decline. It is time to say goodbye to it. Before that, however, we should remember with respect its good motives. The unified school's intention was to create justice and equality. Why it failed, we can see by taking a closer look at the essence of schooling in a historical perspective, and at the relationship between school and justice.

32

The Essence of Schooling and Social Justice

School quality is more than ever crucially important to the survival of individuals, companies and nations. The Norwegian unified school strategy after World War II was a well-meant and ambitious policy for developing the population's skills, simultaneously achieving social and cultural integration, and seeing class distinctions disappear. The progressivist, unified school in Norway had better economic and political framework conditions than in any other country. In addition, to be fair, there are cases where star teachers managed to get incredibly far in achieving knowledge learning, social integration and democracy training simultaneously. Especially, in the first few years after the war, when many, not least socialist teachers, were inspired by the opportunity to make the school an instrument to create the ideal society in a real world.

In light of what has actually happened, there are plenty of indications that the unified school project is no longer valid, in Norway as well as in other countries. Many claim that the very idea of the unified school in crucial ways is a break with the school's historical rationale and people's uniqueness. Problem-and project based learning may be a disaster, when the teacher lacks authority and professionalism. Not only is students' time wasted. Students may also learn that sloppiness and irresponsibility go on without sanctioning. They may as well learn that good results are not important. This is what some educators call a hidden stupidifying curriculum. Sloppy attitudes are especially serious in the demanding school subjects such as mathematics. A stupidifying hidden curriculum is most likely especially harmful for weaker students. They learned more with a teacher like Baard Schoolmaster, one who had clear expectations to them, than left in their ignorance with «responsibility for their own learning». The educational Gyro Gearloose-response to the difficulties of learning mathematics was some time back a serious proposal to drop compulsory maths in school. In practice, the proposal was reality distant, but philosophically justifiable.

In an international perspective, the unified school of progressivist origin is an alien thought, except for the United States and Scandinavia, minus Finland. The English comprehensive schools never embraced «learning by doing». Comprehensiveness extended to efforts to get students of different socio-cultural backgrounds to be in the same school buildings. They maintained academic subject standards clearly. That is still the case in England. In the English population at large, there is a clear recognition of «what schooling is all about».

Historically, the essence of schooling was to develop different people differently. It is not possible to remove the school's unequal-producing character. It can neither be very democratic in practice. A good school is normally hierarchical with wise leadership and wise teachers. Therefore, there must be other venues, than the school, as training fields for practical democracy. The school is inevitably hierarchical, because teachers must have authority in order to gain respect as good teachers. Many blends the concepts of authority and authoritarianism. While it is impossible to be a professional teacher without authority, the teacher should never perform in an authoritarian way.

Authority is the power accepted because it is considered justified, as legitimate. A school where teachers do not have reasonable authority is not justified. The school as a "practicing democracy" seems based on a particular interpretation of Dewey, something along the lines of "learning democracy by doing it". International schools of quality and their teachers do not practice democracy in schools. Most school conscious parents see the school's primary function as making sure that the students most effectively acquire solid and up-to-date academic knowledge. Such knowledge is a key prerequisite for creative problem solving, active learning and ethical responsible consciousness towards society and the environment. In other words, a school providing students with solid knowledge will create essential prerequisites for practising democracy, outside school. The school's significant contribution to democracy is to let everyone have access to as solid knowledge as possible. Knowledge is an important power factor in society. Knowledge acquisition requires active efforts. The progressivist idea that children and youth can get solid knowledge by playing around is a dangerous myth.

If you are trying to investigate the main responsibility for Norway's disastrous school development over the last forty years, it is probably most fruitful to focus attention on the educational researchers, rather than the politicians. Norwegian educational research occurred just before World War II, and almost exploded after the war. Among politicians and others, there was great confidence in such research. To begin with, the research was relatively neutral and psychologically oriented. Eventually it became increasingly ideological. The student-centred and anti-academic foundation laid by progressivism had a fierce increase through the political radicalization of the universities in the 1970s.

For many politically radical education researchers, the progressivist unified school principle was an indisputable premise for their research. The task of educational research was to explain how to reach the goals of the unified school in practice. They forced the terrain to fit with the ideological map. In addition to research results, the universities supplied the teacher colleges with lecturers to convey knowledge about the unified school. Moreover, the universities also supplied the educational bureaucracy with experts to implement the reforms. In this perspective, those who produced so-called scientific knowledge about school development, and trained lecturers for the teacher colleges, they were the main responsible for the content of teacher training and ways of thinking in the educational bureaucracy. Educational researchers often have such strong proximity to practice and to certain values, that they often have difficulties to see consequences of their ideology.

While the progressivist-unified school now appears to be in decline, the international elite schools, as well as English and East Asian schools, indicate which school traditions that are now advancing internationally. The roots of the perception of the school's essence are with Plato and Confucius. Plato's septem artes liberales (the seven free arts or subjects) is the classical curriculum containing three humanity subjects and four natural science subjects. This classic curriculum has throughout history been challenged by encyclopaedism with emphasis on many subjects, of communist polytechnicalism, with theory and practice integrated, and of American progressivism, with the «learning by doing» and rejection of «old European» knowledge.

Today we see internationally a renaissance for Plato's ideas. England is the relevant example of a country in this tradition. There, they have all the time had a curriculum thinking inspired by Plato's ideas. The school's task is to convey subject-based knowledge. Justice occurs by making sure that everybody have access to teaching with quality. You do not reduce quality requirements in order to give the impression that more students have succeeded. Reducing standards is a disservice to those who most need solid knowledge to master their lives, or if you like, to master the class struggle.

Given an acceptance of the view that the unified school has not created the desired justice, and agreeing that education with quality is a human right for the weak, and for the clever students, I imagine intuitively two important measures that will contribute to increased social justice, an improved, but shortened, compulsory school and lifelong learning. To gain access to education with quality is a human right, but it should also be a right for people to drop a mandatory school that is stupidifying.

In a vision, decoupled from political and ideological reality, I envisage an ideal school offer for all. Preschool, primary school and a shortened secondary lower school has a maximum of pedagogical expertise to create optimal knowledge learning for all students, whatever their social and academic backgrounds. The very best pedagogues should serve at these levels of compulsory schooling, preferable on contract and excellent salaries, so that the school (and parents) do not risk being stuck with life long employee incompetence. There should also be an opportunity already after fifth and sixth grade to differentiate between the «theoretical» and «practical» students. Simultaneously with requiring work efforts, there must also be sensitivity to reaching the limits for pressure on students, in order to avoid "the stupidifying school". At the end of the compulsory school age, there should be a real choice between continued schooling and working life. Those choosing working life, have a guaranteed right to a work place, as well as a thick voucher-booklet providing the right and resources for lifelong learning, when the person's real motivation for classroom learning appears, regardless of age.

There are several examples of «late bloomers», those who become intellectually mature later than at so-called normal school age. Even though it is important at school age, with constructive and persistent demands on the student to take the school seriously, most teachers know the extreme difference there is in the learning results, when the student has inner motivation, and when ordered to learn. Largely, it is also a human right for the teacher to avoid impossible learning tasks. The teacher also has a human right to not to be the victim of unmotivated and ill-mannered students who are forced to be at school.

A shortened compulsory school of excellent quality and, a legal right to lifelong learning free of charge when you are motivated, will make optimal justice for the individual, for its opportunities to develop its potential, no matter how strong or frail its ability for abstract thinking. In addition, and very important, my proposal may create the optimal human capital production for Norway as a society. Such production is necessary if the country is going to stay such a strong international economic actor, that it can maintain the world's best welfare state also in the future.

Throughout the most developed part of the world, people are growing increasingly older. Simultaneously, most elderly people also are in better health, have key experiences and considerable capacity for both continued learning and work. At German universities, they have already developed educational programmes for the old people. The point is that people are not really growing old as before; they just live more years, while they continue to be active citizens. They work, travel or take consulting. Thus a new hyphen-pedagogy appears, *Geria-gogikk*. It is a specialization within education as an academic field, where you have research and designing of learning measures for people who have in common that they have reached a certain age, but otherwise are just as diverse as the population at large. In this group of old people, a lot of individual desire to learn can be unleashed. Moreover, the nation is simultaneously, also at this age end extending its human-capital.

To be able to use education policies to achieve greater social justice, you have to begin by looking at the preconditions for the learning culture that developed in Norway after the Golden Age of the 1950s. Another way to gain insight into the distinctive Norwegian learning culture is to compare with other countries. In the first part of this book, I presented a picture of the learning culture in China, and gave specific examples of how this culture had affected great respect for knowledge. In the beginning of the 21st Century, there are several education measures indicating that Norway has a desire to return to the curriculum tradition we had in the golden age. Changes are turtle-like, because changing culture is slow business. In the conclusion part, of my educational travelogue, I am first going to summarize what we can learn from China, and a couple of neighbouring countries, Finland and England, before finally giving my vision for optimal school quality for everyone in Norway.

What Can Norway Learn From Others?

33

What can Norway Learn from China?

The first Norway can learn from China is to have a vision of education as a means to achieve an important value, refinement of human character or morality. Summarized, education can make many people help to create a better society for all. The Norwegian unified school has largely become a place to stay, and has given symbolic certification and a certain amount of technical expertise, more than character formation. From China, we can learn that education contributes decisively to create a strong identity and great mastery, expressed by the commitment and the ability to take advantage of competition. Respect for education and love for education is the central nerve of Chinese patriotism to strengthen the country in difficult times. Such *knowledge patriotism* is perhaps the most important thing we can learn from China. The key factor of the Chinese educational history, I have provided in this book, is a moral philosopher who lived 2500 years ago. He inspired a number of individuals in the 20th Century to take great educational efforts to help to rebuild the nation's self-respect and competence. That was necessary after China' terrible humiliation by Japan and Western imperialist powers.

From China we can learn how important it is to be conscious about our cultural heritage, our philosophical roots, and which curriculum tradition made the foundation for our schools. After the Second World War, Norway switched curriculum tradition. From being part of a European, encyclopaedic knowledge-tradition, we chose to change to an American, pragmatic settler-perception of knowledge and society. How thoughtful was this choice? The American philosopher John Dewey perceived the European cultural tradition as an old elitist knowledge-*threat*, for the democratic and equal American society, to which many poor Europeans had fled. The immigrants came from «the old world» where they were at the bottom of the social hierarchy. Dewey rejected the old, European knowledge heritage. People in the new world were themselves to discover and judge what valid knowledge was. It was this sort of thinking; Norway chose to make the philosophical foundation for its school policies after the war. It has contributed significantly to confusion about what is the school's rationale and function.

The Chinese have acted differently. In China, the same line, the same opinion of what is valuable to learn, was constant for 2500 years. The exception is, when they woke up to their technological backwardness in the 19th and 20th centuries, and realized that they, like the Japanese, as fast as possible, had to learn the scientific thinking and technology that had evolved in the West. They sent talented students to the West, and Western experts came to China. Simultaneously with eagerly picking up useful knowledge and skills from the West, they insisted on retaining their Chinese identity, rooted in Confucianism, the multi-millennial Chinese cultural heritage. From China, we can learn that we should consider looking back to the Norwegian school's golden age, to see what has been lost during the transition to a unified school based on an American progressivist curriculum tradition, and, in order to see what we can regain. Such actions, and even such thinking, may prove difficult in a time of affluent oil economy and the world's best social security system. However, the awareness that we once were a nation with a school focusing knowledge, may be an advantage for us the day there is no more oil, and stronger efforts required. The reward of such awareness is the rediscovery of the kind of school that created business-entrepreneurs, creative scientists and dynamic union leaders in the first part of the 20th Century. The Chinese history tells us about the importance of educational patriotism. From the

Chinese, we can learn the importance of work ethics, never give in, and show stamina when there is competition, even if you do not always win.

From the Chinese, we can learn how important parents are for a child's education. In the beginning of the 20th Century, the Swedish feminist Ellen Key wrote the book *The Child's Century*. She writes about *the child's right to choose its parents*. Key pin points her argument, but her statement really tells everything about what is most crucial for the opportunities a child will have in life. Responsible parents, and especially the mother, is crucial. In the first part of this book, I presented several examples of how this works out in the Confucian world. The Japanese mother who went to school herself, to find out what her daughter had missed when she was ill, and she sought private help to ensure the girl was not lagging behind in her learning of school subjects. The girl from Western China, whose parents helped her to get into Xiamen university, so she could have a better education and a better life than they had had. The parents of the famous professor Pan were able to find the modest money needed for keeping him in the lower secondary school.

In today's Norwegian school, the most serious problem is many parents' lack of interest for the school as a workplace for knowledge acquisition. An example of this lack of interest is how easily parents take their children out of school to go on holiday in the midst of the school year. Their lack of understanding of the school's importance is the darkest effect of the unified school as primarily a place to stay, more than a place to learn. When parents do not consider education as an important value, and school as an essential means to reach this value, the teachers are working in headwind. The very starting point for this book, the motivation for writing it, was to reach out to Norwegian parents and grandparents, to remind them of their responsibilities in relation to what matters most to them, children and grandchildren. I would like to contribute to make them see their responsibilities. Parents' responsibility has increased, because the unified school, without intending it, created considerable disdain for knowledge. Parents and grandparents should also recognize the responsibility following from the possibility that the welfare state may not last forever. They should think that one day their loved ones might themselves be responsible for survival in a tough world. Then it is essential that you believe you *are* something, and that you *know* something. From the Chinese we can learn that we, as parents and grandparents, need to care for the school, that we have no moral right to be quiet, if the school fails in preserving the knowledge responsibility, we have trusted teachers and school leadership.

From the Chinese history, from the Confucius' time, we can learn that the teacher is the linchpin for any society's morality and competence. We can learn to understand that attempts in Norwegian post-war time, to raise teachers' status not only is unsuccessful, it has been destructive. To a large degree, it follows as a side effect of the unified school. Before World War II, Norwegian teachers had high social status. In addition to being teachers, they were politicians, writers and cultural entrepreneurs. In the post-war period, their status has constantly declined. If you ask a lower secondary school student, if he would consider becoming a teacher, he would reply by asking if you think him stupid. Next to making parents become conscious about responsibility in relation to the school, the biggest challenge today is to regain the Norwegian teachers' social status. Teachers' with high social status is crucial for any country with the ambition of being a knowledge nation. As is the case already in China and in Finland.

In the Chinese history, we recognize the Norwegian Baard schoolmaster-character repeatedly. It was such a teacher who *saw* the school girl, Yang Ying. She was the waitress, who later became a billionaire, and established Xiamen international school. It was a Chinese-style Baard schoolmaster, who *saw* the poor boy and rice-cake baker, Pan Maoyuan. He pushed the boy to be able to continue in secondary school. Pan later became the founder of research on higher education in China. The series of such Baard school*masters* is infinite in China. From China (and Finland), we can learn that it is the academic cream of the crop among graduates from secondary school that should become teachers in the compulsory school. These teachers make the foundation for the entire nation's creative powers. Taiwan for many years exempted teachers from paying tax. That tells how important the government considered them to be in creating the economic and political Taiwan Miracle.

Confucius emphasized the rituals and rules of conduct. It has effects in Chinese schools. Teachers meet with great respect and courtesy. We can learn from the Chinese that to show respect for the teacher and the other superiors is important and useful. That does not mean submission and rejection of equality, but acceptance of some useful, social, driving rules that improve interaction between people. American progressivism values highly equality and democracy. It is understandable, because of the discomfort the settlers had experienced at home, in old Europe's nasty class society. The medal of equality, however, has a reverse side. Vulgarity follows easily. It may affect seeing it as «cool» to be rude to the teacher. When the teacher has to be the students' chopping goof, as part of their training to independence and democracy, then the very idea of schooling may be lost. There can be no school of quality without a teacher with authority based in knowledge, and therefore met with respect. Without respect for the teacher, quality learning is close to impossible. If the learning of democracy and independence takes place at the expense of the teacher's self-esteem and authority, you have killed the hen laying the golden eggs. Democracy without knowledge may be a compact majority making poor decisions.

Lessons from Communist China show that streaming of students is necessary. It means a recognition that students are different, some are learning much easier and more effectively than others do. In the lower secondary school, this inequality is impossible to hide, as it can in primary school. There shall also be justice for the clever students. Therefore, streaming according to learning abilities is necessary. This is common sense in all cultures where they primarily see schooling as a means to increased knowledge-appropriation. However, this does not apply to schools based on the progressivist curriculum tradition, such as in the United States and Scandinavia, minus Finland. There has to be other ways of respecting pupils' different learning abilities, than to have everyone in the same class and try to hide the differences. From adolescence and upwards, it is impossible to hide the differences in conditions for knowledge learning. It was, inter alia, this dimension of schooling, the unified school tried to avoid. In vain.

Chinese history teaches us to understand the importance of inequality, how it can be constructive for the community. One key word is meritocracy, leadership by the most qualified. This is of course a challenge for a democratic way of thinking. Since, however, it is a fact that some people are intellectually more adept than others are, it is necessary to find other ways to safeguard democracy, than by hiding inequality. The Chinese conscious commitment to mass and elite education, simultaneously, is a reminder of what the school's opportunities and constraints are, in order to create equality. Since it is essentially impossible to change the basic abilities for learning, the school's contribution to reach goals of equality and justice, cannot go further than to give equal opportunities to quality education, in a lifelong perspective. If a country is able to provide opportunities of learning, *for all*, *free of charge, throughout life*, when people are *motivated*, then that country has done the optimal to create equality and justice for its citizens by *schooling*. Simultaneously, such a country, in return has an optimal production of expertise, which is necessary for the economy we all live by.

Deng Xiaoping underlined in his education policies that everyone, regardless of social background, should have access to the university, as long as the results from secondary school was good enough. This is clear speech, in contrast to unified school thinking. The university cannot give in on academic requirements, when it comes to admission. There will be no good quality (reform) in university education if relaxing the requirements of performance from secondary school. If graduates are not good enough for the university, they have to apply elsewhere. Society as a whole will lose out, if the elite research university deteriorates.

Equality and moral obligations for any school authority, is to ensure that everybody with abilities can move further in the education system. To let everyone, regardless of social background, get this opportunity is fulfilment of a central human right. Simultaneously, this is a very good socio-economic investment. This was Deng's understanding when he designed new education policies for China. These policies for increased competence made the foundation for China today being the world's second strongest economy, and that several hundred millions of people came out of poverty. Put otherwise, the Chinese teach us that it does not make sense to let money prevent young people from education, when they are clever and determined to work hard. They shall have what it takes. That is beneficial for the entire community. In Deng's version of socialism, it is acceptable that some get rich first, in order to create the foundation, that preferably all eventually can become rich together.

The Chinese remind us about something important regarding competition. Competition is something close to a universal phenomenon. The Chinese teach us that competition can be a constructive tool. It is a parallel thinking to how many Chinese people consider «socialist market economy». Market economy is not congruent with capitalism. The market economy can have a socialist equalizing goal. However, the market economy itself is a universal phenomenon, and it involves just competition between vendors in a market. In the Norwegian section of this book, I told about bizarre attempts to remove competition in Norwegian education. They are representative of an attitude that has been, and may still be present the in Norwegian society. The Chinese have shown us that, under certain rules, competition is a central instrument to create dynamism in development. When competition, simultaneously, is a universal aspect of human uniqueness, it is constructive to use competition, consciously, as a tool for development. Many have pointed out the paradox of Norwegian culture; competition not just accepted, but embraced and admired in the sports' context, while judged unfortunate in school. In China and most other countries, this is not a valid view.

Because of the strong influence of Confucius, the Chinese have some values that we had before, but now are either missing, or are severely weakened. An example is persistence. This property has links with competition. Frequently, persistence is necessary to win the competition. This also apply to contexts of schooling and study, e.g. when applying for scholarships or funds for research projects. In China, we see the respect for endurance expressed in the following statement, "It is okay to fail at an examination, while giving up is a shame". This is reminiscent of professor Pan. He failed on the admission tests the first time he applied for the university. It did not knock him out. He examined more thoroughly what the admission tests required, compared the information with assessment of his prior knowledge. Then he realized why he had failed the first time. Next time he succeeded.

China was for thousands of years the world's centre, the Kingdom of the Middle. Then followed humiliation and almost complete colonization, before ascending to new glory. Their history has thoroughly taught the Chinese that they need to be conscious of their own strength and confidence, simultaneously with being open to learning useful things from others. The school's main task is to give students constructive self-confidence and a strong identity. Wise teachers with great authority are essential agents for students to develop such confidence. For Norwegians, this is a lesson learnt from the Chinese. For Norway, however, this is a problem, because the Norwegian teachers today often are just facilitators, not teachers of the Baard schoolmaster type. Strong identity and self-confidence are essential to obtain the other key element of the battle of life, mastery. For Norway, this is a challenging problem.

In an age where the Internet and ICT are inevitable parts of existence, also in the school, we can learn from the Chinese how to manage the technology in a way that serves the school's purpose, and not the reverse, destructive waste of students' time. The principle of "responsibility for your own learning", school democracy and teachers without authority and respect makes it difficult for many Norwegian students not to ruin for themselves, by misusing technology for entertainment also during school hours. Without teachers who are able to control the students' use of the technology, like e.g. the teacher, Mr. Constable, at Xiamen international school did, big investments may be serious losses instead of gains. From the Chinese, we can learn to avoid letting the ICT-logic over-run curriculum logic, and, instead let ICT be a servant for teachers' responsible planning of constructive learning activities.

China's position in the world today, makes Chinese language gaining greater importance. I have mentioned former Prime Minister Gordon Brown in the United Kingdom who saw the challenge, and declared that within a short time all British schools should have partnerships with Chinese schools, to facilitate learning of Chinese. English is still undeniably the world languages no. 1. Nevertheless, Chinese is breathing English's neck. Globally there is a tremendous increase in the number of people learning mandarin. The reason is two-fold, one stimulus is China itself, another reason is other countries' global market thinking, and interest for Chinese culture. China provides the establishment of Confucius institutes all over the world, in order to spread the knowledge of the Chinese language and culture. The market, whether it is individuals who are thinking about career, or businesses who think new business, they all see the necessity to master the language. What Norway can learn, in terms of education policies, is that one should be proactive by getting Chinese language into curricula as a compulsory subject, as early as possible. Young children learn a foreign language easier.

So far, we have observed areas where Norway may have something to learn from China in terms of education. However, it is also important to mention aspects of the Chinese educational culture for which we should watch out. A negative result of Confucius' intense emphasis on learning and knowledge is that the Chinese do not have much respect for practical and vocational education. This is a problem, and Chinese educational researchers now raise a lot of attention to it. China has a similar distribution of the people, when it comes to ability of abstracting, as other countries. It means that they also have the equivalent of those students with scarce, or no motivation for an education consisting primarily of academic subjects. Professor Pan, who worked a lifetime in the particular field of university pedagogy, has in his old age, taken a series of initiatives to strengthen vocational training, which will contribute to giving it higher social status. Such initiatives are important for individuals, and for parts of the business world. However, it will not be easy. The Confucian tradition is stronger than ever. Mao's attempt to change the situation was a failure, and Deng prioritized research and education that strengthened the advanced economy. Another point requiring consideration, are the negative aspects of competition. Although competition in general is inevitable, the schools should be sensitive to situations where it becomes destructive.

Norwegian school patriotism was a main reason for writing this book. Another inspiration was China and the other Confucian countries. Before ending the book with my vision for Norway, I will make a comparative glance. There are also other countries, from which Norway can learn abut school improvement. I will look at two European neighbouring countries, Finland and England.

34

The Finnish School Code

In the last decade, Finland is the world champion of school quality. Until the recent Pisa test, the country enthroned at the top of the world education podium. School researchers internationally have wondered about the reasons for the Finnish success, and have come up with many guesses. Hardly anyone has so far given a convincing explanation. The code has not yet been broken. When a Finnish school researcher four years ago began his presentation at an educational conference in Oslo, he lifted both his hands and said, «Here I guess we have the two reasons why I am invited». In one hand, he held a Pisa-report, and in the other a Nokia mobile phone, and he continued, "You may wonder if there is a connection?" Since then, sceptical Finns had their misgivings confirmed. The Nokia adventure is now history, and the latest Pisa report reported a decline in Finnish achievements. Still, it is a fact that Pisa tests for many years showed Finland to be the world's champion in school achievements for 15 year olds. Modest Finns have since experienced numerous foreign Pisa-tourists. Politicians, bureaucrats and researchers from all over the world have queued to break the Finnish school code, and take it home, to improve their own schools.

What are Pisa-tourists' first dramatic discoveries? It is that recruitment to teacher training is unique, compared to all other countries, and it is one key element of the code. It is the academic cream of the crop from secondary school graduates making recruits to teacher training, and then, to educate the whole nation's potential brainpower, from kindergarten through to secondary school. This fact got strikingly modest attention in different countries' local debates about how they can learn from Finland. In international comparative education, the Finnish recruitment to teacher training is sensational. The quality of recruits to teacher education is the precise point, which ambitious governments should aim at. It is self-evident that when a country succeed in making the most gifted from secondary compete hard to be trained for becoming a teacher in primary and secondary schools, then that country has reached the optimal, in order to provide the best possible school to all its students. The Finnish case is commendable in human rights and equality perspectives, and even more impressive from a financial perspective. Except for forestry, Finland, like Hong Kong, has no natural raw materials. It is by brainpower the country should maintain its welfare state in the future. Because of their quality education, Finns have a built-in power for new thinking and initiative, also when the Nokia adventure is over. The country has a huge human capital.

After secondary school's academic cream of the crop has won in the first competition, to have an opportunity to show that they perhaps are capable, they move on to a series of tests, to be passed in order to see if they actually are suitable for the teaching profession, and if they can collaborate with colleagues. Then they test on research-specific properties, such as curiosity, creativity and innovative thinking in relation to solve unforeseen problems in class. Those who pass all the tests enter a five years research-based master's degree programme at a university. They incorporate in an academic education culture, disparate from the Norwegian teacher training rooted in a next to anti-academic seminar tradition.

So far, we observed the surface of the Finnish school code. To find the core of the code remains. What for most Pisa tourists remains unknown is the foundation of the Finnish school success. *The culture.* Finland is a Scandinavian country, and very similar to its neighbours in many areas, except when it comes to teachers. Many Finns themselves have problems in actually understanding what has created their school success. Finnish educators have virtually insisted that Finland is in the same curriculum company as the rest of Scandinavia, that they are progressivist. The progressivist curriculum tradition is just progressive, something positive, modern, democratic and equal, something better than the old tradition of the class-divided Europe, not to mention that progressivism is a token of being far away from the school traditions of Finland's last colonial master, imperial Russia. When Finnish researchers have recovered from their astonishment caused by foreigners' interest and admiration, they have even felt the pressure to dig deeper to find explanations of why Finland is a «school exception» in Scandinavia and the West as a whole.

The Russian Tsarist Empire is the key word. When Finland was a grand duchy in Russia, the Finnish teachers were the empire's civil servants, with distinct authority and great social respect. The social status then established, Finnish researchers now see as the root of the development that has created today's school success. Since the independence in 1917, the teaching profession's social status influenced recruitment and quality in Finnish teacher education in a way that makes the country fundamentally different from the rest of the West. The teaching profession became the corner stone in the socio-economic development of a poor agricultural country, until reaching its international success in communication technology (Nokia).

The teaching profession continues to have an exceptional high social status. The teachers are popular among people in general. They have solid authority in relation to parents, students, school authorities and society. When a Norwegian research group a few years ago wanted to compare school leader training in five especially interesting countries, Finland was a natural case to include. The problem, however, turned out to be that the country hardly had any such training. Finnish teachers have not needed any professional school administrators to do their teaching job well. They do not need others' evaluation of their work. They very well know themselves what is good teaching in relation to different students. They get authority from respect for what they achieved. These teachers in the public school take care of the interests of students, parents, companies and the whole nation's knowledge needs so well, that there is no need for private schools, which is the case in most other countries. The core of the Finnish school code is Finnish cultural distinctiveness, which further results in a distinctive Finnish school culture. For others to be able to take advantage of the Finnish example, it is necessary to have a certain idea about the nature of Finnish culture. Then it *may* be possible to transfer something useful to your own country's schools. Maybe, because when something has become *culture*, it is extremely difficult to change. To understand the prerequisites of the Finnish school, there is a need to look back, to the country's history, while simultaneously making a glance at Norway.

Finland emerged as a nation state while it was still part of the Russian Empire during the 19th Century. A consequence of the Russian influence was that the Finnish society and culture acquired some features different from the rest of Scandinavia. The particular Finnish cultural character had marks of accepting authority, obedience and a collective mentality. Another aspect making Finland different from their western neighbours is that the country became a fully independent nation only after one of the bloodiest civil wars in modern European history. The relationship with Russia and the civil war may explain the Finns' strong will to achieve consensus on important social and political issues, e.g. educational reforms.

In the years after World War II, the economy has been a particularly important difference between Finland and Norway. Both countries were relatively poor before the war. After the war, Finland had to pay huge war reparations to the Soviet Union, as well as refrain large tracts of land, Norway, firstly, got generous aid from the US for its reconstruction after the war (The Marshall Aid), and secondly, the country enjoyed wealth from off shore oil industry. Although Finland today is a solid welfare state, it occurred at a relatively recent date, compared with the country's Scandinavian neighbours. More typical of the Finnish economy, until three or four decades ago, was that people had to work very hard to make it. Historically, the population mainly consisted of small farmers and forest workers. Finland was primarily a land of scattered villages, and until recently, with very small social differences.

Financially, Finland effectively caught up with its neighbouring countries, and most people currently has a high standard of living. You may now wonder if the relatively recent story of tough economic times, and war reparations to the Soviet Union, developed a stronger work ethic, characterised by efforts and perseverance or *sisu*, in Finnish, than what is the case in the rest of Scandinavia. Moreover, you may now wonder if the sisu will persist, when the Finnish population keep getting increasingly better welfare. May be that increased welfare will make them less hungry for making efforts, and maybe there will appear a more relaxed motivation for education as a key means of individual progress. Like what happened in Norway, who first got the benefit of the Americans' Marshall Aid and then became super wealthy, because of oil and gas. However, it is important to remember that the Finns did not take over the American curriculum tradition, as Norway did. That may still give the Finns an advantage in the global knowledge economy.

A typical feature of the Finnish society is the value attributed to equality in all aspects of life. Equality is an overarching goal. There shall be equality between social groups, genders, and geographic regions. Therefore, it is consensus among all political parties that the country should always follow a policy of continually trying to compensate for social and cultural inequalities in society. Education with the same quality shall be available in every municipality in the country, and it is public. Private schools hardly exist, and if they do, they have their main funding from the state. Large investments in quality education for all was important strategy for social mobility. Everyone should have the opportunity to reach as far as possible in his or her professional ambitions. Several of the aspects of such a policy for social cohesion we find also in Norway. However, the main difference between the two countries is that *the quality of education* as the means to equal opportunities is inferior in Norway.

Russian influence has not only caused harsh economic conditions and pressures to be cautious in Finland's foreign policies. The more than one hundred years under Russian rule has probably influenced Finnish education in distinct encyclopaedic direction, from Germany, via Russia. There is also reason to believe that the special feature of Russian culture and mentality have made the Finns more obedient and set to accept authority, than has been the case with their western Scandinavian neighbours. Implicit in such Russian influence, was a general high regard for teachers, and readiness to follow their advice and requirements.

The synthesis of various features of Finnish culture and Finnish society has brought forth a distinctive Finnish *educational culture*. The first important feature is a teacher education with curriculum and organizing based in an encyclopaedic tradition. The other important characteristic is that the recruits to teacher education is the intellectual cream of the crop from secondary school. The third feature is that economic and political conditions have taught the Finns to work hard, to persevere and to find common solutions, in order to survive in a political tension field between East and West. The result of this distinctive educational culture is one in international comparison unusually high social status of the teaching profession, in the compulsory school. Such status involves a general high regard for teachers in the Finnish society, from students, parents, politicians and the business community.

Finland's repeated top rankings in the Pisa tests reinforce respect for those who create such a quality education, the teachers, and for the education sector itself. The special education-culture has made Finland unique in the international educational landscape. The questions that simultaneously inevitably arises are will this educational culture persist? Or, will "The Finnish Pisa-Tower be leaning increasingly more"? Will increasing prosperity lead to weaker motivation for learning and, consequently, deteriorating school results? Alternatively, will the cultural nature ever be so strong that it resists the negative impacts of welfare? Such questions makes it extra interesting to observe Finnish school development in the years ahead. May Finland be heading west, towards a progressivist school? Is it possible to se a Finland marked by welfare indulgence, and hence that Finnish students becoming more committed to thrive, than of working hard at school?

When the Finnish school example has become so interesting for other countries, it is also because it is a quality school for most people, or those who Europe often called the working class. My next comparative glance, at England, is at a school system that is interesting and important of a completely different reason. There you find the schools preferred by parents who have money and awareness of school quality. As Confucius said: «When a person has become rich, what does he need in addition? Knowledge". Many people around the world regard English private schools as the world's best. They definitely have model effects for the current international elite schools. School researchers in general are mostly concerned about schooling for ordinary people. Nevertheless, the English elite model is advancing globally, because this type of school meets the needs of a growing group of rich, education-conscious people. This fact makes it worthwhile to make a glance at it.

35

England - Elite Schools for All?

England is Norway's close neighbour on the other side of the North Sea, but when it comes to school tradition, we are on different planets. We turned extra far from each other in the time after World War II. The King and many Norwegians had exile in England during the war. However, they did not return home with new ideas about schooling. That is, however, what Norwegians fleeing to the United States did. In 1976, as a student of international education, I visited the Schools' Council in London. It resembled the Norwegian Council for Innovation in Education. The English, especially the Labour Party, was busy raising school quality for the entire population. Like Norway, Labour had the intention to reform the school to counter class distinctions. In England, such reforms resulted in the formation of the comprehensive schools. They are similar to the first version of the unified school in Norway, the branch-divided lower secondary school. The great difference between reforms in the two countries is that in England, the most accomplished students would have their own branch. These schools were in the tradition similar to the Norwegian real school. They were grammar schools. The reason for the difference between the two countries was the strength of an academic curriculum in England, in the essentialist tradition. It had dominated the country's education history for ages.

Another reminder of English uniqueness, I experienced a few years ago, when a Norwegian television team made a programme about schools at various places in Norway and England. The intention of the programme was to have an informal comparison of schools in the two countries. In a sequence, the Norwegians meet with English parents having their 11-year-old son at a boarding school. He only goes home during the holidays. What I remember best from the programme, was how shocked the Norwegians were learning about this long absence from home. The continued discussion between the Norwegians and the English about curriculum and method confirmed my impression that England and Norway are on different education planets.

In England, it is the Labour Party, which has been politically most eager to improve school offers. In 2005, the party under Tony Blair's leadership had a general election victory for the third time in a row. Education reforms were an important issue of the election campaign. In advance of the election, Norwegian educators at the University of Oslo had a visit by a group of young Labour politicians. They came from the Education Team in The Prime Minister's Strategy Unit, in the Cabinet Office. Their purpose of going to Norway was to collect ideas for the educational reform they worked on, in England. Like other foreigners, they had a positive impression of Norway, the school included. They talked with a number of Norwegian politicians, not least from their sister Norwegian Labour Party, and with a variety of education people. What they wanted to discuss with educational researchers at the University of Oslo, was some wonderings they had after their talks with politicians and practitioners. They had trouble understanding what the Norwegians actually thought about school quality. Especially, they were amazed that all students, independent of abilities could be in the same class at the lower secondary level. How was that possible? What did the parents think? In the discussion, we tried to explain, by giving the English a small insight into the particular Norwegian educational history. Afterwards, they thanked very politely for the talks. However, I think they left the University of Oslo still puzzled by the nature of the Norwegian school. The talks implied however, a side effect, the Norwegian gained insight in what was the main points of the educational reform, the Labour Party presented before the general elections in 2005.

One important goal of the reform was to increase parental involvement in school. In England, parents' possibility to choose between different school offers is a platitude. The challenge for policymakers was how to help «weak» parents, when they were going to choose. Labour's reform proposal was, additionally, support for measures to enhance school awareness among underprivileged socio-economic groups. Parents should also have stronger involvement in the governance of the school, and the evaluation of it. Another goal was to reform the leadership structure of the school. Academically successful primary schools should be able to opt being free-schools, by a simple decision in the school's board of directors, after consultation with the parents. There would also be more flexibility in the leadership structure, like having smaller boards, or "customized" leadership, as well as strengthened parental influence.

Such reforms indicate a very different mind-set than in Norway, when it comes to the parents. Formally, there is great emphasis on cooperation between school and home in Norway, but cooperation on academic matters is limited to quite a few parents. The difference in views on free-schools shows that the Labour Party in England in 2005 had more in common with the Norwegian Conservative Party's school policies, than with the Norwegian Labour Party. One reform goal was to make it easy to establish new free-schools, and it was going to be easier for academically successful free-schools to expand. The English agency corresponding to the Norwegian Education Directorate, OFSTED, should reform to become more sensitive to complaints from the parents. In Norway, this challenge is «solved» by the Parents' Commission for the compulsory school level. The Norwegian commission seems more like a helper for the Directorate, than as an interest organization for Norwegian parents.

The final most important reform goal, announced in Labour's election manifesto, applied to academic quality. Academic standards should increase, in order to guarantee that all students leave school functional in reading, writing and arithmetic. Quality teachers would be available to all students, especially the socially underprivileged. Based on the tests at age 11, 14 and 16, in English and math, there would be additional time and resources for students with special needs. The testing and evaluation scheme is dramatically different from what you find in Norwegian schools. In Norway, even modest attempts to get to a more valid and reliable evaluation of what students actually learn, still elicit resentment from both researchers and the Teachers' Union.

These education reform goals from England in 2005, emphasizes in particular three important aspects. First, they tell that England is still profoundly rooted in the essentialist curriculum tradition. The second message is that academic quality is what schooling is all about. The third is the importance of parents. Without full commitment from the parents, the school is in a much weaker position. Essentialism is an elitist school tradition. The special dimension of Labours' policies is that elite school quality becomes an equality value; everybody shall have access to elite school quality. A school is not just a place to stay. The good school is a place where all students are aiming towards knowledge. The English school is a place, where you strive to reach as far as possible in the direction of an academic standard, set in the elitist tradition. Also working class children shall get as much as possible of elitist school quality. All political parties in England have the same perception of school quality. Over the centuries, wealthy private schools set and maintained the standard for school quality. It is to such quality-schools several labour party leaders send their children. Tony Blair is one of them. Only the best is good enough for your most precious.

The wealthy parents in England have always used lots of money to give those most important to them, the best possible preparation to master the struggle of life. It has been a tradition since the middle ages. It all began with the universities. Oxford and Cambridge, established in the early 1100-hundreds. As with other universities at the time, they were a continuation of the learned tradition in the monasteries. Those who wish to study at the Oxbridge universities needed to prepare before admission. Preparation took place in private schools. The regular English public school is not of particularly ancient date. Private schools were for the wealthy, who wanted to qualify their hopefuls for one of the two universities. The two are among the world's ten top universities. Cambridge is among the best in the world in science and technology subjects. The university has had both Newton and Darwin as students. Oxford's weight is the humanities and social sciences in modern times. The philosopher John Locke was a student at Oxford. The university has fostered 27 Nobel prize-winners and 26 prime ministers. The last is the current, David Cameron.

The private education system in England, which is still going strong, starts with the preparatory schools. They correspond to primary level. They have excellent teachers. Therefore, the school fees, parents have to pay are high. The classes are small. Students receive individual follow up by teachers who are highly academically qualified and employed, because they can document solid practical-educational experiences from previous schools, and proof of having made students successful learners. From the prep schools, students go on to private lower secondary, and, finally, upper secondary. Their common name, even today, is «public schools», which literally means public school. For foreigners it is confusing to have both a public and a "private public" school. The latter, the private, have very high school fees that parents have to pay. The explanation of the confusing concept "public" has to do with the origin of this private school. Several hundred years ago, they started as a public school offering for the poor, but clever children. Only condition for admission was that the student was clever. Since they were open for all clever students, they were public. That is why these private schools are still called "public". They had very high academic quality, and became increasingly attractive among the wealthy. Today, they are private brands, establishing offshoots in the educational market in other parts of the world, e.g. East Asia. Some of the most famous schools are Eton and Harrow. Cameron is an «Etonian».

For students from the age of eleven, the private schools in England are boarding. The students live at the school. This is an important aspect for understanding the nature of, and the creation of what is quality in the English school. Quality rests on three legs: academic standard, socio-emotional care and sport. Together these three legs will affect an educated man, also named "the English gentleman", a person who is knowledgeable, wise, and considerate towards others - well behaved. A brilliant illustration of the English quality school is Harry Potter's Wizard school, Hogwarts. If you replace the wizardry subjects with common subjects from the humanities, mathematics and natural science, there will emerge a picture of a quality school that rests on these three legs. Academic subjects, and skilled teachers who know the subject and are skilled to convey it, is the first leg. This leg also includes systematic testing and rigorous examinations. The library is very important. These are indications of the strong academic aspect of the English school. It has its roots in Plato's philosophy and his understanding of human psychology, specifically expressed in his opinion of his elitist, republican state.

The other leg is the social and emotional part. The students live in different homelike "houses" at the school. Harry Potter lives in Gryffindor. In the house, they live like a family. Simultaneously, academic interests integrate into social life. A student is a house leader, the prefect. The house teacher has the particular responsibility of monitoring the connection between what takes place in the «House» after school hours, with what with what happens in classes at school time. Life in school and outside school constructively integrates. Students learn to take responsibility for specific tasks and for each other. There is friendship and there are conflicts that need to be resolved, and there is competition with the students from the other houses, such as Slytherin. For Harry Potter, the school and his friends there, is the good life. The life he is longing for during the long, boring summer vacation.

The third leg is sports. In China, sports were not particularly important on campus. In England, they are very important. It also applies to Hogwarts. Author J. K. Rawling has invented the sport of Quidditch. Its similarity with English football is striking. The same competition, the same emotional involvement and team building come to expression. The sport leg of English schools has several implications. One is physical education affecting a health benefit. Another is collaboration, learning to act as a team. It requires leadership in active action. It is all about winning battles and reaping glory, trophies. There is the view, that English military leaders in the time of the British Empire had prepared their successes on the battlefield, while playing cricket at Eaton or Cambridge.

Combined, these three legs, the academic, the socio-emotional and sports make a holistic education that will create the ideal, strong, moral man. It is not difficult to see that this ideal is far away from that of American settlers or participants in the Norwegian Lofoten Islands' Project, focusing local culture. However, this English school ideal exists. It is real. It is advancing in the world today, expressed not least evident in the international elite schools. Plato's conception of human psychology and his subsequent classifying of people has met with attacks, since the 1600's by encyclopaedic subject-centred school, in the 1900's by the polytechnic socialist school, and by the American progressivist school. Still, the ideas of the old master are as alive as ever. He survived in England. In the knowledge economy of globalization, he has renewed validity. The same applies to his contemporary Chinese colleague, Confucius. Xiamen international school was a meeting point, in terms of impact from the two ancient philosophers. They died thousands of years ago, but their thinking is actively framing the motivation of today's parents and educational politicians, for the latter, more and more. However, the politicians in different countries still cannot move faster with reform policies than the curriculum culture the population is stuck in, allows.

For the record, I must add that the literature has many accounts of a darker side of English boarding schools. The author Roald Dahl is one example. Life at school could sometimes turn brutal. This also comes forward in the Harry Potter books. The movie *Dead Poets' Society*, with actor Robin Williams, is also an example of how things can go deadly wrong in a boarding school. Despite such darker sides, it is incontestable that the English model, with a private preparation school and boarding school, is stronger than ever. The fact that the model now so strongly influences the growing international market for elite schools makes it useful for Norwegians with an interest in education quality to familiarize with it. Finland and England have reached similar quality measures by rather different means. In England, essentialist elite values are the starting point. Values and morale will set the standard for school quality. In Finland, the starting point is the common people's dream of moving up the social ladder in the encyclopaedic-democratic tradition. The equality value is the standard for all. The common denominator for the Finnish equality school and the English elitist school are subjects conveying solid academic knowledge. China reflects a third track, pursuing, simultaneously, both elite and mass education with quality. Norway can learn from both Finland, England and China.

36

An Optimal Knowledge School for All

I have come to the last chapter of my educational travelogue. It started with a patriotic desire, to reach those of my fellow Norwegian citizens, whom I think have the strongest motive for an optimally good school, parents and grandparents. Through a long life, close to Norwegian school development, I have seen how schools have increasingly become poorer. The Norwegian public school has fallen in relation to the Golden Age, just after the Second World War, and it has become worse in comparison to other countries. Such level lowering of the school is threefold dangerous. A poor school affects the young, the businesses and the nation. The cures applied have not helped. The recent Pisa report was a slap in the face of the *Knowledge Promotion*, the recent curriculum reform to improve schools.

Simultaneously, there are glimmers of hope. What has happened in the schools of Oslo capital municipality, in recent years, is a positive example. Still, furious reactions from key local stakeholders to what Oslo is trying, show how ingrained the progressivist unified school culture still is. Culture is extremely difficult to change. Something turned *culture* sits fixed in the spinal cord-reflex. It sits glued into the brain as a fixed frame for how to perceive all other existing things. It is unshakable until there are mental earthquakes in your life that force structures in the brain to change. As happened with the Chinese, when Deng Xiaoping said, «It is good that some get rich before others». He interrupted the Chinese thinking along Mao's naive and idealistic socialism. Instead, he attached to the old culture of Confucianism, about the necessity of knowledge, and to the thinking that characterized Chinese education patriots early in the 20th Century. The businessman Tan, who founded Xiamen university is one outstanding example.

This travelogue is my educational project report to parents and grandparents, triggered by two intentions. Firstly, I like to contribute to making these key people in children's and young people's lives familiar with what is educational quality internationally. Then they can advise their loved ones in the best way. Second, I like to challenge them to think about other people, those who may not be as conscious, or have many resources. I want conscious parents and grandparents to help change the educational culture in their context, by taking moral responsibility to see that everyone, no matter how modest the intellectual starting point is, get access to a knowledge school with quality. This involves taking a position on education *policies*, and support policies that contribute to a better knowledge school for all, and, in particular, for those who do not have strong parents and grandparents backing them. Access to a good knowledge school is most important for those who do not have rich parents. This was the teacher's message to the poor rice cake-baker parents in South China. Against odds, their son got the opportunity to continue schooling. He later became a professor, and created a new university institute and a new discipline. Now 95, he works hard gearing up vocational education. It is also very important.

However, we must dare to recognize that people are different, in terms of prerequisites for learning something abstract, simultaneously with recognizing that all people are equal, and shall experience justice through equal opportunities to life-long learning. An old bookseller who stopped by the school's staff room, commented on learning, "You can lead a horse to the stream, but you cannot force him to drink". He took the point. What is essential for a good school is a leadership who can find teachers making students themselves wanting to learn. That is what the 22 years' old American teacher did in English lessons at the Xiamen international school, when she inspired 11-year-olds to find it cool to write short stories, having Alexander the Great and Mandela as heroes in the same story. The greatest challenge for the heart-warm, humanist Norwegian parents and grandparents, themselves products of the unified school culture, is to realize that primarily applying the school as an instrument for social and cultural integration was incorrect. Such attitudes must give way to seeing that the purpose of the school is to make *all* students acquire as much *knowledge* as possible. The latter is the school's essence and has been its historic mission, since Plato and Confucius. England shows that Plato not only survived the three, recent Western curriculum traditions, but also is challenging them even in our time.

A holistic perception of a knowledge school, involves attention to three basic categories: the curriculum, which tells what students will acquire in the classroom, the school organization, which is the tool for implementing the curriculum, and the school's surroundings, which includes all the factors that affect what happens in the school organization. My *vision* for a knowledge school in Norway is *unrealistic*, both politically and practically. I do *not* take the existing Norwegian reality, in terms of private schools and employment conditions for teachers and leaders, as my point of departure. Instead, I like to present a vision of the optimal knowledge school, based on my experiences and observations in China, Hong Kong, Xiamen international school and our neighbouring countries, Finland and England. Based on these observations, I will choose the best from four curriculum-traditions: Encyclopaedism, Essentialism, Confucianism and Progressivism. My ideal school, then appearing, will only exist on the drawing board. The benefit may be that such a school picture provides people with a basis for comparisons of existing school offers, as well as provide ideas as to what might be possible to change, in the difficult world of reality. Three major preconditions for my optimal school vision is that there firstly, is a *school market* outside the public school, secondly, that a shortened *teacher education* is linked to the university's disciplinary departments, and that highly paid headmasters and teachers are hired on *contract*.

THE SCHOOL ORGANIZATION

The school's board of directors consists of people who have high levels of expertise on education and economy, as well as representatives of the parents. The institution or person who provides the essentials of the school's funding is chairperson of the board. The model is Xiamen international school. Since the school exists for the interests of students and parents, no one, neither leaders nor teachers, can have permanent employment. Lifetime employee incompetence is treason against students and parents. Employees who have to leave, because of incompetence, should have a proper safety net on their way to another job. The headmaster is on a three years' contract. The salary is competitive with leadership positions in the business world. The board, every year makes an evaluation of the headmaster, and renewal of the three years' contract only occurs if the board and the parents think the school has delivered satisfactory. The headmaster has the responsibility to hire and terminate teachers. Appointments take place with the help of a professional recruitment company. Teacher salary is very high. Teachers will have a bonus when delivering extraordinary results. The teachers have one-year contracts, renewed as long as the headmaster deems the teacher's efforts satisfying, in terms of how well students reach learning objectives, and in relation to their parents' expectations.

The board ensures agreement with an accreditation firm, that every five years will evaluate how well the school organisation is implementing the curriculum. If the school does not work optimally, it will have a fixed deadline to correct weaknesses in order to retain its certification as an accredited school. The board ensures proper buildings, equipment, and all facilities required to keep a high standard of teaching. The library is first class. A student board is unnecessary. Students learn about democracy at school, but practice it in forums outside of school. A good school is inevitable hierarchical, but not authoritarian.

THE CURRICULUM

At the lower secondary level, there is organizational differentiation. The students go to classes according to ability. There are good opportunities to change to another class, depending on efforts and results. An effective testing system will make it clear when results are too poor. Then, students might benefit from repeating a class level. If the students do very well, they can skip a class level. Students who are struggling get extra professional follow-up. The curriculum includes in addition to ordinary subjects, mandatory Chinese, German, French, and moral philosophy. Common to all the subjects are their knowledge centring. Knowledge is the essential precondition for students' gaining competence and moral consciousness. Learning of rules of conduct and courtesy are important. The teacher is a role model. He must live as he teaches.

The school has first class textbooks, with relevant learning materials. The teacher is superior in determining teaching method, whether it is lecture, group work or project work. Objective tests come frequently. They are crucial means to improvement of learning. A tutorial guide explains the purpose of the tests, and their design. In addition, the parents have to familiarize with this guide. This system worked perfectly well at Xiamen international school. Students use the Internet actively in their learning, but under clear teacher control, and the Internet does not replace the library. Students are stimulated to compete in their academic work, and, simultaneously, to learn cooperation, and see how it pays off. Physical education, or sports and sports activities have a central place. To establish the school's own team in several sports are important, and, as well, that the school team has the opportunity to compete with other schools.

THE SCHOOL'S SURROUNDINGS

An essential prerequisite for quality elevation of Norwegian schools is that the public school get the opportunity to see and learn from other types of schools, on how to achieve quality. A main strategy to bring about such learning is to make use of market mechanisms and competition. Deng Xiaoping said, "It doesn't matter if the cat is white or black, as long as it catches mice." The occasion was his introduction of «socialist market economy». In addition to applying the market principle, he considered education and research the most important prerequisites for successful national economic development. Thus, China went from being a backward developing country to become the world's second-largest economy.

The Norwegian welfare state is so strong and well intended that it makes many key figures in society think it a good idea to park people of 70 years or more. They think these oldies do not know their own good. The old should not accept such thinking. They do not have to ask for permission to work, from neither the employers' powerful association, nor, the equally strong workers' trade union. The old should decide themselves about how they like to use their energy and creative force. Among the retired, there is great expertise and financial resources. Here you may find grandparents who would like to use the money they do not really need any more, on measures that would make the public school increase its quality. These retirees can become educational patriots.

One example of how such patriotism could play out is to stimulate creation of international elite schools in Norway, completely privately and commercially based, with high tuition fees. It is uncertain, whether there are sufficiently many school-motivated parents in progressivist Norway that will pay for first class education. That we do not know. However, we do know that many parents support their secondary school leavers with hundreds of thousands crowns for buying a special bus to carry the drunken youths around during the Russ Celebration, just before the final examinations. It means, the money is there, and you could instead use it for education purposes, if you think education an important value. If elite schools appear in Norway, they would act as showcases for quality schools. The existence of such schools would have learning effect for Norwegian parents in general, and for the public school. Parents then will have the opportunity to prioritize their resources on a quality-school, on their children's most important life insurance.

Another change strategy for parents and grandparents is to make active use of the existing free-school alternatives, which are already legally present in the country. The engagement that often comes with such schools, whether the background is religious or new educational ideas, often involves better teachers, more enthusiastic leadership and parents who engage in what is going on at school. It is also important, eventually, to open up for commercially driven free-schools. As shown, both in China and England, there is nothing indicating that the quality will be lower, if profit is part of the school owner's motivation. The Chinese multi-billionaire, who established Xiamen international school, demanded hefty tuition fees of the parents. That was not just to get money to build schools for the poor in Western China. When parents pay high fees, they expect quality, and they care more.

Only parents and grandparents can change the Norwegian school for the better. Occasionally, there pops up a politician, who has the powers and creativity to change basic terms for understanding what schooling is all about. That is what minister of education, Kristin Clement, did from 2001 onwards. However, that is an exception in a society, often controlled by "the power of ignorance", or twisting Ibsen's words, a society controlled by the darker side of "the compact majority". It is parents and grandparents, perhaps especially the latter, after they have turned retired free citizens, who can make a difference. Besides being active as advisors and tutors for their own grandchildren, they can use their energy to challenge the still existing progressivism, by joining boards or commissions that pertain to the school, whether it is public or private. Something bolder would be to create an alternative to the State's Parental Commission for the compulsory school. It is entirely possible to create a non-state, private interest organization that can speak "truth to state power". Such an independent Parents' and Grandparents' School Commission could work both as a think tank to improve the school, and as a pushing force on politicians. The grandparents would not just use their time to play with the grandkids, but take a moral social responsibility to achieve a better knowledge school, not least for those who need it the most.

Can Norway learn from China?

When I now feel like a Norwegian education patriot, I cannot help thinking about Yang Ying, the school-clever poor girl, who at the age of 15 worked long days producing bricks, with a salary $ 0.70 per day. At 17, she was a waitress in Xiamen. Simultaneously, she used her brains, because she in primary school had one particular teacher, one that *saw* her. When her parents, because of poverty, wanted her to end schooling, he refused to let her go. He made math Ying's favourite subject. The waitress became a multi-billionaire. Deng Xiaoping had introduced market economy. First, she used profits to establish two elite schools in Xiamen, one for Chinese, and one for foreigners. Later, she built schools for the poor in Western China, established centres for blood donation in the countryside, and she gave money to blood cancer research, initially, one million US dollars.

Thinking about my own country, and the tragic school development I have witnessed during fifty years, reason cannot prevent the following question: Is there currently a Norwegian Yang Ying?

Background Literature

Bell, Daniel A. (2008) *China's New Confucianism. Politics and Everyday Life in a Changing Society.* Princeton: Princeton University Press

Bergersen, Arne and Arild Tjeldvoll (1983) *Skole uten rektor?* (School without a headmaster?) Oslo: Didakta Publishing Company

Castells, Manuel (1996) *The Information Age: Economy, Society and Culture. Volume 1: The Rise of the Network Society.* Oxford: Blackwell

Castells, Manuel (1997) *The Information Age: Economy, Society and Culture. Volume 2: The Power of Identity.* Oxford: Blackwell

Castells, Manuel (1998) *The Information Age: Economy, Society and Culture. Volume 3: End of Millennium.* Oxford: Blackwell

Elias, John L. & Sharan Merriam (1980) *Philosophical Foundations of Adult Education.* Malabar: Krieger Publ. Co.

Fukuyama, Francis (2011) *The Origins of Political Order.* New York: Farrar, Strauss and Giroux

Fukuyama, Francis (2014) *Political Order and Political Decay.* New York: Farrar, Strauss and Giroux

Hodneland Wang, Lei (1999) *The Chinese "Paradox": High Academic achievements versus "unfavourable" Learning Conditions – a Cultural Study.* Master thesis. Oslo: University of Oslo

Homes, Brian & Martin McLean (1989) *The Curriculum. A Comparative Perspective.* London: Routledge

Johansen, Kari & Arild Tjeldvoll (1989) *Skoleledelse og skoleutvikling* (School leadership and School Development) Oslo: Solum Forlag

Kissinger, Henry (2012) *On China.* New York: Penguin Books

Confucius (1989) *Samtalar* (Conversations). Oslo: Det norske samlaget

Levinson, Joseph R. (1968) *Confucian China and Its Modern Fate: A Triology.* Berkeley: University of California Press

MacRae, Donald G. (1974) *Weber.* London: Fontana

Norsk samfunnsvitenskapelig datatjeneste (2005) Europa-undersøkelsen om det gode liv: Nordmenn vil nyte, europeerne vil yte (The Europe-survey on the good life: Norwegians will enjoy, the Europeans will provide). Bergen: NSD-new No. 1/2005

Tjeldvoll, Arild (1977) Pedagogisk-psykologisk tjeneste? (Educational-Psychological Services?) Oslo: Department of Educational Research, University of Oslo

Tjeldvoll, Arild (1978) "Ungdom og flytting i en utkantkommune – et eksempel" («Youth and emigration in a remote district - an Example», in *Norsk Pedagogisk Tidsskrift*, No 2, 1978

Tjeldvoll, Arild (1979) "Skole, samfunn og lærer"(«Local communities, School and Expertise») in Anton Hoem, et al. (ed.) (1979) *Society-oriented Education*. Oslo: University Press

Tjeldvoll, Arild (1980) Læreryrket i forandring. Fra skolemester til folke-adjunkt (*The Teaching Profession Changing. From Schoolmaster to Folk-adjunct*) Oslo: University Press

Tjeldvoll, Arild (1992) "Enhetsskolens exit?" ("Exit of the Unified Schoiol Idea?"). Oslo: *Mercator*, 11/92

Tjeldvoll, Arild (1995) «The Language of Education. The Coherence of Educational Rationales, Systems, Cultures and Paradigms" in Daun, Holger et al. (Eds.): *The Role of Education in Development. From Personal to International Arenas*. Stockholm: Stockholm University, Institute of International Education

Tjeldvoll, Arild (1997) «The Service University in service-societies: The Norwegian Experience» in Jan Currie and Janice Newson (Eds.) (1997) *Globalization and The University: Critical Perspectives*. Thousand Oaks: Sage Publications

Tjeldvoll, Arild (1998) *Education and the Scandinavian Welfare State in the Year 2000: Equality, Policy and Reform*. (Ed.). New York: Garland Publishing

Tjeldvoll, Arild (1999) "Students' Morale and Morality in the Service University" in *Uniped*. Tromsø: The Norwegian Council of Higher Education.

Tjeldvoll, Arild (2000) *Torsten Husèn – Conversations in Comparative Education*. Bloomington, IN., USA: Phi Delta Kappa Educational Foundations

Tjeldvoll, Arild (2002) "The Decline of Educational Populism in Norway" in *European Education*, Volume 34, No. 2, 2002

Tjeldvoll, Arild (2002) "Norwegian Education – Oscillating between Equality and Quality" in *European Education*, Volume 34, No. 3, 2002

Tjeldvoll, Arild (2002) "The Service University in the Knowledge Economy of Europe" in Dewatripont, M., F. Thys-Clemet, L. Wilkin (2002) (Eds.) *European Universities: Change and Convergence?* Bruxelles: Universite Libre de Bruxelles

Tjeldvoll, Arild (2003) «The Norwegian Unified School – a Paradise lost?» w. Anne Welle-Strand. In: *Journal of Education Policy*, 2002, VOL. 17. NO. 6, 653-686

Tjeldvoll, Arild (2004) "Globalisation and University Quality Improvement: The Effect of Globalisation to the University Service Quality and Organisation". In (Chinese language) Fudan: *Education Forum* 2004/3

Tjeldvoll, Arild (2004) *Xiamen International School – Ambition Excellence.* With Anne Welle-Strand and Jenny Stretton, Oslo: Norwegian School of Management BI (Also in Chinese)

Tjeldvoll, Arild (2004) «Service University Development and Lithuanian Idealist & Rationalist Legacies», in *Social Sciences* Nr. 2, 2004

Tjeldvoll, Arild (2005) «School Leadership Training under Globalisation: Comparisons of UK, US and Norway». With Christopher Wales and Anne Welle-Strand, in *Managing Global Transitions International Research Journal.* Volume 3, Number 1 Spring, 2005

Tjeldvoll, Arild (2005) *Pan Maoyuan – A Founding Father of Chinese Higher Education Research*. Trondheim: Norwegian University of Science and Technology's Department of Teacher Education. Academic Reports Number 24, 2005. Also in Chinese

Tjeldvoll, Arild (2006) «How to build creative universities in China?» In *Chinese Education Daily*, Beijing, Nov 6th, 2006 (in Chinese)

Tjeldvoll, Arild (2007) "Concepts of a service university", in David Bridges et al. (Eds.) (2007) *Higher Education and National Development – Universities and societies in transition*. London: Routledge

Tjeldvoll, Arild (2008) "School Management: Norwegian Legacies Bowing to New Public Management", in *Managing Global Transitions International Research* Journal, Vol. 6, no. 2, summer 2008

Tjeldvoll, Arild (2008) "Elite Universities – Conditions for being Innovative", in *Jinangsu Gao Jiao*, No. 1, 2008 (in Chinese)

Tjeldvoll, Arild (2008) "Finnish Higher Education Reforms", in *European Education* Vol. 40, No. 4 (p 91-107)

Tjeldvoll, Arild (2009) "Limits to Education Policies as Social Policies" – *Journal of Comparative Education*, Taipei 2011

Tjeldvoll, Arild (2009) "The HEAD-ache in Norway", in *European Education*, Vol. 41, Issue 3, 2009

Tjeldvoll, Arild (2009) "Higher education restructuring battle: Norway and Taiwan compared", in Bulletin of *Taiwan National Institute of Educational Resources and Research*, Vol. 44

Tjeldvoll, Arild (2009) "Teacher Quality. Finland and Norway Compared Within the Frame of Western Curriculum Philosophies", in *Proceedings from The Annual Conference of the Comparative Education Society*, Taiwan 2009

Tjeldvoll, Arild (2010) "The Service University", in *Managing Global Transitions International Research Journal*, Winter issue 2010

Tjeldvoll, Arild (2011) "Change Leadership in Universities: The Confucian Dimension", in *Journal of Higher Education Policy and Management – special issue on leadership and change in higher education in Asia Pacific*, edited by Professor Philip Hallinger, Hong Kong Institute of Education and Professor Arild Tjeldvoll, National Chi Nan University, College of Education.

Zhang Weiwei (2012) *The China Wave. Rise of a Civilizational State.* Hackensack: World Century.

Can Norway Learn From China?

China soon has the world's largest economy.
Can a substantial explanation be the population's strong willingness to learn?

When China joined the Pisa surveys (2009), Shanghai's 15-year-olds were top in the world. The same was the case in Pisa 2013.

Chinese students abroad, are those that complete the fastest. Is willingness to learn, China's strongest soft power? Can Norway learn from China about school quality?

A common denominator for those who analyse the global economic competition is that individuals and nations' level of knowledge is the power source number one. Importance of knowledge for individuals', companies' and nations' identity and mastery is the overall frame for this book.

Focus is on a learning culture that both provide formation (morality) and education (competence). Concretely, attention is on educational policies, curriculum traditions and schools as instruments, to achieve the culture that results in both education and character formation.

The book is an educational travelogue based on the author's experiences with school and education in Norway and internationally during seventy years.

Arild Tjeldvoll (b. 1939) is a retired professor from the University of Oslo. His research has included international education in general, and higher education and leadership in particular. He has had affiliated positions and longer research stays at universities in the United Kingdom, the United States, Sweden, Lithuania, Zimbabwe, South Africa, China, Finland, Hong Kong and Taiwan. Tjeldvoll has initiated several international research networks. His practice includes teaching in special school, lower secondary school, upper secondary school and university. He has been headmaster of a lower secondary school, a private upper secondary school and head of the Department of Educational Research, University of Oslo. In retirement, he is advisor for the establishing of graduate studies in education at the National University of Vietnam.

www.ingramcontent.com/pod-product-compliance
Lightning Source LLC
Chambersburg PA
CBHW061423040426
42450CB00007B/877